HISTORICAL ATLAS OF THE MIDDLE EAST

HISTORICAL ATLAS OF THE MIDDLE EAST

G.S.P. FREEMAN-GRENVILLE

SIMON & SCHUSTER

A Paramount Communications Company

New York London Toronto Sydney Tokyo Singapore

Cartography: Lorraine Kessel
Designed and produced by Carta, Jerusalem

Academic Reference Division
Simon and Schuster
15 Columbus Circle, New York, NY 10023

A Paramount Communications Company

Library of Congress Cataloging-in-Publication Data
Freeman-Grenville, G. S. P. (Greville Stewart Parker)
  Historical atlas of the Middle East / G.S.P. Freeman-Grenville:
[cartography, Lorraine Kessel].
       p.   cm.
  Includes bibliographical references and index.
  Contents: Introduction – The Arab period – The Muslim world –
Crusaders and Muslims – The further spread of Islam –The Ottoman
world – The twentieth century.
  ISBN 0-13-390915-8
  1. Middle East–History–Maps.   I. Kessel, Lorraine. II Title.
G2206.S1F7 1993 <G&M>
911'.58–dc20
                                              93-9294
                                                CIP
                                                MAP

PREFACE

This *Historical Atlas of the Middle East* is for the general reader, and has 113 maps with commentaries covering the whole period from earliest historical times until 1993. "Middle East" is a word on everyone's lips, but not an easy one to define. An American admiral, Alfred Thayer Mahan, coined it in 1902. He used it as a convenient shorthand expression for the area between India and Arabia, centering on the Persian Gulf.

The term has become more flexible than that, as the centers of power and their range of influence have shifted from time to time. At one moment the Egypt of the Pharaohs is in power in the Levant; at another a Persian dynasty rules from Afghanistan to the Nile Delta and Valley. When Alexander the Great founded Alexandria he created a pivot for eastern and western commerce, and so it remained under Rome, and then Byzantium, with the Persian Empire as a counterweight. Alexandria became by far the most populous Jewish city in the world, and then the most influential in the development of Christian thought. When Islam emerged upon the world stage, the scene expanded from the Arabian peninsula first to Syria, Iraq and Persia, and then westward from Egypt to the Atlantic. For a time it embraced Spain and briefly parts of France. Early on it extended down the African coast as far as Mozambique, and crossed to India, whence eastward to Malaysia and Indonesia. It reached across southern Russia overland to China, and later across the Sahara. Its earliest centers in the Arabian peninsula were soon displaced by Damascus and then Baghdad; but, with the decline of the Caliphate, Cairo became the commercial center, and, with the university mosque of al-Azhar, became the intellectual powerhouse of Islam, which it remains to this day, with students from every Islamic country in the world. After 1518 the whole vast region from the Moroccan border to the Persian boundary fell under Ottoman Turkish dominance, succeeded only by the brief Anglo-French domination which terminated in 1957. It was in this period that Israel reemerged after an eclipse of more than two millennia, and, at the same time, new, oil-rich states among Arabs whose fathers had been Bedouin. It is only within this fluctuating kaleidoscope pattern that contemporary events can be viewed.

There are a number of differing conventions for the transliteration of Arabic and other tongues in the region. So far as geographical names are concerned the conventions of the *Webster's New Geographical Dictionary* have been followed. These names have varied over the centuries, and where a given place has had more than one name (e.g. Mecca, Macoraba; Medina, Yathrib) this has been indicated in the index by a double entry, e.g. Mecca (see also Macoraba).

The Select Bibliography includes only a proportion of the works consulted. The bibliography of the Middle East includes many thousands of books and articles, and to these the bibliographies in the *Encyclopaedia of Islam*, and those in the Cambridge *Histories*, are useful guides. P.K. Hitti, *A History of the Arabs*, gives short accounts of the Arab geographers, of whom the *Encyclopaedia of Islam* has longer entries. For brevity, journal articles have for the most part been excluded, together with works in languages other than English, except where there are no relevant English translations. For works in Greek or Latin works in the Loeb Classical Library have been used, unless otherwise stated.

My thanks are once again due to Lorraine Kessel for her admirable maps, and to the all but myriad number of persons who have instructed me and shown me kindness in the course of travels in the lands this atlas portrays.

Sheriff Hutton,
York

G.S.P.F.-G.

TABLE OF CONTENTS

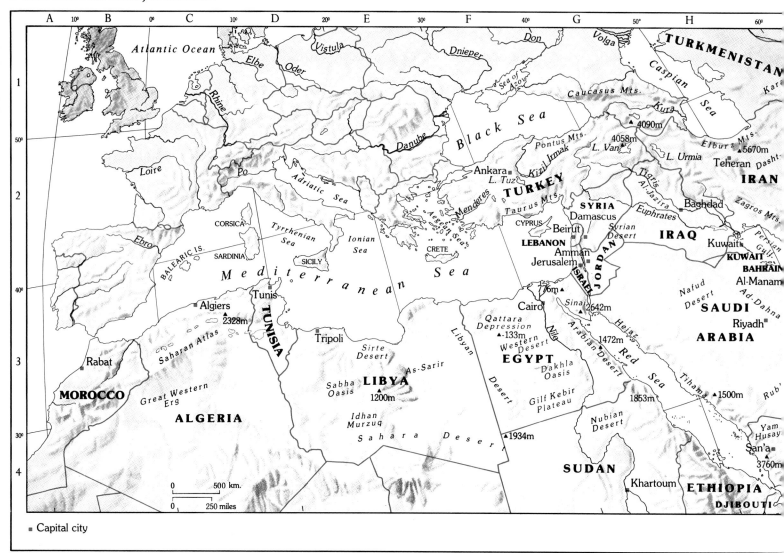

- ■ Capital city

1. THE MIDDLE EAST, PHYSICAL

Rudyard Kipling was wrong when he wrote:
Oh, East is East, and West is West,
and never the twain shall meet...
for the Middle East is a land bridge across which
civilization after civilization has passed. Originally
defined as scarcely more than Mesopotamia, its
kingdoms spread ideas both eastward and westward.
At one time the power of Persia stretched from the
present Pakistan border to Libya, Egypt, and Nubia
(Sudan); at another, Islam and the power of the
Arabs stretched from the Atlantic to the Kirghiz
steppe and the Indus River.

Fire and tools were the first products of civilization.
It was the people of Urartu in the Armenian
mountains who first mined and manufactured

metal, practices that rapidly became known in the
Zagros Mountains and in Egypt, Nubia, and Ethiopia.
The search for metal lured the Levantine Phoeni-
cians, to Spain and even Britain.

Commercial enterprise necessitated the keeping of
records. Thus it was in Syria that the art of cursive
writing was developed by Semitic-speaking peoples,
whose alphabets are ancestral to numerous present-
day writing systems.

It was in this same geographical area that four
great religions evolved. If the Mosaic concept of the
unity of God has priority, it was the Persian seer
Zarathustra (Zoroaster) in the sixth century B.C., who
first taught the concepts of immortality, the Last
Judgment, and the activity of God through the Holy

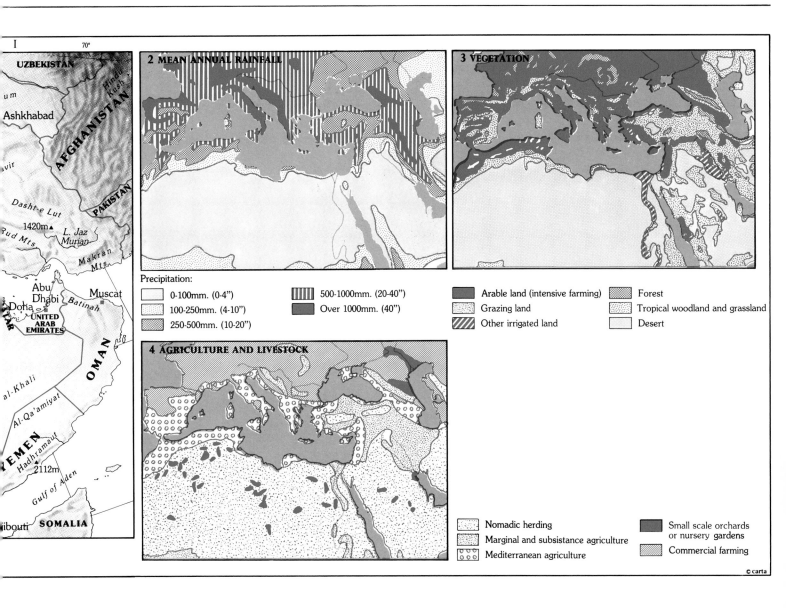

2 MEAN ANNUAL RAINFALL

3 VEGETATION

Precipitation:

- 0-100mm. (0-4")
- 100-250mm. (4-10")
- 250-500mm. (10-20")
- 500-1000mm. (20-40")
- Over 1000mm. (40")

- Arable land (intensive farming)
- Grazing land
- Other irrigated land
- Forest
- Tropical woodland and grassland
- Desert

4 AGRICULTURE AND LIVESTOCK

- Nomadic herding
- Marginal and subsistance agriculture
- Mediterranean agriculture
- Small scale orchards or nursery gardens
- Commercial farming

© carta

Spirit — concepts that found their way into Judaism, and from Judaism into Christianity and Islam.

Herodotus claimed that it was Egypt that taught Greece religion. Be that as it may, it was in the following century that the Greeks under Alexander carried Hellenism as far east as India and established Alexandria on the northern shore of Africa as a world center, not merely of commerce but also of philosophy and learning.

The first kingdoms evolved around river systems. The gradual desiccation of the Sahara forced men into the Nile Valley. In Mesopotamia a similar effect was produced; fertile soil was washed down each year from the northern mountains, as the Nile brought down soil from the mountains of Ethiopia.

Shortly before the beginning of the first millennium B.C., the Arabian camel was domesticated and bred throughout the whole desert area, providing, with the horse, a primary means of land transport. By this time shipping and ports had evolved in the Persian Gulf and the Red Sea as well as the Mediterranean. Under the Persian ruler Darius, the utility of linking the Mediterranean to the Nile and the Red Sea was perceived, and the first canal begun.

With the discovery of the rich oil fields in the Zagros Mountains, Mesopotamia, the Persian Gulf, and Arabia, the region took on immense economic importance during the twentieth century, in addition to the commercial and cultural significance that it had had for four-thousand years.

5. THE ANCIENT MIDDLE EAST, c.2050 TO 1000 B.C.

In ancient Mesopotamia, a series of city-states arose. Perpetually at war with each other, none achieved superiority for any great length of time, save Babylon and Assyria. The earliest city-states in the Middle East had arisen long before, but, in the absence of written records, their history is largely closed to us. Although Jericho was fortified by 9000 B.C. we have only an archaeological record of artifacts. By 3000 B.C. a group of city-states had come into being in southern Iraq with a common Sumerian language that had been committed to writing; these are the first written records. It is to this group that we owe the beginning of Middle Eastern history, properly so called. Their religion was pantheistic; their system of government was theocratic, with a priest-king whose will was absolute. In architecture, their greatest achievement was the ziggurat, and in agriculture, the use of irrigation canals. It is this area that the Bible names the Garden of Eden.

By 2400 B.C., these city-states were displaced by Akkadian rulers of Semitic origin, who made Babylon their capital. Under these rulers a monotheistic form of religion developed, together with a coded legal system whose origins can be traced to the small kingdom of Ur. Under the great law-giver Hammurabi (1792–1750 B.C.) the tribal law of revenge was replaced by fines, a legal concept that persists to our day. This code of laws marked the beginning of modern Syria and Iraq. Between 1595 and 1300 B.C., the Hittites of Indo-European origin took over the territory. A warlike people, they encountered a civilization more sophisticated than their own and were absorbed by it. Around 1300 B.C. the Semitic Babylonians, so long under a conquering heel, overthrew them, creating an empire that stretched as far as the Levant and, for a time, into Egypt.

6. ANCIENT EGYPT

By the fourth millennium B.C. the gradual desiccation of the Sahara had forced substantial populations into the relatively small cultivable lands on either side of the Nile. The annual flooding of the Nile, which brought down the rich silt on which their agriculture depended, compelled these populations to form strict administrative structures. Knowledge of this organization and the art of metallurgy had been brought from western Asia. By 3100 B.C. two kingdoms had evolved: Lower Egypt, that is, the Delta, and Upper Egypt, based in Thebes. Shortly before 300 B.C. these kingdoms were united.

In the south the boundary reached the First Cataract, below which the whole river is navigable. Under the Old Kingdom (2700–2200 B.C.) the capital was shifted to Memphis, in the region of modern Cairo. Here the Pyramids bear mute witness to a highly sophisticated development of mathematics, engineering, medical science, and religion.

None of this development would have been possible without a lively foreign trade with the Levant, and even the mysterious PWNT, possibly Somalia, from which — along with southern Arabia — came the immense quantities of frankincense used in temple worship.

Between around 2250 and 1750 B.C., under the Middle Kingdom, there was some expansion into Palestine. There followed two centuries under the Hyksos. Under Akhenaton (c.1367–c.1350) religion was reformed and a new capital built at Thebes. During the twelfth century B.C. Egypt suffered raids by the Sea Peoples, but independence was preserved until Cambyses II of Persia seized the country in 525 B.C. Except for a brief interval, the Hyksos ruled until Alexander the Great swallowed Egypt up into his vast empire (see map 10). To him Egypt owes the creation of Alexandria as a port, which was to become the pivot of trade between East and West.

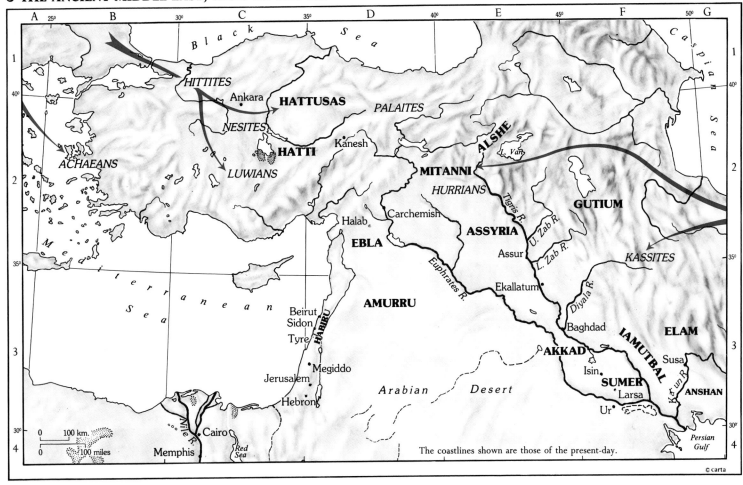

The coastlines shown are those of the present-day.

© carta

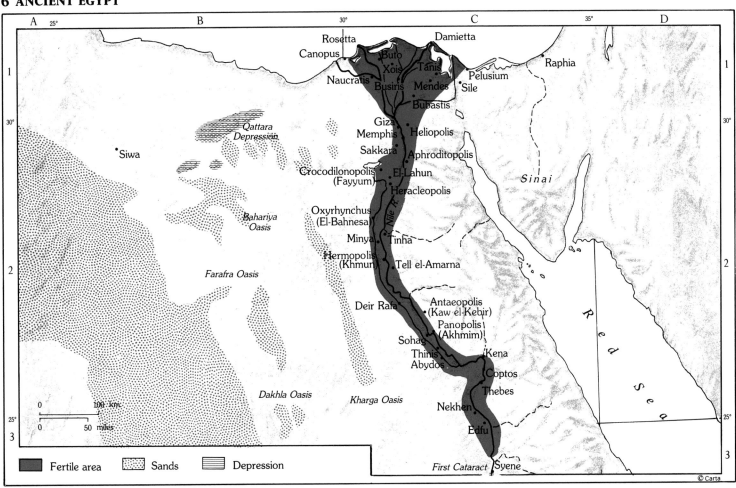

Fertile area Sands Depression

© Carta

7. THE SEABORNE EMPIRE OF THE PHOENICIANS

The Phoenicians are also known as Canaanites and Sidonians in the Hebrew scriptures. In northern Africa, where they set up trading colonies, they are known by the name of their principal colony, as Carthaginians. Their language was unquestionably Semitic, as was that of their Levantine neighbors. Their distinctiveness was neither racial nor linguistic, but as dwellers on the Levant coastland with a preference for peninsulas and islands, they were distinct in their development of the arts of navigation and long-distance commerce. In their hinterland, present Lebanon, they were fortunate in possessing huge forests, which provided not only ships' timbers but also wood for export to, for example, Solomon's Israel. Timber was also sent to Assyria and Egypt, and supplied ships that traded in the Red Sea and perhaps with Yemen or Somalia. Through a series of entrepôts, merchandise from India was reaching the Levant by the tenth century B.C.. In the ninth century B.C. the Phoenician cities — each apparently self-governing — were under Assyrian control. Not until the eighth century did the Assyrians impose direct rule.

The *Annals* of Tyre record that in the seventh year of King Pygmalion's reign (814–813 B.C.) his sister fled and founded Carthage in Libya. Phoenician colonization long antedates this period. The founding of Gades (Cádiz) is traditionally dated in 1110 B.C. and Utica in 1101 B.C.; some African cities are said to have been founded earlier. These dates are highly debatable, as are ninth-century inscriptions in Cyprus and at Nora in Sardinia. By the term *colony* is here meant a trading settlement, not the political domination of a people by alien immigrants. The classical Greek authors maintain that the Phoenicians monopolized trade in the Mediterranean before the maritime expansion of Greek trade. Precise chronological evidence for Phoenician expansion is highly tenuous, but it is certain that by 509 B.C. Carthage and Rome had entered into a treaty relationship, defining their respective areas of trade. In north Africa the Carthaginian-Phoenicians increased in number, as evidenced by the necropolises in their numerous settlements. In the fifth century B.C., because Greek traders cut off communications with northern Europe at Marsalia (Marseilles), long voyages were undertaken past Spain and Gaul as far as Cornwall in southwest Britain in search of tin. During this time a Carthaginian, Hanno, is claimed to have circumnavigated Africa. The tale has been greatly disputed, and he may have reached only the Gulf of Guinea, itself no mean feat. The principal object of these voyages was to obtain gold, silver, and tin, which were transported via the trans-Saharan trade routes as far as the gold-bearing areas, later known as Guinea. The Phoenicians established the first seaborne trading empire, a loose-knit system that linked the prosperity of western Africa and the Mediterranean with the cities of the Euphrates and the Tigris.

When Rome dominated all Italy in 272 B.C., it came into inevitable conflict with Carthage. Three wars (264–261; 209–206; and 201–146), known as the Punic Wars, ended with the destruction of Carthage and the absorption of northern Africa into the Roman orbit.

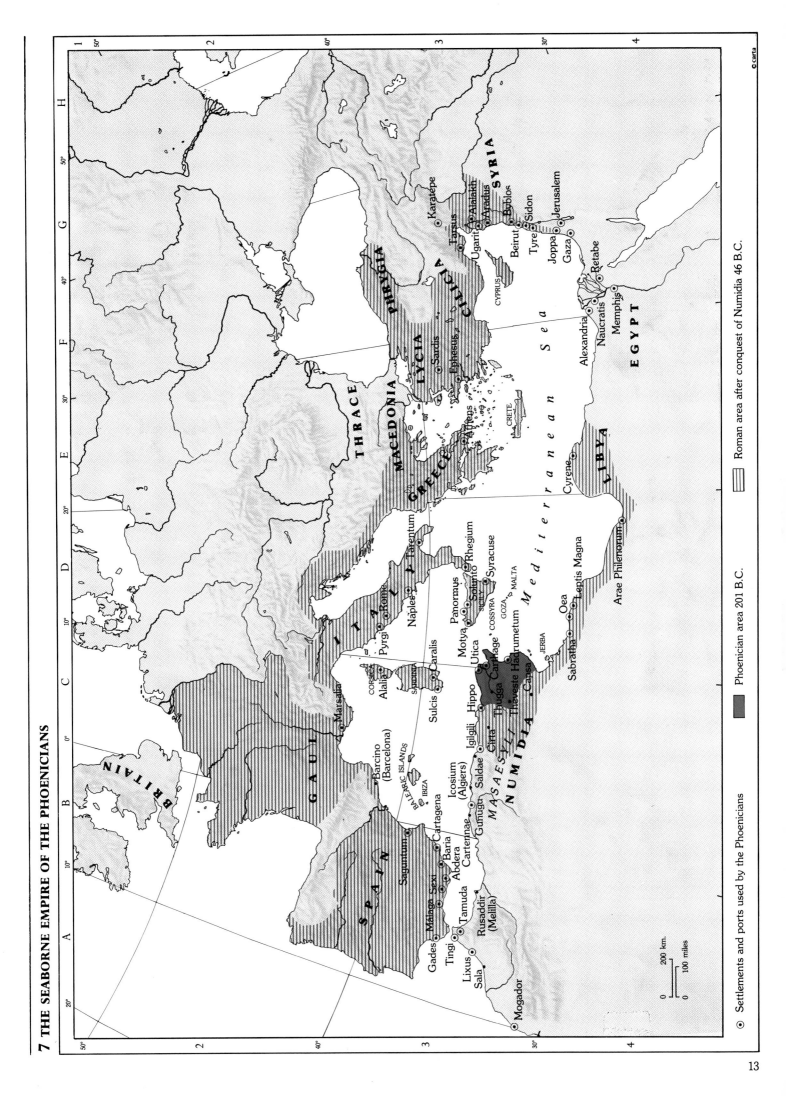

7 THE SEABORNE EMPIRE OF THE PHOENICIANS

BRITAIN

GAUL

SPAIN

Marsalia

Barcino (Barcelona)
BALEARIC ISLANDS
IBIZA

Saguntum
Cartagena
Malaga Sexi
Baria
Abdera
Cartennae
Icosium (Algiers)
Saldae
Gumugu
Cirta

Gades
Tingi
Lixus
Sala
Mogador
Tamuda
Rusaddir (Melilla)

CORSICA
Alalia
SARDINIA
Sulcis
Caralis

ITALY
Rome
Pyrgi
Naples
Tarentum

THRACE
MACEDONIA
GREECE
Athens
Rhegium
Syracuse

PHRYGIA
LYCIA
Sardis
Ephesus
CRETE

CILICIA
Karatepe
Tarsus
Ugarit
Alalakh
Aradus
Byblos
Beirut
Tyre
Sidon
Jerusalem
Joppa
Gaza
CYPRUS

SYRIA

EGYPT
Alexandria
Naucratis
Memphis
Retabe

Mediterranean Sea

Motya
Utica
Carthage
Hippo
Panormus
Solunto
SICILY
MALTA
GOZA
COSSYRA
Thugga
Theveste
Hadrumetum
Capsa
JERBA
Sabratha
Oea
Leptis Magna

NUMIDIA
MASAESYLI
MASSYLII

Igiligii

LIBYA
Cyrene
Arae Philenorum

© carta

200 km.
0
100 miles
0

◉ Settlements and ports used by the Phoenicians

Phoenician area 201 B.C.

Roman area after conquest of Numidia 46 B.C.

13

8. ANCIENT ISRAEL AND NEIGHBORING KINGDOMS, 10TH TO 6TH CENTURY B.C.

The Palestine of the Bible which occupies the western horn of the Fertile Crescent and links the land masses of Africa and Asia, has been the scene of constant migration, struggle, and conquest. It was a collection of small city-states, up to around 1800 B.C., when a group of nomadic herdsmen — 318 fighting men with their families, flocks, and herds — migrated under the leadership of Abraham from Ur in Chaldaea. They settled near Hebron. Around 1500 B.C. famine forced their descendants to migrate to Egypt, from which they returned around 1250 B.C.

The returning Israelites were loosely organized under tribal leaders. These "Judges," as they were called, had been primarily settlers of tribal disputes; now they emerged as war leaders. Philistine immigrants and native Canaanites had a technological superiority in their knowledge of the use of iron and war chariots. The Israelites were thus forced to unite under a king, Saul (reigned about 1020–1000 B.C.), and to learn the art of war from their enemies. Under David (reigned about 1000–961) the kingdom was consolidated, and Jerusalem became the religious as well as civil capital. Under Solomon (reigned 961–922) a splendid temple, palaces, and other public buildings were erected. The expansion was the result of a great increase in foreign trade with Syria, Egypt, southern Arabia, and perhaps Somalia.

On Solomon's death, the kingdom split into northern and southern segments, possibly representing an ancient division among the tribes. In both kingdoms prophets arose, crying out against injustice and preaching a renewed moral system. In 721 B.C. Israel, the northern kingdom, was seized by Assyria; Judah became a vassal of Egypt at the end of the seventh century. In 605 B.C. Egypt fell to Babylon, and around 597 Jerusalem also surrendered. Some three-thousand citizens were deported. Nevertheless, unabashed, the Jews revolted in around 595/4. The Babylonians again besieged the city. When it fell after eighteen months, it was sacked and Solomon's Temple was destroyed. Numerous citizens were deported to Babylon in 587 B.C. and again in 582, taking their religion and culture with them.

9. THE EMPIRE OF PERSIA

Early in the first millennium B.C., Aryan peoples migrated from north of the Caspian Sea into the south-western part of modern Iran, which borders the Persian Gulf. These people were absorbed into an already existing civilization that dated back to around 4000 B.C. This area was later known to the Greeks as Persis, and to the Arabs as Fars. Here grew the great cities of Persepolis, Pasargadae, and Susa. In the north their kinsmen, the Medes, had settled south of the Caspian Sea in the region of modern Azerbaijan, with a capital at Ecbatana (Hamadan). They took Nineveh from the Assyrians in 612 B.C. and destroyed their empire.

Some sixty years later, in 550 B.C., an obscure Persian, Cyrus II, succeeded in gaining a hegemony over the Medes, and then absorbing neighboring Assyria, Mesopotamia, Armenia, and Cappadocia. Finally, in 538 B.C., he took Babylon, whence he allowed the Jews to return from exile. His successor, Cambyses II, extended the conquest to Egypt, but his successor failed to conquer the Greek states.

This huge and ramshackle empire was held together by satraps, or local governors, and by a constitution remarkable for the stability of its laws and the extent to which the "Great King" was constrained by convention "that altereth not." Thus in Babylon the "Great King" was a Babylonian monarch, in Egypt he was a pharaoh. The governors, virtual kings wielding both civil and military authority, were nevertheless subject to scrutiny by inspectors, who were known as the "king's eye" and the "king's ear." The governors were responsible for a comprehensive taxation system based on a survey of the whole empire, on lines similar to the Domesday Book. Perhaps the greatest binding force was language; Aramaic was the official language of record, displacing local languages, including Hebrew, except for religious purposes. The system of satraps gave way to the consolidated empire of Alexander the Great.

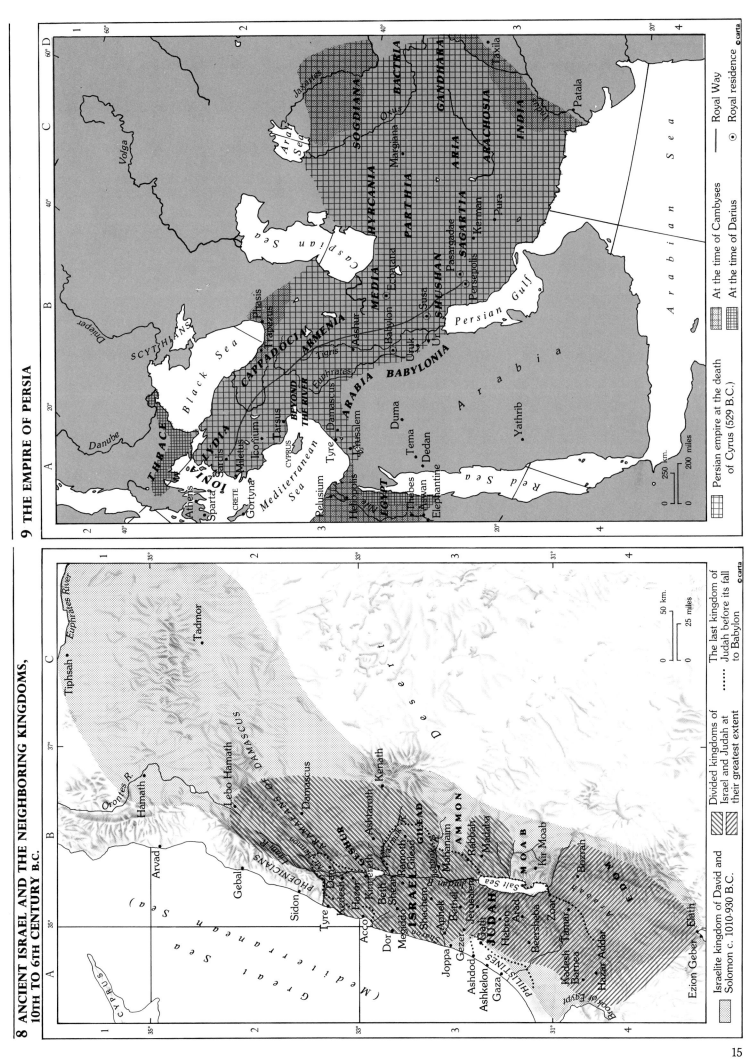

**8 ANCIENT ISRAEL AND THE NEIGHBORING KINGDOMS,
10TH TO 6TH CENTURY B.C.**

Israelite kingdom of David and
Solomon c. 1010-930 B.C.

Divided kingdoms of
Israel and Judah at
their greatest extent

The last kingdom of
Judah before its fall
to Babylon

9 THE EMPIRE OF PERSIA

Persian empire at the death
of Cyrus (529 B.C.)

At the time of Cambyses

At the time of Darius

Royal Way

⊙ Royal residence

15

10. THE EMPIRE OF ALEXANDER THE GREAT AND ITS DIVISION AMONG HIS SUCCESSORS

Alexander the Great's short life (353–323 B.C.) and reign (336–323 B.C.) mark a crossroads in European and Asiatic history. In a Mediterranean and Oriental world fragmented among many small powers, he moved the centers of Hellenic civilization from Greece and Macedonia as far as the Punjab, instituting a Hellenic cultural empire that was effective from Gibraltar to the Hindu Kush in Afghanistan. Alexander was the greatest general the world had yet seen, and few have ever equaled him. He initiated a new age that, in the form of Greek monarchies, was the precursor of the Roman Empire and of Christianity as a world religion. This achievement survived in different cultural forms in empires in both East and West, as Byzantium and the caliphate, Charlemagne and the Ottoman empire, in Imperial Russia and Austria, and the transitory empires of Britain and France.

The map displays his achievements in Greece and Asia Minor, and then in the Levant, Egypt, and northern Africa. The road to his real goal, the conquest of Persia, now lay open. The defeat of the Persians at Gaugamela was decisive, and, as an act of revenge for earlier Persian wars against Greece, Xerxes' palace at Persepolis was burnt. Media was occupied in 330 B.C.. Adopting the Persian title "Great King," he campaigned in central Asia and, in 327 B.C., India.

His conquest was not one of destruction. Rather, it was of the foundation of cities and the organization of commerce. He had a special interest in geography, exploration, and natural history. Administration was conducted through satraps, governors on the Persian model. Strictly controlled, between 326 and 324 B.C. over a third of them were accused of corruption and superseded.

Alexander's final aims are not known. His untimely death at the age of thirty led to the breakup of the empire under his principal generals. The Seleucids failed to hold the East together. In Egypt the Ptolemies reigned as Pharaohs from Alexandria. In the West, the Roman star had yet to rise.

11. ROME IN THE MIDDLE EAST

During the second century B.C. Rome slowly developed influence in Asia Minor. By around 90 B.C., after various diplomatic and military setbacks, Mithradates, the king of Pontus, had created an empire on the Black Sea that stretched as far as India and challenged Roman commercial supremacy in western Asia Minor. Following several wars, in 70 B.C., Pompey made Syria a Roman province, while Lucullus drove Mithradates out of Asia Minor into Armenia. Asia Minor was now Rome's chief source of revenue.

From 57 to 55 B.C. Judaea rebelled against Rome, which had come face to face with the Parthian empire (see map 9). In 40 B.C., in an attempt to reinforce indirect rule, Herod was made King of Judaea. After 30 B.C., Rome became the direct ruler of Egypt. From 27 B.C., when Octavian was proclaimed emperor as Augustus, until the Arab invasion in the seventh century A.D. (see map 19), the whole area of the Levant was organized under a constitutional government. Arabia proper was never conquered, but the Roman frontier was to some extent secured by the client kingdoms of Ghassan and Nabataea. In the north, Armenia and Parthia presented continuous problems. The optimum frontier was the Euphrates. In an area that had become deeply Hellenized under Alexander's successors (see map 10), the Jews stood alone in declining to acknowledge the state religion of the Pantheon and the deified Roman emperors. Their rebellion in A.D. 67 resulted in the devastation and ruin of Jerusalem, but not of the great trading city of Alexandria. By A.D. 72, the Euphrates was again Rome's frontier. In A.D. 73, Masada, the last Jewish stronghold, fell as the defenders committed mass suicide. After a further rebellion, Jerusalem was rebuilt as a Roman colony in A.D. 135.

In the following centuries, the long struggle between Rome and its successor, Byzantium, continued. Christianity, which was to change the character of world civilization (see map 13), blossomed, with Alexandria as its intellectual center until it suffered partial eclipse at the hands of Islam (see maps 14 ff.).

10 THE EMPIRE OF ALEXANDER THE GREAT AND ITS DIVISION AMONG HIS SUCCESSORS

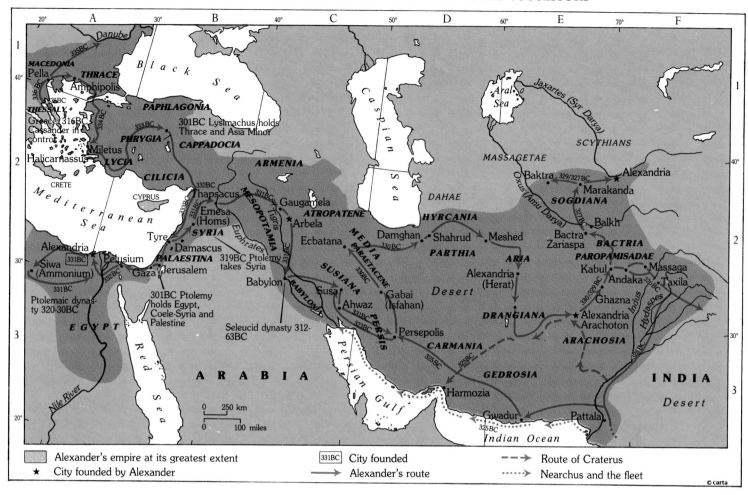

	Alexander's empire at its greatest extent	331BC	City founded		Route of Craterus
★	City founded by Alexander	→	Alexander's route		Nearchus and the fleet

11 ROME IN THE MIDDLE EAST

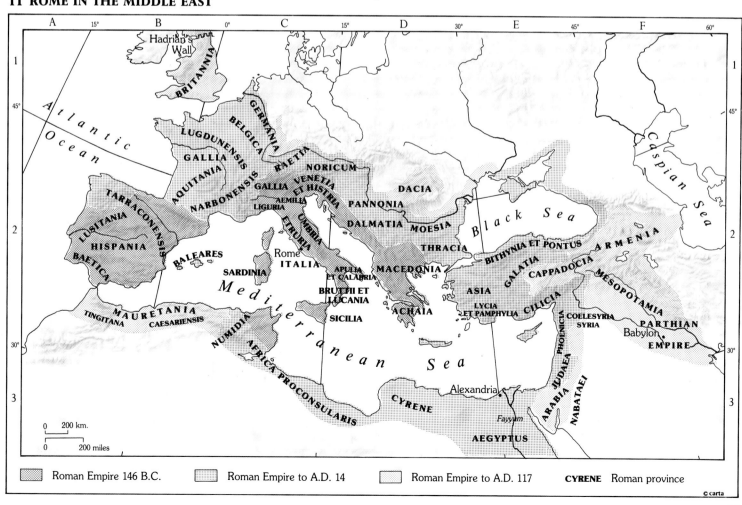

Roman Empire 146 B.C.   Roman Empire to A.D. 14   Roman Empire to A.D. 117   **CYRENE** Roman province

12. COMMERCE WITH THE MIDDLE EAST, c. A.D. 50

Already by 1000 B.C. ships sailed the Indian Ocean from ports in the Persian Gulf. They traded with southern Persia and western India, and with Indian vessels voyaging in reverse. Farther west Pharaohs had already traded down the coast of the Red Sea to Punt, possibly northern Somalia. By 116 B.C., Eudoxus of Cyzicus had sailed to India and back — a practice that Strabo would regard as normal in A.D. 6.

Written around A.D. 50, the anonymous *Periplus of the Erythraean Sea* presents a report on Egyptian and Arab trade in the Indian Ocean, in which Aden was an important entrepôt. Finds of Roman coins and pottery in India attest to a greatly increased volume of trade, which under the emperor Augustus extended down the eastern coast of Africa, as well as to India and, possibly, China. These voyages were seasonal and regular and had access on arrival at Egyptian ports to organized land transport services using camels and donkeys. Similar services were found in the southern Arabian ports whence caravans set off for the Levant and Syria.

Although records are in Greek, this was simply the lingua franca of the time; the operators were Egyptians and Arabs, who often settled abroad as agents, intermarried locally, and learned the local languages. The principal bases of this commerce were luxury goods — ivory, tortoise shell, rhinoceros horn, spices, frankincense, precious stones, fine cloth, silk and pepper — in demand in the Mediterranean region and distributed by long-established sea and land routes used for ordinary commerce. It was the Roman emperor Tiberius who complained that "the ladies and their baubles are transferring our money to foreigners." Nevertheless, to India went expensive manufactured cloth, glass-ware, copper, tin, lead, cosmetics, silver, wine, with slaves and slave girls.

13. THE EXPANSION OF CHRISTIANITY, FIRST TO FOURTH CENTURIES

Before the sudden emergence of Islam most of the Middle East was Christian. During its first two centuries relatively small areas had been converted, either from Judaism or from pagan cults. These areas were chiefly urban — potent areas of theological development where Jewish concepts of monotheism and Greek philosophy met and coalesced. Aside from these intellectual levels, the new religion offered all, without distinction of race or social status, a spiritual life in sacraments accessible to all and the promise of resurrection to eternal life.

Alexandria, in which a catechetical school had been founded before 155, was the leading center of advanced study by the early third century. Rome, Carthage, Lyons, and cities in Asia Minor had similar centers. In Palestine, Origen, the most brilliant and original thinker the church had yet seen, taught chiefly in the capital, Caesarea Maritima. Here, in the early fourth century Eusebius Pamphili, the first ecclesiastical historian, became bishop.

At a popular level, a monastic movement was born — first in Egypt, then Palestine, then throughout the Roman world — devoted to ascetical exercises, the psalms and the scriptures. Antony of Egypt gave inspiration to the first monasteries, to which Pachomius later gave order and discipline. To these monks, and their routine of prayer, manual work, and study, the contemporary world owes its schools, universities, and hospitals.

Under Constantine the Great (reigned 306–337), Christianity became a state religion. His motives have been variously assessed, but his concern was genuine. The institution of church councils, an agreed canon, or rule, of scripture, a recognized calendar, and systematic theology all spring from Alexandrian thought and teaching. Imperial involvement had its dangers, and local reactions emerged as separatist, heretical movements, weakening the entire body and providing an effective opening for Islam.

12 COMMERCE WITH THE MIDDLE EAST, C. A.D. 50

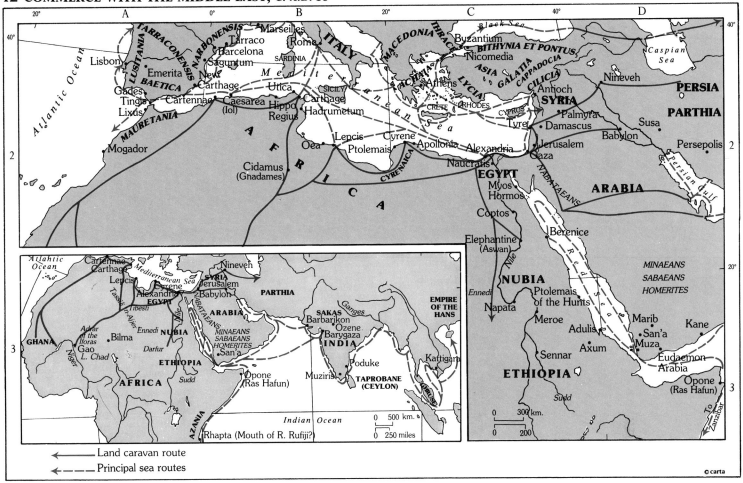

Land caravan route
Principal sea routes

13 THE EXPANSION OF CHRISTIANITY, FIRST TO FOURTH CENTURIES

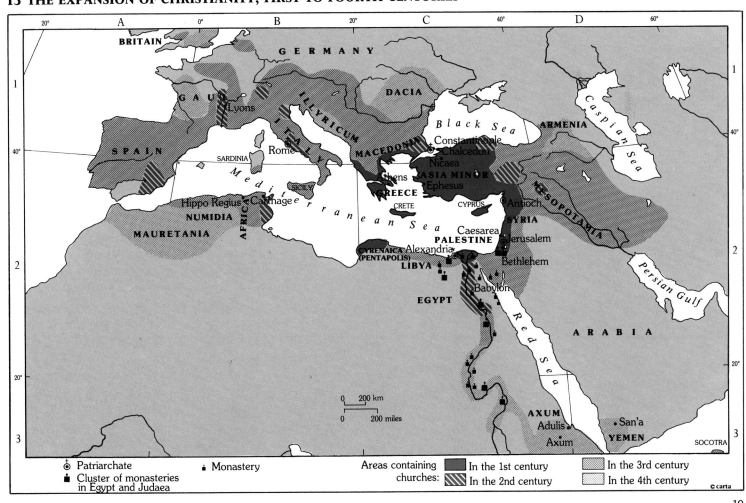

⊕ Patriarchate
■ Cluster of monasteries in Egypt and Judaea
▪ Monastery

Areas containing churches:
In the 1st century
In the 2nd century
In the 3rd century
In the 4th century

14. ARABIA FROM THE BIRTH OF THE PROPHET MUHAMMAD C. 570 TO THE CALIPHATE OF ABU BAKR

The birth of the Prophet Muhammad is traditionally dated in 570 or 571. In that year an army from Persia occupied Yemen, and an Axumite (Aksumite) army from Ethiopia, which had occupied Yemen from 525, attacked Mecca. It is known as the Year of the Elephant, for their force included an elephant, never before seen in Arabia. Ten years before, a fifty-year peace had been made between Byzantium and Persia. In 572, the emperor Justin II refused to continue the annuity to Persia, and war ensued until 591. Persia took the stronghold of Dara in 574, and Byzantium had to secure a year's truce by the payment to Persia of 45,000 gold pieces. In the following year the Axumites were finally evicted from Yemen by the Persians, who made it a viceroyalty. The rest of Arabia was divided among a number of petty kingdoms and nomadic tribes with shifting allegiances. Among the most prominent were Tadmor (Palmyra), Ghassan, Lakhm, Nabataea, and in the far south the ancient line of Himyar. Many of these kingdoms and tribes were clients of Persia. In the Hijaz and Najd the vast majority of the inhabitants were nomads, with poetry as their only expression of art. Mecca is located in the Hijaz, and Medina in an enclave between Hijaz and Najd. Some idea of the historical situation is conveyed in map 15, Claudius Ptolemy's map of Arabia. Originally composed around 150, this map underwent numerous recensions until his *Geography* reached its present form in around 450. It is thus impossible to ascribe a precise date to it.

Muslim historians refer to the time before the Prophet as al-Jahiliyah, the Days of Ignorance. If, as now, the Bedouins had little or no idea of religion, in southern Arabia there were elaborate cults with ornate temples. In Petra and Palmyra, the sun god and astral deities were popular. Natural objects, trees, wells, caves, and stones, were conceived as sacred. At Mecca, Arab authors believed that the well Zamzam had given water to Hagar and Ishmael, and that in the Ka'aba was a black meteorite, the Black Stone, which had been given to Ishmael by the angel Gabriel, who instructed him in the ceremonies of the pilgrimage. In this sanctuary numerous deities were worshipped, of whom Allah, the principal but not the only god of the Meccans, was believed to be the creator and provider of all good. In addition to Jewish settlements in the north, there were colonies of Christian and Jewish merchants, with Medina as the principal settlement of Judaized clans of Arab and Aramaean origins. Among Christians, heterodox as well as orthodox beliefs were present, and parallels to Muhammad's teaching can be found in a variety of Christian sects.

Muhammad's adult life falls into two distinct periods. From A.D. 610 to 628 he taught in Mecca; in 628 until his death in 632, he resided in Medina. It was in this latter period that he emerged as a ruler and lawgiver. In 630, he made the pilgrimage to Mecca and smashed the many idols in the sanctuary, said to have numbered 360. In 631, his secular power had developed to the point that he was able to conclude treaties with Christian and Jewish tribes and to receive delegations of allegiance from almost all Arabia. In the following year, he again made the pilgrimage; he died three months later, in June 632. The suddenness of the Prophet's death was catastrophic, and the unification of Arabia that had begun had to be renewed under the caliph Abu Bakr (r. 632–634) in the so-called secession, or apostasy, wars. These had the effect not only of completing unification, but also of training and coordinating armies for the period of conquest that was to follow, even though this was hardly the primary intention.

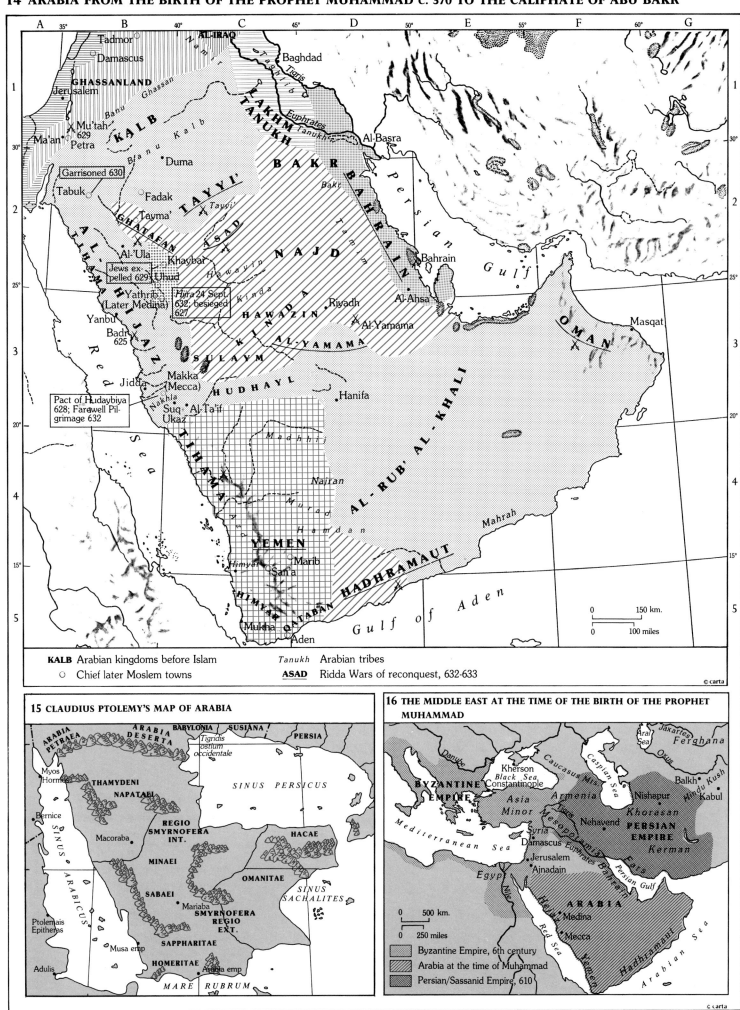

14 ARABIA FROM THE BIRTH OF THE PROPHET MUHAMMAD C. 570 TO THE CALIPHATE OF ABU BAKR

Tadmor
Damascus
GHASSANLAND
Jerusalem
Ma'an
Mu'tah
629
Petra
AL-IRAQ
Baghdad
KALB
LAKHM
TANUKH
Banu Ghassan
Ghassan
Banu Kalb
Duma
Garrisoned 630
Tabuk
Fadak
BAKR
Al-Basra
BAHRAIN
Tayyi'
ASAD
NAJD
Bahrain
Al-Ula
Khaybar
Jews expelled 629
Uhud
Yathrib
(Later Medina)
Hijra 24 Sept 632; besieged 627
Yanbu
Badr 625
SULAYM
Makka (Mecca)
Jidda
Pact of Hudaybiya 628; Farewell Pilgrimage 632
Nakhla
Suq Ukaz
Al-Ta'if
HUDHAYL
Hanifa
Kinda
HAWAZIN
Riyadh
Al-Yamama
AL-YAMAMA
Al-Ahsa
OMAN
Masqat
Persian Gulf
TIHAMA
Madhhij
Najran
Murad
Hamdan
YEMEN
Marib
Himyar
San'a
HIMYAR
Mukha
QATABAN
Aden
HADHRAMAUT
AL-RUB' AL-KHALI
Mahrah
Gulf of Aden
Red Sea

0   150 km.
0   100 miles

KALB Arabian kingdoms before Islam
○ Chief later Moslem towns

Tanukh Arabian tribes
ASAD Ridda Wars of reconquest, 632-633

© carta

15 CLAUDIUS PTOLEMY'S MAP OF ARABIA

ARABIA PETRAEA
ARABIA DESERTA
BABYLONIA
SUSIANA
PERSIA
Tigridis ostium occidentale
Myos Hormos
THAMYDENI
NAPATAEI
SINUS PERSICUS
Bernice
REGIO SMYRNOFERA INT.
HACAE
Macoraba
MINAEI
OMANITAE
SINUS ARABICUS
SABAEI
SMYRNOFERA REGIO EXT.
SINUS SACHALITES
Ptolemais Epitheras
Mariaba
SAPPHARITAE
Musa emp
HOMERITAE
Arabia emp
Adulis
MARE RUBRUM

16 THE MIDDLE EAST AT THE TIME OF THE BIRTH OF THE PROPHET MUHAMMAD

Danube
Jaxartes
Aral Sea
Ferghana
BYZANTINE EMPIRE
Kherson
Black Sea
Constantinople
Caucasus Mts.
Caspian Sea
Oxus
Balkh
Hindu Kush
Asia Minor
Armenia
Nishapur
Kabul
Mediterranean Sea
Syria
Mesopotamia
Damascus
Euphrates
Tigris
Nehavend
KHORASAN
PERSIAN EMPIRE
Kerman
Jerusalem
Ajnadain
Egypt
Nile
Fars
Bahrain
Persian Gulf
Red Sea
ARABIA
Medina
Mecca
Yemen
HADHRAMAUT
Arabian Sea

0   500 km.
0   250 miles

▦ Byzantine Empire, 6th century
▨ Arabia at the time of Muhammad
▩ Persian/Sassanid Empire, 610

© carta

21

17. SEMITIC LANGUAGES AND THE DEVELOPMENT OF THE ART OF WRITING

Before 3000 B.C., different forms of pictographic writing had evolved, chiefly in Egypt and Mesopotamia. In these forms, small pictures stood for objects and concepts. Around 1700 B.C., there developed syllabic systems, in which each sign represented a syllable. Thus, in the cuneiform (Latin, *cuneus*, a wedge = form) system that developed in Mesopotamia, almost six-hundred signs were used. Some of these signs had more than one sound-value; some retained a pictographic type of function.

So large a repertoire of signs is obviously inconvenient, as the Chinese system seems to Westerners. It is unknown who first devised the first alphabetic script. There have been many different views, often held with tenacity, but no final conclusion. According to Greek legend, Kadmos, son of Agenor, king of Phoenicia, brought the use of letters to Greece from Phoenicia. Whoever it was, certainly this person was a Semite, for he isolated consonantal sounds and ignored vowels, although later, in Aramaic and Hebrew, and yet later in Arabic, signs to indicate vowels were occasionally used.

The term *Semitic*, was introduced by the German philologist August Ludwig von Schlözer in 1781. It was chosen in the belief that those who spoke a particular group of languages were descended from Shem, son of Noah, as recorded in Genesis 10. This classification was made on a wholly geographical basis and included peoples who did not speak Semitic languages, Elamites and Lydians, and ignored others who did speak them. Among those excluded were Canaanites, who spoke a language closely akin to ancient Hebrew, and the peoples of Arabia and Ethiopia.

The ancient Semitic languages resemble one another as closely as do the Romance languages in Europe. They share easily definable characteristics: the predominance of triconsonantal roots, the similar formation of nominal and verbal stems, the use of personal pronouns to inflect verbs, and the use of two principal tenses — incomplete and completed time. These characteristics, with, of course, many local differences, persist to this day over a wide range of languages, all of them ultimately descended from Ur-Semitic (or primitive Semitic), now long extinct.

The earliest of these languages, known as old Akkadian, was in use in Iraq between 2400 and 2200 B.C. Although derivatives of it survived long after, it eventually gave way to another Semitic language, Aramaic, the official language of the Persian empire of Cyrus II (see map 9). Parallel to Aramaic were the languages of Canaanitic origin: Phoenician and Punic; the language of Carthage; Hebrew; and the speech of certain adjacent peoples, such as the Moabites and Edomites. These two branches are known as West Semitic (derivatives of Canaanite) and East Semitic (derivative of Aramaic), the latter being the first to disappear. From Canaanite, modern Hebrew is a descendant; and from Aramaic, a number of existing a languages and dialects descend. South Semitic forms a separate branch, from which descend northern and southern pre-Islamic languages, together with classical and modern Arabic in all its forms, the languages of Ethiopia, and small, archaic language groups in Yemen and Socotra.

17 SEMITIC LANGUAGES AND THE DEVELOPMENT OF THE ART OF WRITING

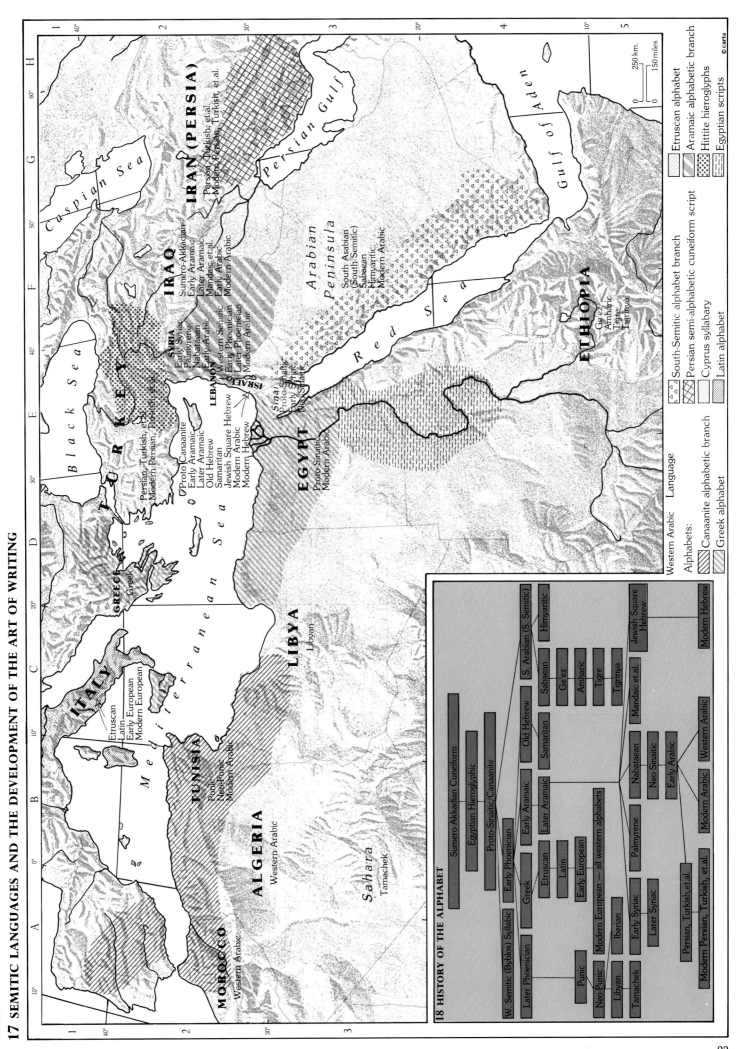

© carta

Language   Western Arabic

Alphabets:

Canaanite alphabetic branch

Greek alphabet

South-Semitic alphabet branch

Persian semi-alphabetic cuneiform script

Cyprus syllabary

Latin alphabet

Etruscan alphabet

Aramaic alphabetic branch

Hittite hieroglyphs

Egyptian scripts

IRAN (PERSIA)
Persian, Turkish, et al.
Modern Persian, Turkish, et.al.

IRAQ
Sumero-Akkadian
Early Aramaic
Later Aramaic
Mandaic et.al.
Early Arabic
Modern Arabic

SYRIA
Early Syriac
Palmyrene
Nabataean
Early Arabic
Modern Arabic

LEBANON
Western Semitic
Early Phoenician
Later Phoenician
Modern Arabic

ISRAEL
Proto-Canaanite
Early Aramaic
Later Aramaic
Old Hebrew
Samaritan
Jewish Square Hebrew
Modern Arabic
Modern Hebrew

EGYPT
Proto-Sinaitic
Modern Arabic

Sinai
Proto-Sinaitic
Early Syriac
Neo-Sinaitic

ETHIOPIA
Ge'ez
Amharic
Tigre
Tigrinya

Arabian Peninsula
South Arabian
(South Semitic)
Sabaean
Himyaritic
Modern Arabic

TURKEY
Persian, Turkish, et al.
Modern Persian, Turkish, et.al.

GREECE
Greek

ITALY
Etruscan
Latin
Early European
Modern European

TUNISIA
Punic
Neo-Punic
Modern Arabic

LIBYA
Libyan

ALGERIA
Western Arabic

MOROCCO
Western Arabic

Sahara
Tamachek

Caspian Sea

Persian Gulf

Gulf of Aden

Red Sea

Black Sea

Mediterranean Sea

250 km.
150 miles

18 HISTORY OF THE ALPHABET

Sumero-Akkadian Cuneiform

Egyptian Hieroglyphic

Proto-Sinaitic/Canaanite

Early Phoenician

Early Aramaic

Later Aramaic

S. Arabian (S. Semitic)

Himyaritic

Sabaean

Ge'ez

Amharic

Tigre

Tigrinya

Old Hebrew

Samaritan

Mandaic et.al.

Jewish Square Hebrew

Modern Hebrew

Greek

Etruscan

Latin

Early European

Modern European — all western alphabets

Nabataean

Palmyrene

Neo-Sinaitic

Early Arabic

Modern Arabic

Western Arabic

Persian, Turkish, et.al.

Modern Persian, Turkish, et.al.

Early Syriac

Later Syriac

W. Semitic (Byblos) Syllabic

Later Phoenician

Punic

Neo-Punic

Libyan

Tamachek

Iberian

19. THE ARAB CONQUEST OF SYRIA, IRAQ, AND PERSIA

By A.D. 629 and 630, Arabs from the peninsula had raided Byzantine territory in southern Syria. In 633, regular operations began with as many as nine-thousand men. This army was later expanded to 22,500. Amr ibn al-As led along the coastal route via Aylah. Yazid I ibn Abi-Sufyan attacked southern and southeast Syria. The generalissimo Abu Ubaydah ibn Jarrah proceeded along the ancient trade route to Damascus. On 4 February 639, the Byzantine troops facing Yazid I were almost annihilated; around the same time, Khalid ibn al-Walid led a raid into Iraq and seized al-Hira (Hira). He then turned northwest and, after a brilliant forced march, outflanked the Byzantine army. He defeated the Byzantines at Ajnadain on 30 July 634, laying almost all Palestine open. After a further Byzantine rout in January 635, Khalid laid siege to Damascus. After the city surrendered in September, all the great cities of Syria fell.

The emperor Heraclius's army of fifty-thousand men was defeated decisively at the battle of the Yarmuk on 20 August 636. Only Jerusalem and Caesarea held out — the former until 638, the latter until 640. The superficiality of the Hellenization of Syria was now exposed: an Arab ruler was preferable to an alien.

In Iraq the Arabs left behind by Khalid were almost annihilated by a Persian force near al-Hira on 26 November 634. On 31 May or 1 June 637, an enlarged Arab army defeated the Persian force in southern Iraq, whose inhabitants had sentiments similar to their Syrian fellow Semites. Later in June, the Arabs made a triumphal entry into Ctesiphon. They now possessed the most sophisticated capital in the east and endless booty. Garrisons were established at al-Kufa and Basra. In the Persian highlands, the Sassanian dynasty of Yazdagird III stood out, but all was over when, in 641, al-Mawsil (Mosul) was captured, and the Persian army was annihilated at Nehavend.

20. THE ARAB CONQUEST OF EGYPT

It was obvious to Amr ibn al-As that as long as the Arab left flank was exposed to Byzantine forces in Egypt, the conquests of Khalid ibn al-Walid in Syria and Persia were insecure. Amr had known Egypt well from caravan trading in his youth, and now he took advantage of the caliph Umar I's visit to Jerusalem to seek permission to cross to Egypt.

In December 639, Amr and four-thousand cavalrymen reached al-Arish via the route that Abraham had taken and that later Cambyses II, Alexander, the Holy Family, and, finally, Allenby would take. Napoleon would take this route in reverse.

In January 640 al-Farama (Pelusium) fell after a month's siege. Amr at once marched on Babilyun (Babylon), where a Roman fort dominated the peak of the Nile Delta, the present-day Old Cairo (see map 48). Shortly thereafter, he was reinforced by ten-thousand men, thus bringing an army of fourteen-thousand against the twenty-five thousand Byzantines. Amr attacked at 'Ayn Shams (Heliopolis) in July 640. The patriarch Cyrus tried to buy peace and failed. The fortress capitulated on 6 April 641.

Amr still had to take the Delta. Nikiu fell on 13 May, but Alexandria, the commercial capital of the world, lay ahead. Alexandria was a splendid city, garrisoned by fifty-thousand men and backed by the whole Byzantine navy. On 8 November the Byzantines capitulated. The Coptic population of native Egyptians had no love for the Byzantines, and the poll tax exacted by the Muslims was less onerous. In spite of their numbers the Byzantines had no stomach to fight an enemy that had so often defeated them.

Amr had now to provide an administration. (For his mosque and buildings, see map 48.) A camp was set up with a defensive ditch, whence its name al-Fustat, the fosse. The old Pharaonic canal connecting the Nile with the Red Sea was reopened, and trade could flow between the Red Sea and the Mediterranean. The Byzantine administrative system was maintained for the Coptic clerks could hardly be replaced by warriors from the desert.

19 THE ARAB CONQUEST OF SYRIA, IRAQ AND PERSIA

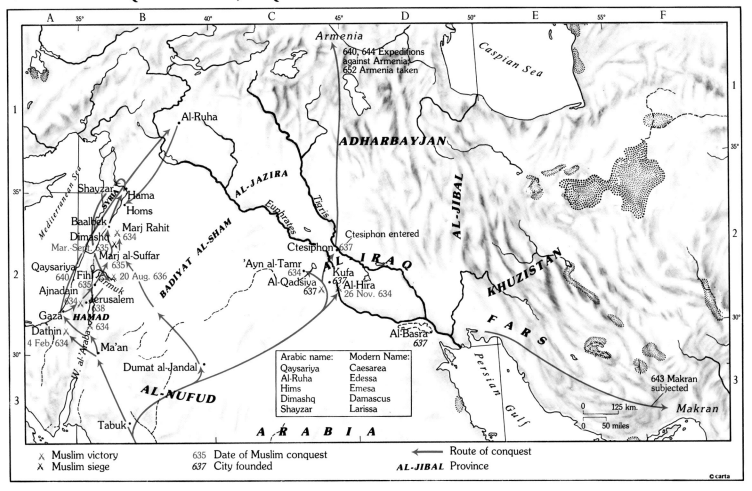

Arabic name:	Modern Name:
Qaysariya	Caesarea
Al-Ruha	Edessa
Hims	Emesa
Dimashq	Damascus
Shayzar	Larissa

× Muslim victory   635 Date of Muslim conquest   ← Route of conquest

✗ Muslim siege   637 City founded   AL-JIBAL Province

© carta

20 THE ARAB CONQUEST OF EGYPT

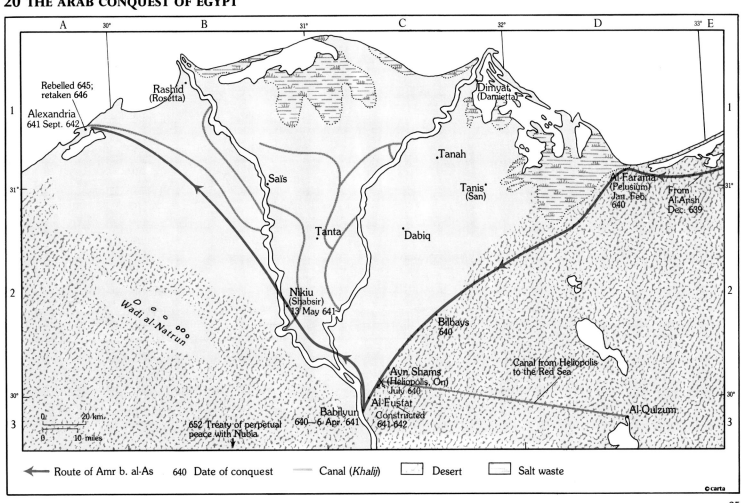

← Route of Amr b. al-As   640 Date of conquest   Canal (*Khalij*)   Desert   Salt waste

© carta

21. THE ARAB CONQUEST OF NORTH AFRICA AND SPAIN

Although Alexandria had been acquired, the Byzantine fleet presented a continual threat. In 649 a Muslim fleet was built for the Egyptian rulers in Alexandria, enabling the seizure of Cyprus. A struggle for mastery continued into the ninth century (see map 26).

It remained to secure Egypt's western flank. In 642–643 Amr ibn al-As led his cavalry into the Libyan Pentapolis, or Cyrenaica. Barca (Barqa) was occupied without difficulty, and several Berber tribes submitted to him. Amr's brother Abdullah pushed further to Tripoli and then into the Byzantine province of Africa, receiving tribute from Carthage. In the south a treaty was made with the Nubian kingdom of Dongola, providing the Arabs with an annual tribute of slaves.

In the west no attempt at further conquest was made until 670, when Uqbah ibn Nafi founded Kairouan (Arabic, Qayrawan, from Persian, *karwan*, caravan) as a military base. Here his splendid mosque still stands. Uqbah advanced westward until, according to tradition, his horse was stopped by the Atlantic. Under the governorship of Hassan ibn al-Numan al-Ghassani, the Byzantines were driven from Carthage in 698; Hassan now had to face Berber resistance, led by a prophetess (Arabic, *kahinah*) until she was defeated by treachery. His successor, Musa ibn Nusayr, subdued the north African coast. In 711 his lieutenant, Tariq ibn Ziyad, a Berber freedman, led a raid into Spain, crossing at Gibraltar, which carries his name (Arabic: Jabal al-Tariq, the mountain of Tariq).

A wholesale campaign of conquest began. On 19 July 711, Tariq's twelve-thousand men defeated Roderick's army of twenty-five thousand. Thereafter the conquest was virtually a ceremonial parade, and by the end of the summer Tariq held half of Spain. Acting out of jealousy, Musa put Tariq in chains, and recalled him. On the same grounds, the caliph recalled Musa to Damascus, which he entered in 715 with four-hundred Visigothic princes and a huge retinue of slaves and prisoners bearing booty. The Arabs had seized the fairest of the Byzantine provinces.

22. THE UMAYYAD CALIPHATE

Muhammad left no constitutional arrangements for a successor. As prophet he could have none. The first three caliphs succeeded simply as senior tribal elders. Ali, the fourth caliph, was acclaimed because he was Muhammad's first cousin and the husband of his daughter Fatima, introducing the prospect of hereditary legitimacy which led to a quarrel between the Sunnites and Shi'ites, the traditionalists and sectarians. The latter supported Ali, who was murdered at the instigation of Muawiyah, governor of Damascus and leader of the Sunnites, on 24 January 661.

The new dynasty, proclaimed in Jerusalem, established Damascus as capital. Under this dynasty, north Africa was added to the caliphate (map 21), and Khorasan and Turkestan were raided. Muawiyah had substantial administrative abilities and gave order and discipline to the army. The civil service was reorganized on Byzantine lines, and a period of stability was inaugurated. An immense free-trade area was now open to commerce.

Under the reigns of his grandson, Abd al-Malik ibn Marwan (685–705), and his four sons (705–743) the Islamic empire reached its greatest extent, from the Atlas Mountains and the Pyrenees to the Indus River and even into China. This area far surpassed that of the Roman Empire and even the empire of Alexander the Great. Khorasan, Sughd (Sogdiana), Khwarizm, and Farghana were the crossroads of east-west trade. Trade with India after the conquest of Sind (711–712) enabled the magnificence of the Umayyad mosques and palaces. The Dome of the Rock in Jerusalem, among the most splendid of man's architectural achievements, belongs to this period.

The Umayyad state was now an Arab state; Arabic was the official language, and there was an Arab currency, postal service, chancery, and judiciary. An immense construction program included new irrigation canals. Though the desert austerity of the Muslim population now gave way in this period of prosperity to drunken debauchery and lechery, poetry, music, and other cultural values survived.

21 THE ARAB CONQUEST OF NORTH AFRICA AND SPAIN

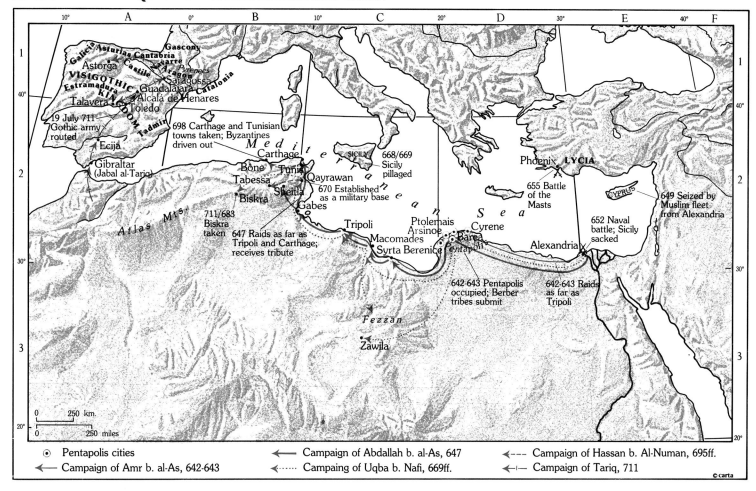

⊙	Pentapolis cities	←	Campaign of Abdallah b. al-As, 647	←--- Campaign of Hassan b. Al-Numan, 695ff.
←	Campaign of Amr b. al-As, 642-643	←·····	Campaing of Uqba b. Nafi, 669ff.	←—I Campaign of Tariq, 711

22 THE UMAYYAD CALIPHATE

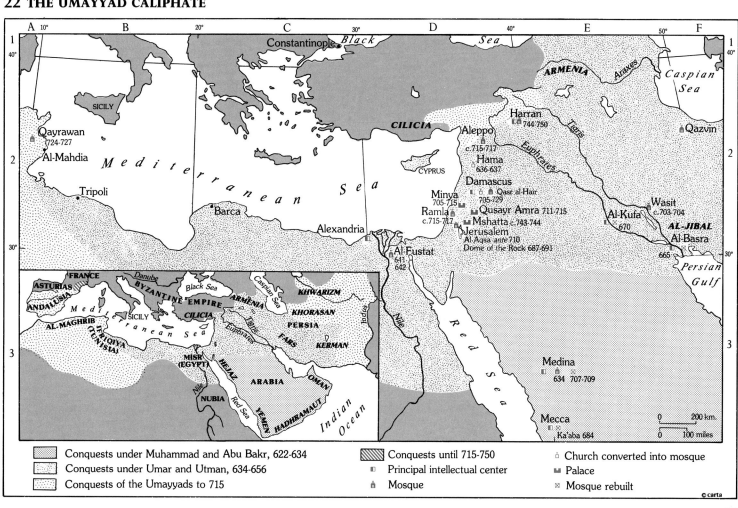

▓ Conquests under Muhammad and Abu Bakr, 622-634		▨ Conquests until 715-750	⌂ Church converted into mosque
⠿ Conquests under Umar and Utman, 634-656		▫ Principal intellectual center	▪ Palace
⠿ Conquests of the Umayyads to 715		⌂ Mosque	⊠ Mosque rebuilt

23. THE ABBASID CALIPHATE

Even during the reign of Yazid II (720–724) the caliph was accustomed to pass his time hunting, wining, and in the harem. Poetry and music were more entertaining than the Koran (Qur'an) and affairs of state. Hence when the descendants of al-Abbas, an uncle of the Prophet, pressed their claim to the throne, they rapidly gained adherents, especially among the Persians. Thus it was in Khorasan that Abu al-Abbas was first proclaimed caliph in 750. The new dynasty lasted 508 years with Baghdad as its capital and in shadow form in Cairo until 1517. After the ninth century, however, caliphs reigned rather than ruled.

The Abbasid caliphate was a theocratic state. The caliph wore the *burdah* (cloak) of the Prophet at his accession and on state occasions. As in medieval Europe, the caliph was surrounded by canon lawyers, among whom were Persians and other non-Arabs. Though Spain slowly began to be lost to the caliphate (see map 25), by 762, when Baghdad was founded (see map 27), the empire was solidly established. As described in *One Thousand Nights and a Night*, the reign of Harun al-Rashid (786–809) launched an era of prosperity in which the arts and sciences blossomed.

The weakness of this highly bureaucratic state lay in its army. The Arabs had never had a standing army with discipline, training, and tradition. A caliphal bodyguard provided a nucleus of infantry, archers, cavalry, engineers, and naphtha-throwers. Persians from Khorasan formed this nucleus until 833, when they were replaced by Turks. By 836 these were the terror of Baghdad. The caliph built a new capital at Samarra (map 28), where the habits of the Roman Praetorian Guard were speedily reproduced. The empire slowly dissolved into governorships, often with the hereditary title of sultan, with the caliph no more than a shadow.

24. ARABS IN THE MEDITERRANEAN IN THE 9TH CENTURY

During the ninth century, two Muslim powers — in the east the Abbasid caliphate, in the west the Aghlabids from Ifriqiya (approximately modern Tunisia) — disputed Byzantine supremacy in the Mediterranean. In 797 the caliph Harun al-Rashid had campaigned in Asia Minor as far as Ephesus and Ankara; and this démarche against the Byzantines was undoubtedly related to the caliph's relationship with Charlemagne between 797 and 806. In the eastern Mediterranean pirates from Crete raided the Aegean Islands and in the tenth century the Greek coast. These operations were random and with merely temporary consequences.

In the western Mediterranean the Aghlabids prosecuted a war of quite different character. The founder of the dynasty, Ibrahim ibn al-Aghlab (r. 800–811) was the Abbasid governor of Ifriqiya, who declared himself independent within a year of his appointment. Thereafter no Abbasid authority was exercised in the area.

The Mediterranean was now surrounded by Islamic powers on the west, south, and east. It was logical that the successors to the Carthaginians would dispute control of the central Mediterranean, and this began under Ziyadat-Allah I (r. 817–838) with an expedition against Byzantine Sicily in 827. The conquest of Sicily was not achieved until 902. What began as piratical raids resulted in permanent settlements in Sicily, Sardinia, and in much of Italy south of Naples. In 846 a landing at Ostia failed to take Rome, but the basilicas of St. Peter and of St. Paul's outside the Walls were pillaged. In 849 the Arab fleet was destroyed off Ostia, but this was a temporary setback. In 866–867 Malta, the key to the central Mediterranean, was taken, and from 872 until 882 Pope John II found it prudent to pay tribute. In 882 John II was murdered by the Roman nobility. Two short papal reigns followed, and then in 885 to 886 the Byzantines reoccupied southern Italy under Pope Stephen V.

23 THE ABBASID CALIPHATE

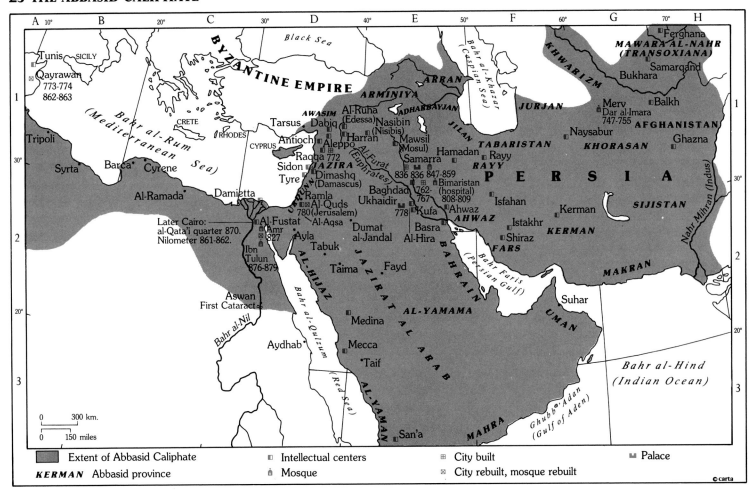

Extent of Abbasid Caliphate
KERMAN Abbasid province
▫ Intellectual centers
⌂ Mosque
⊞ City built
⊠ City rebuilt, mosque rebuilt
▬ Palace

© carta

24 ARABS IN THE MEDITERRANEAN IN THE 9TH CENTURY

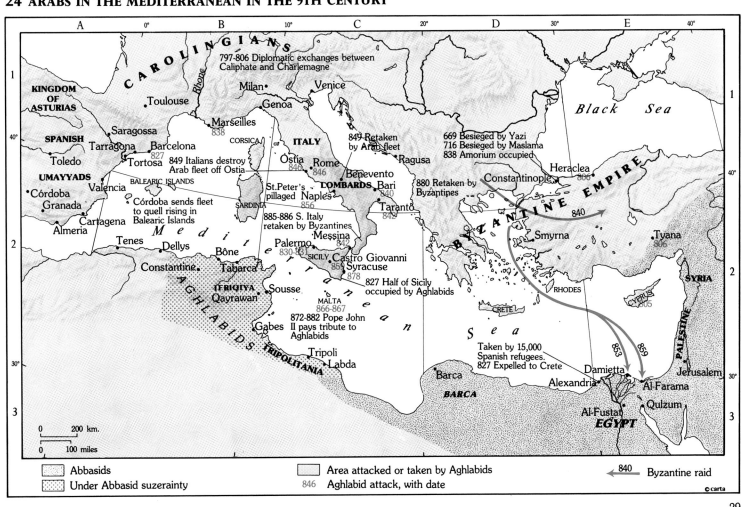

Abbasids
Under Abbasid suzerainty
Area attacked or taken by Aghlabids
846 Aghlabid attack, with date
←840 Byzantine raid

© carta

25. THE UMAYYAD SPAIN AND THE EMIRATE

All but the northwest corner of the Iberian Peninsula was in Arab hands by 715 and answerable to the caliph in Damascus. About 717 or 718 France was raided as far as Narbonne; an attempt on Toulouse was defeated. In 732 Abd al-Rahman al-Ghafiqi stormed Bordeaux and advanced on Tours. After a day of battle with Frankish forces under Charles Martel, the Arabs slipped away during the night. It was not so much a victory as the beginning of an ebbtide. In 759 the Arabs relinquished Narbonne and finally withdrew from France.

The capital of the emir, or lieutenant-governor subject to the provincial governor at Kairouan, was at first in Seville and then in Córdoba. The emirate was torn between factions of Arabs from Syria and Yemen and the Berbers from North Africa. In 755, following the overthrow of the Umayyads in Damascus by the Abbasids, the Spanish Umayyad emirate declared its independence. Abd al-Rahman I, a survivor of the Umayyad massacre by the Abbasids, seized power in Córdoba. Many years of struggle among Arabs of different origins, Berbers, Goths, Hispano-Arabs, Numidians, Syrians, and the earlier mixed populations of the peninsula followed. The zenith of Moorish Spain was signified in 788 by the building of the Great Mosque of Córdoba, with its forest of columns and arches, splendid mosaics, and monumental outer court. Though transformed into a cathedral in 1236, it is still known as la Mezquita (mosque in Spanish). Córdoba now rivaled Baghdad as a cultural center and mediated Eastern culture and barbaric Europe. Whereas the rulers were Muslims, the majority of the population remained Christian, affecting Arab culture. In 854 a Christian writer remarked:

Our Christian young men with their elegant airs...are...intoxicated with Arab eloquence...knowing nothing of the beauty of the Church's literature, and looking down with contempt on the streams of the Church that flow forth from Paradise....Hardly a man in a thousand can write a letter to inquire after a friend's health intelligibly [in his native language] but can learnedly roll out grandiloquent periods in the Chaldaean tongue.

26. ISLAMIC DYNASTIES IN THE EAST, 9TH TO 11TH CENTURIES

After the murder of the caliph al-Mutawakkil by his guard in December 861, the history of the caliphate presents a confused picture of disintegration and unstable rule by a series of puppets of the Turkish troops. Spain, North Africa, Egypt, and the Levant had long been lost. At one time in the mid-tenth century, three former caliphs, all blinded, could be seen in Baghdad begging for bread.

From 945 until 1055 a succession of *amirs al umara* (emirs above all emirs) ruled, making and unmaking caliphs. The Buwayhids had come from the southern shores of the Caspian Sea, and in the first half of the tenth century they had taken Persia and Iraq. They preferred Persia as a residence, and Baghdad was governed as a province from Shiraz. Under Adud al-Dawlah, Buwayhid power was at its zenith; he assumed the title of the ancient rulers of Persia, *shahanshah*, underlining the essentially Persian character of the Shi'ite dynasty. This character is also reflected in the building of mosques, shrines, hospitals, public buildings, and canals. The Bimaristan al-Adudi, a hospital in Baghdad with a teaching faculty, was the most sophisticated of its time. Tolerant to all, the Buwayhids repaired even churches and monasteries.

Buwayhid power was swept away by the advent of the Seljuq (Seljuk) Turks. Family quarrels were tearing apart the Buwayhids when the Seljuq Tughril Beg entered Baghdad in 1055. This family had originated in the Kirghiz Steppe of Turkestan; it then settled near Bukhara and fought its way into Khorasan and finally through Persia to Isfahan. As the Turkomans entered Baghdad, the last Buwayhid governor fled. The caliph al-Qa'im hailed Tughril as "King of the East and West" and invested him with the title sultan ("he who has authority"), the first time that this title was used in Islam.

25 THE UMAYYADS IN SPAIN AND THE EMIRATE

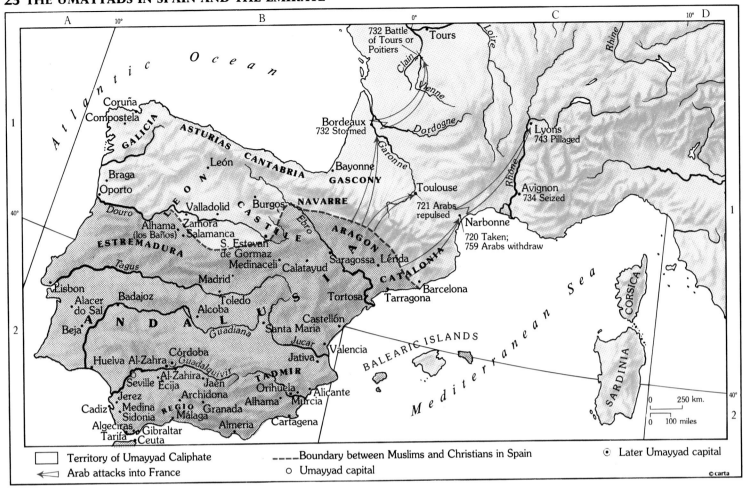

Territory of Umayyad Caliphate

Arab attacks into France

- - - - Boundary between Muslims and Christians in Spain

o Umayyad capital

⊙ Later Umayyad capital

732 Battle of Tours or Poitiers
Tours
Bordeaux 732 Stormed
Lyons 743 Pillaged
Bayonne
GASCONY
Toulouse
Avignon 734 Seized
721 Arabs repulsed
Narbonne 720 Taken; 759 Arabs withdraw
Coruña
Compostela
GALICIA
ASTURIAS CANTABRIA
NAVARRE
León
Braga
Oporto
Valladolid
Burgos
ARAGON
CASTILE
Zamora
Alhama (los Baños)
Salamanca
S. Estevan de Gormaz
Medinaceli
Saragossa
Lérida
CATALONIA
ESTREMADURA
Tagus
Madrid
Calatayud
Barcelona
Tarragona
Lisbon
Badajoz
Toledo
Alcoba
Tortosa
Alacer do Sal
Castellón
ANDALUS
Guadiana
Santa Maria
Beja
Jucar
Jativa
Córdoba
Valencia
Al-Zahra
Huelva
Guadalquivir
TADMIR
Al-Zahira
Jaén
Orihuela
Alicante
Seville
Ecija
Archidona
Alhama
Murcia
Jerez
REGIO
Granada
Cartagena
Cadiz
Medina Sidonia
Málaga
Almeria
Algeciras
Gibraltar
Tarifa
Ceuta

BALEARIC ISLANDS
CORSICA
SARDINIA
Mediterranean Sea
Atlantic Ocean

250 km.
100 miles

© carta

26 ISLAMIC DYNASTIES IN THE EAST, 9TH TO 11TH CENTURES

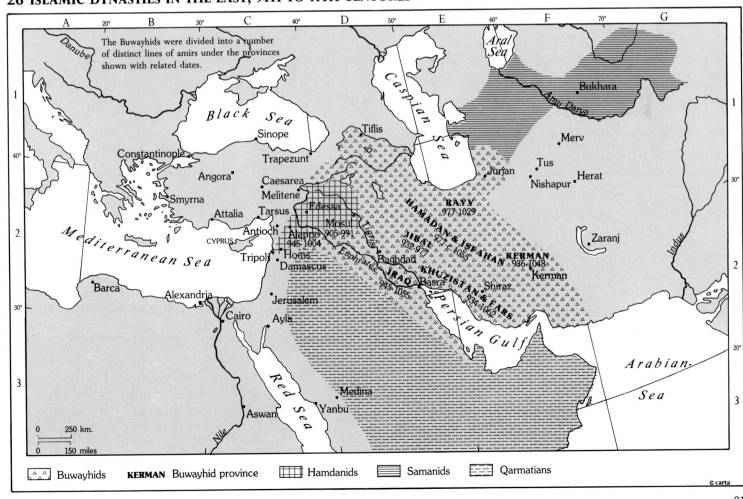

The Buwayhids were divided into a number of distinct lines of amirs under the provinces shown with related dates.

Danube
Aral Sea
Black Sea
Caspian Sea
Bukhara
Sinope
Amu Darya
Constantinople
Trapezunt
Merv
Tiflis
Angora
Caesarea
Jurjan
Tus
Nishapur
Herat
Smyrna
Melitene
RAYY 977-1029
Attalia
Tarsus
Edessa
HAMADAN & ISFAHAN 977-1055
Zaranj
Antioch
Mosul 905-991
JIBAL 932-977
Aleppo 945-1004
Baghdad
KERMAN 936-1048
Tripoli
Homs
Euphrates
Damascus
Tigris
IRAQ 945-1055
KHUZISTAN & FARS 934-1062
Kerman
CYPRUS
Basra
Shiraz
Barca
Mediterranean Sea
Alexandria
Persian Gulf
Jerusalem
Cairo
Ayla
Arabian Sea
Red Sea
Medina
Nile
Yanbu
Aswan

250 km.
150 miles

△ Buwayhids **KERMAN** Buwayhid province ▦ Hamdanids ≡ Samanids ⋮ Qarmatians

© carta

31

27. THE CITY OF BAGHDAD, 9TH CENTURY

Khatib al-Baghdadi, described his native city as the "navel of the universe." It was indeed a commercial center and the capital of the Abbasid caliphate until it was overtaken by Fatimid Cairo (see map 48) and subsequently razed by the Mongols in 1258.

The caliph al-Mansur chose the site for his capital in 762 for military, economic, and agricultural reasons. Originally a small Persian settlement during the Achaemenid dynasty, it was at the crossroads of river and caravan routes to east and west and north to south. Situated on a fertile plain, it was traversed by irrigation canals that afforded rich cultivation and water supplies to a substantial human population and their cattle. With Basra as a port of transit, smaller vessels came up river. The Tigris similarly brought commerce from the north. It was healthy and free from mosquitoes.

Baghdad was planned initially as a round city, with a high defensive wall. Inside were empty spaces for maneuvers and then a second wall. The caliphal palace, located in the center, was surrounded by yet a third wall, which enclosed the great mosque and official buildings. High officials and officers lived between the third and second walls. Outside were suburbs, provided for different ethnic groups — Arabs, Khwarizmians, and Persians — and different vocations — soldiers, merchants, and craftsmen. Each had its own mosques, shops and markets. Altogether they formed on the west side of the Tigris a remarkable example of town planning, for which a team of architects with 100,000 craftsmen and laborers was employed.

On the east side of the Tigris a palace and mosques were provided for the caliph's heir, al-Mahdi, with houses for his officers and a commercial quarter. Poets celebrated the splendid palaces and houses, the wonderful furnishings, restful gardens, and green countryside.

After civil disorder in the early ninth century Turkish mercenaries were recruited as caliphal guards. The Turks soon fell foul of the Arabs in the army, and for this reason al-Mutasim and other caliphs resided at Samarra from 836 until 892. Baghdad, however, remained the center of commercial and cultural activity and continued to grow in extent outside the walls.

In 892 the caliph al-Mutamid returned to Baghdad. He and his son, al-Mutadid (892–902) rebuilt the palace and added other palaces, prisons, and a racecourse. Al-Muktafi's palace, built between 901 and 907, was an architectural curiosity for it had a high dome, on which he could ride on a donkey. Al-Muqtadir added palaces, a zoo, and a silver tree with eighteen branches, on which silver and silver-gilt birds shrilled and sang. The lion house had a hundred beasts.

There were numerous markets — fruit, meat, cloth, flowers, gold, books, with a special one for Chinese merchandise only. The volume and scope of trade necessitated a banking system. There were innumerable mosques and baths. Many mosques had *madrasas* (residential teaching colleges) attached. Culturally, the city was also important for its schools of law and translation, hospitals, and libraries. There were numerous *ribats*, built during the twelfth century as hostels for Sufi religious ascetics and mystics. The most outstanding of the mystics was al-Ghazzali, a Persian by birth, whose teaching had influence on Thomas Aquinas.

In the last century of the caliphate there were numerous floods and fires. Weak government brought in its train riots and pillage, and irrigation was neglected. On 10 February 1258 the city fell an easy prey to the Mongol army of Hulagu Khan. Estimates of those killed vary from 800,000 to two million. In 1261 the last caliph of Baghdad was carried off to Cairo as a prisoner of the Mamluk Baybars, but the city lived on a half life under local, Turkoman, Persian, and finally Ottoman rulers.

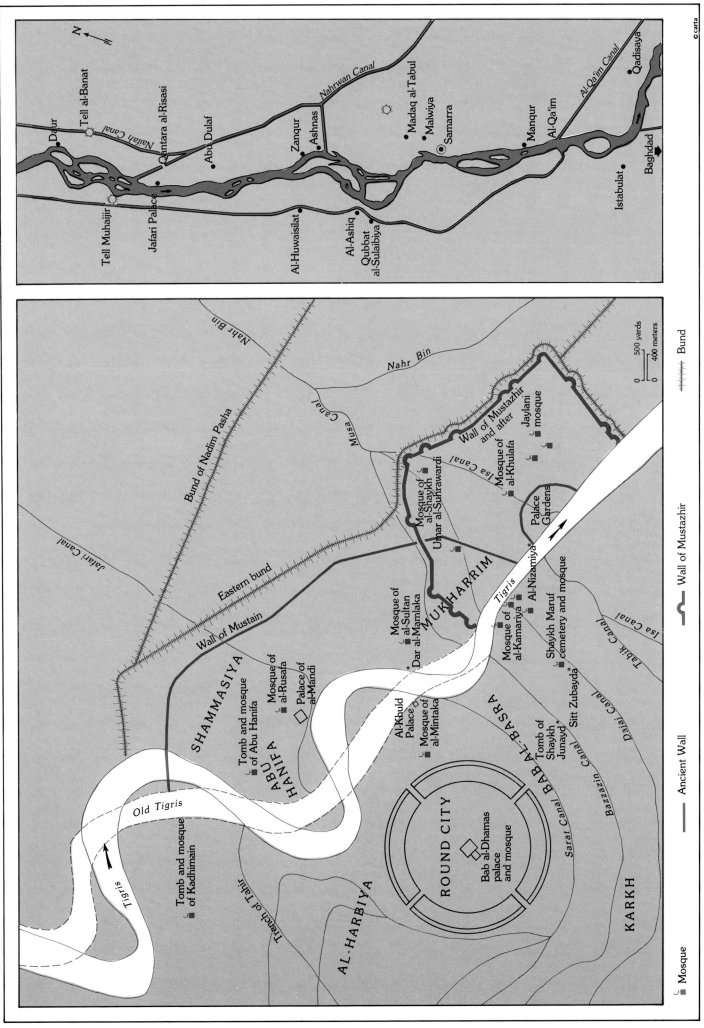

27 THE CITY OF BAGHDAD, 9TH CENTURY

ROUND CITY

Bab al-Dhamas palace and mosque

AL-HARBIYA

KARKH

Trench of Tahir

Old Tigris

Tigris

Tomb and mosque of Kadhimain

ABU HANIFA

SHAMMASIYA

Tomb and mosque of Abu Hanifa

Mosque of al-Rusafa

Palace of al-Mandi

Al-Khuld Palace

Mosque of al-Mintaka

BAB AL-BASRA

Tomb of Shaykh Junayd

Sitt Zubayda

Shaykh Maruf cemetery and mosque

Mosque of al-Kamariya

Al-Nizamiya

Palace Gardens

Tigris

MUKHARRIM

Mosque of al-Sultan

Dar al-Mamlaka

Wall of Mustain

Eastern bund

Bund of Nadim Pasha

Jafari Canal

Nahr Bin

Nahr Bin

Musa Canal

Isa Canal

Mosque of al-Shaykh Umar al-Suhrawardi

Mosque of al-Khulafa

Jaylani mosque

Wall of Mustazhir and after

Tabik Canal

Isa Canal

Dajlal Canal

Bazzazin Canal

Sarat Canal

500 yards
400 meters

Bund

Wall of Mustazhir

Ancient Wall

Mosque

28 THE CITY OF SAMARRA, 9TH CENTURY

N

Daur

Tell al-Banat

Qantara al-Risasi

Nailah Canal

Tell Muhajir

Jafari Palace

Abu Dulaf

Zanqur

Ashnas

Nahrwan Canal

Al-Huwaisilat

Al-Ashiq

Qubat al-Sulaibiya

Madaq al-Tabul

Malwiya

Samarra

Manqur

Al-Qa'im

Al-Qa'im Canal

Istabulat

Baghdad

Qadisaya

© carta

33

29. DYNASTIES IN NORTH–WEST AFRICA, 757 TO 976

As the Battle of Poitiers (1356) marked the turn of the tide of Arab expansion in Spain and France, Berber nationalism, latent even in Roman times, began to reassert itself in north-west Africa by the mid-eighth century. In the region of Sijilmasa the Midrarite dynasty dominated the region from 757 until 976, as did the Rustamids at Tahert from 776 until 906; in the region of Fez (Arabic, Fas) a dynasty founded by Idris ibn Abdallah, a great-great-grandson of the caliph Ali, ruled from 788 until 974. In what is now Tunisia (with some of Algeria) Ibrahim ibn al-Aghlab was appointed governor by Harun al-Rashid in 800. He and his descendants ruled as virtually independent sovereigns from 800 until 909.

From their capital at Kairouan the Aghlabids dominated the western Mediterranean. Following raids that began around 827, Sicily was conquered in 902, followed by the fall of Malta and Sardinia. The Great Mosque of Kairouan, erected between 670 and 675, replaced an earlier, humbler building. In it the Koran has been recited continuously by day and by night ever since, and from it went out teachers, who now transformed an outwardly Christian, Latin-speaking province into an Islamic, Arabic-speaking province. Nominally the Aghlabids were subject to the Abbasid caliphs in Baghdad and used the title of emir only. This subjection was of trifling importance in practice, and for western Muslims Kairouan became a fourth holy city, ranking only after Mecca, Medina, and Jerusalem. At the same time the Tunisian cities provided a link with western Africa south of the Sahara — a region rich in gold and salt, essential to the prosperity of Cairo (see map 37). In 909 the Aghlabids were swept aside by the Fatimid dynasty (see map 36).

30. TULUNIDS (868-905) AND IKHSHIDIDS (935-969) IN EGYPT

The disintegration of the Abbasid caliphate that had occurred in the west eventually reached Egypt. Ahmad ibn Tulun, whose father was a Turkish slave from Farghana, had the advantage of an education in Baghdad. He was sent to Egypt in 868. Shortly after becoming governor he ignored the caliph in Baghdad and made himself independent. Egypt thus became an independent state for the first time and was able to enjoy its own revenues. Since the rule of Amr ibn al-As (map 20) Egypt had had more than a hundred governors for an average of two and a half years each, lining their own pockets and transmitting the residue to the caliph. In 877 Ibn Tulun, as he is usually known, added Syria to his domains, with a naval base at Acre. A new capital was built beside al-Fustat, with a great mosque that still exists, together with other magnificent buildings, including a hospital.

Khumarawayh (r. 884–895) who succeeded Ibn Tulun, was a sybarite and an idler, whose wine-swilling habits earned him the contempt of the orthodox. On his death it was thought appropriate that, by coincidence, as his body was lowered into the grave, the Koran readers chorused: "Seize ye him and drag him into the mid-fire of hell." Under his feeble successors the Abbasid caliphs regained Egypt and Syria without difficulty in 905. Thirty years later another Turkish dynasty of Farghana origins, the Ikhshidids (r. 935–969), gained the throne. They speedily regained Syria, and then the province of Hejaz, and its chief towns of Medina and Mecca. Under the reigns of Muhammad al-Ikhshid's two sons, the real ruler was an Ethiopian eunuch and former slave soldier, Abu al-Misk Kufur. He took pleasure in his table, and the daily order for his kitchen, the Arab authors claim, included 100 sheep, 100 lambs, 250 geese, 500 chickens, 1,000 pigeons, and 100 jars of confectionery. A year after his death, the Fatimids seized Egypt.

29 DYNASTIES IN NORTH-WEST AFRICA, 757 TO 976

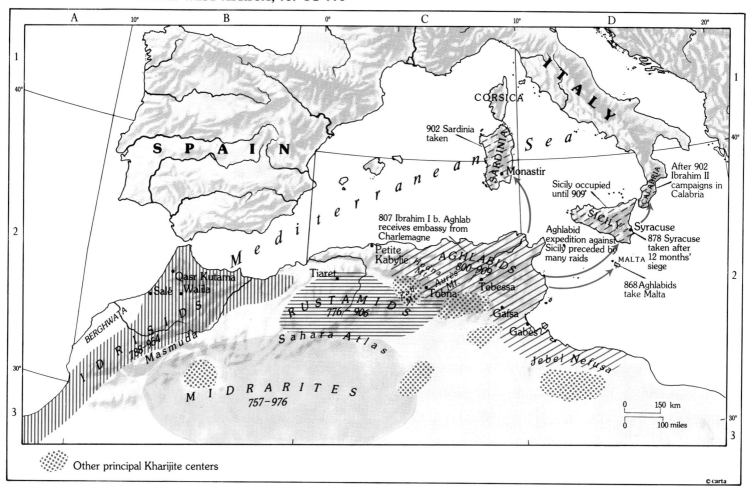

902 Sardinia taken

CORSICA

ITALY

SARDINIA
• Monastir

Mediterranean Sea

SPAIN

807 Ibrahim I b. Aghlab receives embassy from Charlemagne

Sicily occupied until 909

After 902 Ibrahim II campaigns in Calabria

CALABRIA

SICILY

Aghlabid expedition against Sicily preceded by many raids

Syracuse
878 Syracuse taken after 12 months' siege

MALTA

868 Aghlabids take Malta

Petite Kabylie

AGHLABIDS 800-909

• Qasr Kutama
• Salé • Walila

Tiaret •

Hodna Aures Mt.

738 Mt.

Tobna •

Tebessa

BERGHWATA

IDRISIDS 788-974

Masmuda

RUSTAMIDS 776-906

Sahara Atlas

• Gafsa

Gabes •

Jebel Nefusa

MIDRARITES 757-976

0 ___ 150 km
0 ___ 100 miles

⊙ Other principal Kharijite centers

© carta

30 TULUNIDS (868-905) AND IKHSHIDIDS (935-969) IN EGYPT

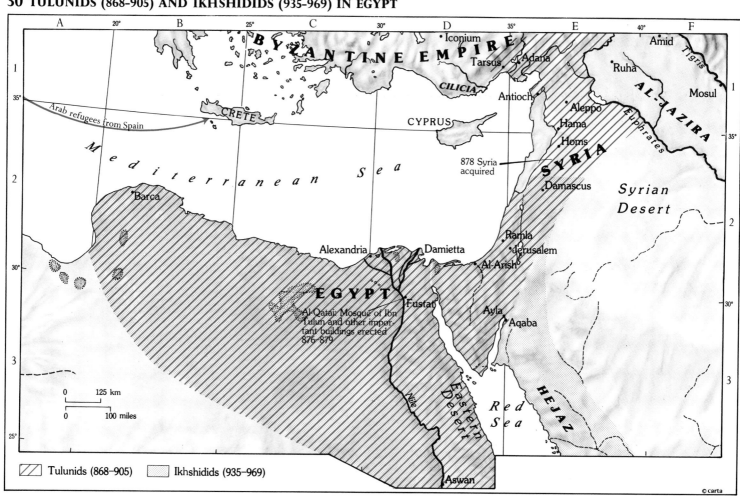

BYZANTINE EMPIRE

• Iconium
Tarsus • Adana

CILICIA

Antioch •

Amid •

Ruha •

AL-JAZIRA

Tigris

Mosul •

Arab refugees from Spain

CRETE

CYPRUS

Aleppo •

Hama •
Homs •

SYRIA

Damascus •

Mediterranean Sea

• Barca

878 Syria acquired

Syrian Desert

Alexandria •

Damietta •

Ramla •
Jerusalem •

Al-Arish •

EGYPT

Fustat

Al Qatai, Mosque of Ibn Tulun and other important buildings erected 876-879

Ayla •
Aqaba •

Nile

Eastern Desert

Red Sea

HEJAZ

Aswan •

0 ___ 125 km
0 ___ 100 miles

▨ Tulunids (868-905)   ⊙ Ikhshidids (935-969)

© carta

35

31. THE TAHIRIDS (820-872), SAFFARIDS (867-908), AND SAMANIDS (874-909)

In the same way that states split off and developed independently from the caliphate in Egypt and the Maghreb, other states grew up east of Baghdad. The first was the quasi-independent state of the Tahirids. Tahir ibn al-Husayn, the descendant of a Persian slave, was made governor of all the lands east of Baghdad in 820. In 822 he omitted mention of the caliph's name in the Friday prayer, substituting his own. His capital was at Merv (Marw). His successors extended his kingdom as far as India, transferring the capital to Nishapur (Naysabur).

In 872 they were superseded by the Saffarids, who took their name from Ya'qub ibn al-Layth al-Saffar (r. 867–878), a coppersmith (Arabic, al-saffar) who had turned brigand. His abilities and chivalrous conduct attracted the attention of the governor of Sijistan, who made him his commander. Ya'qub succeeded his master and ruled almost all Persia and Afghanistan as far as India.

In Transoxiana and part of Persia, the Samanids, a family of Zoroastrian origin from Balkh, ruled from 874 to 909. The dynasty took its name from Saman, a Zoroastrian nobleman. His great-grandson Nasr (r. 874–892) was founder of the dynasty, but it was his brother Isma'il (r. 892–907) who seized Khorasan from the Saffarids in 900. Under Nasr II (r. 913–943) the kingdom was extended to include Sijistan, Kerman, Jurjan, al-Rayy, and Tabaristan, Transoxiana, and Khorasan. Outwardly the Samanids professed allegiance to the Abbasids, but in all other respects they were independent. Bukhara, their capital, together with their leading commercial city, Samarqand, became centers of learning and art, almost overshadowing Baghdad. Persian and Arabian scholarship was protected, and it was in Bukhara that the young Ibn Sina (known in the West as Avicenna) acquired the knowledge of medicine, philosophy, poetry, and philology that caused the Arabs to acclaim him "shaykh and prince of the learned." In 994 the Samanid territory was conquered by the Ghaznavids (map 38).

32. QARMATIAN, SHI'ITE, AND OTHER DYNASTIES, 860-1281

Tradition reports that the Prophet Muhammad said, "The Israelites have been divided into seventy-one or seventy-two sects, and so have the Christians, but my community shall be divided into seventy-three." True or false, by the ninth century opposing sects had formed, with the same fissiparous consequences that are observable in sixteenth century Europe, where also they took on a political form.

A basic division was between Sunni and Shi'ite, between traditionalists and believers in the prescriptive right of the descendants of Ali to the caliphate. A new major division appeared in 827 when a rigid puritanical Mu'tazilite judge asserted that the Koran had been created, as opposed to the orthodox belief that it is the identical representation of a celestial original. Shortly thereafter Baghdad proclaimed the former position to be law, and the caliph al-Ma'mun instituted an inquistion.

In the mid-tenth century the orthodox creed was reestablished in Baghdad, and scholastic theology developed. Its greatest exponent was Abu Hamid al-Ghazzali, a professor at Nizamiyah college. To him is owed the development of Sufism and the mystical practices of the Islamic fraternities, similar in many respects to Christian religious orders. These fraternities contributed significantly to the spread of Islam beyond its Middle Eastern home as far as the Atlantic and sub-Saharan Africa and to Malaysia and China.

In opposition to this orthodoxy the Ismailis, who today claim the Agha Khan as their leader, spread their esoteric doctrines by means of underground missionaries. From the Ismailis in the mid-ninth century Hamdan Qarmat, an Iraqi peasant, organized a secret society that preached a form of communism and set up an independent state in the Persian Gulf. From this society were derived the doctrines that formed the seed of the Fatimid movement in North Africa (map 36). In the eleventh century the Qarmatian movement engendered the Nusayris in northern Syria, while the Fatimids were the progenitors of the Druze in Lebanon and later the neo-Ismailis or Assassins, of Alamut and Syria, both borrowing greatly from Christianity. The Ithna'ashari Shi'ites in Persia and the Zaydites of Yemen represent a middle course, nearer to the Sunni doctrine, and more tolerant of other sects.

31 THE TAHIRIDS (820–872), SAFFARIDS (867–908), AND SAMANIDS (874–909)

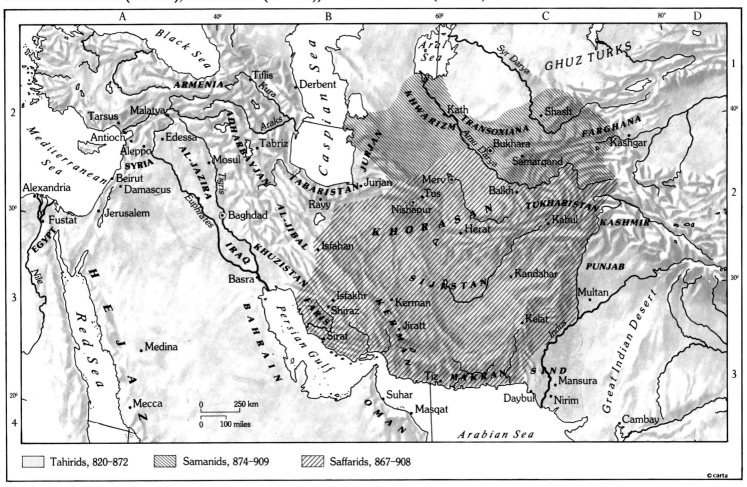

| Tahirids, 820–872 | Samanids, 874–909 | Saffarids, 867–908 |

32 QARMATIAN, SHI'ITE, AND OTHER DYNASTIES, 860–1281

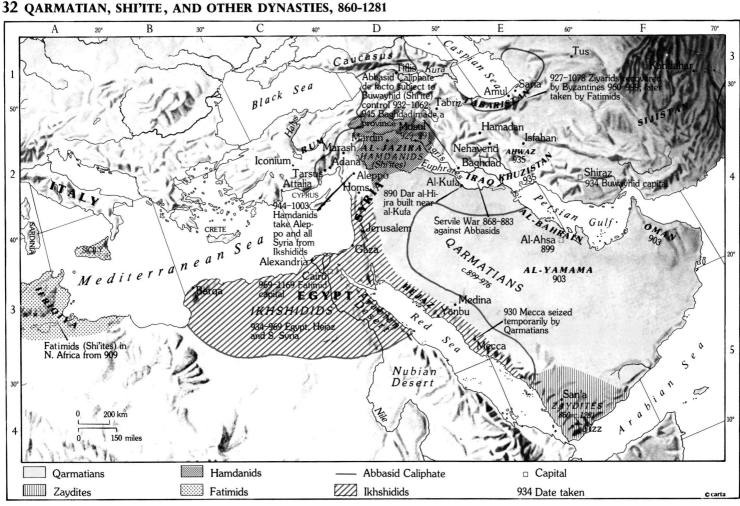

| Qarmatians | Hamdanids | — Abbasid Caliphate | □ Capital |
| Zaydites | Fatimids | Ikhshidids | 934 Date taken |

33. THE WORLD AS KNOWN TO AL-MAS'UDI (D. 956); THE WORLD AS DEPICTED BY IBN HAWQAL, C.988

Abu al-Hasan Ali ibn al-Husayn ibn Ali ibn Abdallah al-Mas'udi, usually known as al-Mas'udi, was the most remarkable traveler, historian, geographer, and writer of the tenth century. He is believed to be the descendant of an eminent Companion of the Prophet Muhammad. He was born in Baghdad around 893–898. Nothing is known of his immediate forbears, education, or means of livelihood, but his very extensive travels suggest that he was engaged in commerce. His surviving works show that he was a scholar. He was born at a time when it was considered meritorious among Muslims to travel in order to acquire religious knowledge. He was a Shi'ite, but nothing suggests that he engaged in missionary activity, nor, for that matter, in diplomacy. His interests were not confined to Islam. Unlike other Muslim scholars, he was interested in non-Muslim communities — Christians, Jews, Manichaeans, Sabaeans, and Zoroastrians. He was not less interested in heretical sects, and he recorded his debates and discussions with their learned adherents. He also took an interest in flora and fauna, in meteorology and dendrology, in tides, minerals, merchants, warriors, ordinary sailors, ancient monuments, and tombs — all of which and more receive mention in his works in a random manner and without any appearance of planning. He made the pilgrimage to Mecca and took the opportunity to attend lectures on genealogy. In Cairo he attended the Coptic festival of the Epiphany, in which Muslims participated with Copts in celebrating not only the visit of the Magi but also the baptism of Christ.

Though it is not possible to construct an itinerary of his journeys because many of his references are simply incidental and given without dates, it is known that in 914–915 he was in Persia and then India. In

Persia he was particularly interested in Zoroastrians. In India he had extensive contacts with merchants in the Indus valley, many of them Arabs from Iraq and Oman. Although some of his remarks suggest that he visited Ceylon and even China, this is unlikely, for his accounts appear to be based on the work of others. In 916 he visited Qanbalu, which possibly refers, as recent archaeology and numismatics show, to Pemba Island off Mombasa. From there he sailed to Suhar, then the capital of Oman. He also describes Siraf and Basra, where he probably acquired his knowledge of China.

After further travels in Syria and on the Byzantine frontier, which included the Christian shrines in Jerusalem and Nazareth and Jewish scholarship in Tiberias, he traveled to Armenia and near the Caspian Sea, thus acquiring a knowledge of the Black Sea and southern Russia. In 941 he was in southern Arabia, in the mountainous country of northern Yemen, Hadhramaut, and Oman. The last fifteen years of his life were spent in Egypt, where he died around 956.

The great age of systematic Arab geography, of which al-Mas'udi was one of the forebears, began with Abu Zayd al-Balki (d. 934), whose work al-Istakri elaborated around 950. Al-Balki's work even had colored maps. At his request Ibn Hawqal (fl. 943–977), who had traveled in Spain, revised his maps and text, later rewriting the whole book. Other contemporaries were al-Maqdisi (also called al-Muqaddasi), whose name implies that he was born in Jerusalem, and al-Hamadani, who was also an archaeologist. These laid the foundation for the later work of twelfth-century geographer and cartographer al-Idrisi (see map 47) and the great geographical encyclopaedia of Yaqut.

34 THE WORLD AS DEPICTED BY IBN HAWQAL, c.988

Principal places mentioned in his *Meadows of Gold*

AL-SIN

Khanfu (Canton)

SARANDIB (CEYLON)

AL-HIND

Kanbaya (Cambay)
Sandjan (Sindan)
Thana (Tana)
Sopara (Subara)
Chaul (Saymur)

Multan

Al-Mansura

Bahr al-Hind

Al-Daybul

Bahr Fars

ARDH AL-TURK

KHORASAN
SIJISTAN (SISTAN)
FARS
KERMAN
KHUZISTAN
Istakhr
Siraf

Isfahan
Hamadhan
Baghdad
Mosul
Qumis
TABARISTAN
Jurjan
Abaskun
Bakuya
Ardabil
Bardha'a
Tarabzunda

ARDH AL-RUS

ARDH AL-KHAZAR

Itil

Bahr al-Khazar

Bab al-Abwab
Tiflis

ARDH AL-RUM

Constantinople

Bahr al-Rum
(Bahr Buntus wa Mayitas)

Adana
Tarsus
Antakiya
Halab
Damascus
Jerusalem
Al-Basra

Al-Quizum

Suhar
HADHRAMAUT
Ma'rib
San'a

AL-AHSA

Medina
Mecca

Bahr al-Quizum

Al-Bahr al-Habashi

Bahr al-Habashi

ARDH AL-HABASHA

ARDH AL-ZANJ

JAZIRA AL-KHADHRA
Qanbalu
ZANJBAR

Alexandria
Al-Fustat

Aswan

Tarabulus

al-Rum

ARDH AL-SAQALIBA
(Land of the Slaves)

Kuyaba (Kiev)

Salunika
(Thessalonika)
Athina
(Athens)

ARDHJA AL-IFRANJA

Bariza (Paris)

Rumiyya (Rome)
Bari
Nabuli (Naples)
Palermo

Tulaytila (Toledo)

Córdoba

Qadis (Cádiz)

Bàhr al-Rum

Tunis
Al-Qayrawan

IFRIQIYYA

Sijilmasa

500 km
250 miles
0

© carta

39

35. THE UMAYYADS IN SPAIN, 950-1050

Abd al-Rahman III al-Nasir (r. 912–961) succeeded to the emirate in 912, and proclaimed himself caliph on 16 January 929. By then the Abbasid caliphs were virtually prisoners of their Turkish mercenary guards, and in North Africa the Fatimids (see map 36) had already laid claim to the caliphate. It was politically important that al-Andalus (Arabic name for the Arab possessions in Spain) should not give the appearance of acknowledging superior. Moreover, the latter years of the reign of Abd al-Rahman's predecessor and grandfather, Abd Allah (r. 888–912), had been years of unrest and rebellion in many provinces, and it was imperative that he restore order and reassert unity. There were also external enemies: in the south, the Fatimids; in the north, the Christian kings of the Asturias and of Léon; in the east, the ancient kingdoms of Aragon and Navarre.

Córdoba, which now had the most splendid court in Europe, had half a million inhabitants, seven-hundred mosques, three-hundred public baths, and a palace with four-hundred rooms and thousands of guards and slaves. Outside the city was the summer palace of al-Zahra. Partly destroyed in 1013, it still has a haunting beauty. An army of more than 100,000 recruits comprised eastern Europeans, so-called Slavs, from which comes the word "slave." The city's yearly revenue was 6,245,000 gold dinars. The army took a third; public works took another third, while a third was put in reserve. Despite the prosperity of his caliphate, al-Rahman, as he died amidst so much magnificence, remarked that he had had only fourteen days of happiness in his life.

His successor, Hakam II (r. 961–976), was a scholar and patron of learning. The Great Mosque of Córdoba housed a university that drew students even from al-Azhar in Cairo and the Nizamiyah in Baghdad. The library contained 400,000 books. Here, for a brief period, was the intellectual capital of the Islamic world.

It was but a short moment of greatness. A son and six nephews followed Hakam II, under whom the caliphate foundered and dissolved into petty states.

36. THE FATIMIDS IN NORTH AFRICA AND EGYPT, 904-1171

The Fatimid dynasty was the only major Shi'ite dynasty in Islam. Whereas orthodox Sunni Muslims hold that the first three caliphs were constitutionally elected, the Shi'ites hold that a divine right of succession to the caliphate vests in descent from the Prophet's daughter Fatima and her husband Ali. By the mid-ninth century the Shi'ites had elaborated an intricate theological system, in which God is always incarnate in a spiritual leader, or imam, who must be a descendant of Fatima and Ali. Accordingly, in Persia and Lebanon the Ismailis and the Assassins evolved, and in North Africa Ubayd Allah al-Mahdi declared himself imam.

Ubayd Allah seized Kairouan from the Aghlabids and Morocco from the Idrisids (map 29). In 914 he took Alexandria, and in 916 his troops devastated the Delta. Sicily, Malta, Corsica, Sardinia, and the Balearic Islands soon fell within his control. He established his capital at al-Mahdia, near Kairouan. Finally, in 969, a Fatimid general took al-Fustat, establishing the caliph al-Mu'izz in Egypt. Shortly thereafter, Mecca and Medina, and all Syria were added. Only Islamic Spain and the Abbasid territories near Baghdad were excepted.

Al-Mu'izz's successor, al-Aziz (r. 975–996), now controlled all the trade routes of the eastern Mediterranean, trading as far as India and eastern and western Africa. A luxurious building program in Cairo was financed by this commerce, of which the most lasting acheivement was the foundation of the university mosque of al-Azhar, later to become the intellectual center of orthodox Sunni Islam. Al-Aziz's son al-Hakim was an insane megalomaniac, and his caliphate followed by a series of youths in the hands of viziers, who tried in vain to control a mercenary army of Turks, Berbers, and Sudanese. The regime was brought to an end in 1171 by Saladin (Salah al-Din), a commander of Kurdish origin (see maps 45 and 46).

35 THE UMAYYADS IN SPAIN, 950–1050

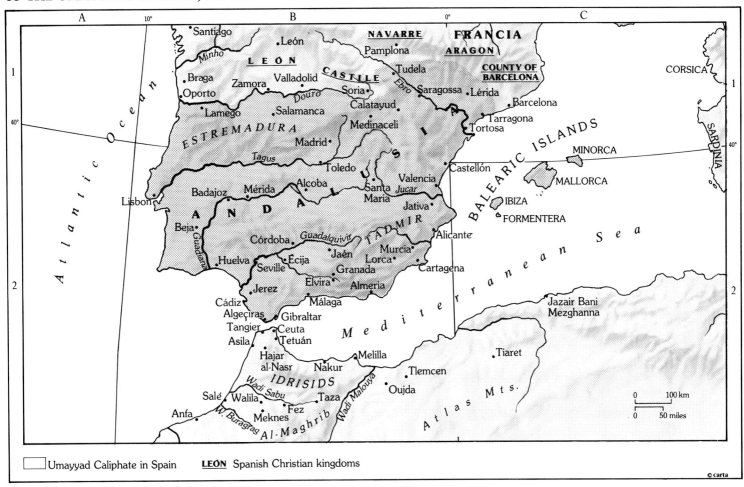

Umayyad Caliphate in Spain   **LEÓN** Spanish Christian kingdoms

36 THE FATIMIDS IN NORTH AFRICA AND EGYPT, 904–1171

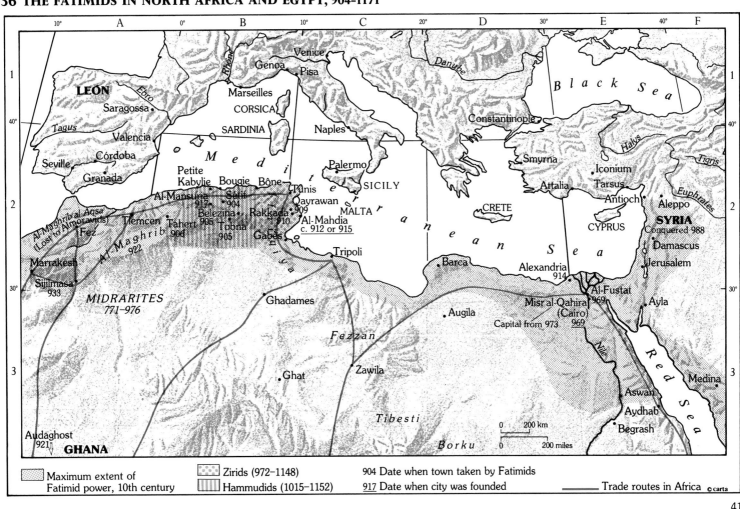

▨ Maximum extent of Fatimid power, 10th century	▦ Zirids (972–1148)	904 Date when town taken by Fatimids
	▥ Hammudids (1015–1152)	917 Date when city was founded
		▬ Trade routes in Africa ©carta

37. NORTH–WEST AFRICA AFTER THE FATIMIDS, 11TH AND 12TH CENTURIES

After 1043 the Fatimid possessions showed obvious signs of disintegration. Fatimid power in Syria shrank before the Seljuqs, and in north–west Africa small principalities reverted to allegiance to the Abbasids in Baghdad. From 1050 to 1052, the Banu Hilal and the Banu Sulaym tribesmen from Nejd and then from Upper Egypt, moved westward and ravaged Tripoli and Tunisia. During this period, Sicily was taken by the Normans, who likewise raided the African coast. In 1055–1056, the Almoravids (Arabic, al-Murabitun) from the Sahara (see map 40) seized Morocco, with its western trade routes, which led to the gold of Ghana and the salt of Teggazza.

The Fatimid caliph al-Mu'izz made the Sanhaja Berber Bulugin ibn Zairi governor in Tunisia and Tripolitania. He and his son paid tribute to Cairo. Under Badis (r. 996–1016), the people became more anti-Shi'ite in sentiment, with the result that al-Mu'izz (1016–1062) threw off the Fatimids and proclaimed allegiance to the Abbasids. At the capital, Mansura, an important textile industry developed, while the seaports of Tunis, Sousse, al-Mahdia and Gabès had an active trade with Egypt, Sicily, Italy, and Spain.

The Hammadid kingdom stretched from near Algiers to the foothills of the Aurès Mountains. It had been set up in 1014 when Hammad, brother of the Zirid emir al-Mansur, broke with his nephew, the emir Badis, and paid fealty to the Abbasid caliph. The capital, Qal'a Beni Hammad, had been founded in 1007, but it was no more than a citadel, for the warlike Beni Hammads, of Sanhaja Berber origin, were fully occupied in resisting the encroachments of the Zenata. These, which at one time had owed allegiance to the caliph in Córdoba, were but bands of rival tribesmen, thus bringing all Morocco into a state of anarchy.

38. THE CONQUEST AND DOMINIONS OF MAHMUD OF GHAZNA (997-1030) AND SUCCESSORS

In 962, Alptigin, a Turkish slave who had risen to be governor of Khorasan, seized Ghazna (present-day Ghazni) from its native rulers and developed what became an empire that extended throughout Afghanistan and the Punjab. The founder of this dynasty was Subuktigin, a slave, who was Alptigin's son-in-law and successor (r. 976–997). His empire extended from Khorasan to Peshawar. His son Mahmud (r. 999–1030) became the most distinguished scion of this dynasty. Between 1001 and 1024 he conducted seventeen campaigns into India, annexing the Punjab, Multan, and part of Sind. This established Muslim influence in the Punjab and brought fabulous riches, the spoils of Hindu temples, to Ghazna. He was the first Muslim warrior to receive the title *Ghazi* for his leadership in war against unbelievers. In the west he took the Persian province of Iraq, including Rayy and Isfahan, from the Shi'ite Buwayhid dynasty. In the north and Khorasan, he held Tukharistan, with its capital Balkh, and parts of Transoxiana and Sijistan.

Ghazna now became a center of culture, with an academy and other magnificent buildings. Mahmud's wealth enabled him to become the patron of poets and men of learning, of whom the most distinguished were the scientist and historian al-Biruni, the historian al-Utbi, and the Persian poet Firdawsi, who had to flee for his life when, as a reward for his sixty-thousand-verse epic *Shahnameh*, he received only 60,000 dirhems instead of the expected 60,000 dinars, and responded with a satirical poem.

The Ghaznavid dynasty, which continued until 1186, marks an important turning point in Islamic history, for it was the beginning of Turkish dominance in Islam, presaging the Seljuq sultanates and the Ottomans.

37 NORTH-WEST AFRICA AFTER THE FATIMIDS, 11TH AND 12TH CENTURIES

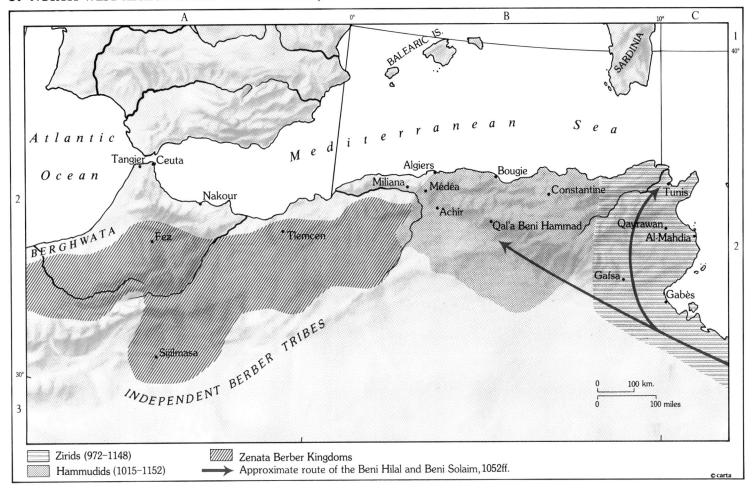

Zirids (972-1148)
Hammudids (1015-1152)
Zenata Berber Kingdoms
Approximate route of the Beni Hilal and Beni Solaim, 1052ff.

© carta

38 THE CONQUESTS AND DOMINIONS OF MAHMUD OF GHAZNA (997-1030) AND SUCCESSORS

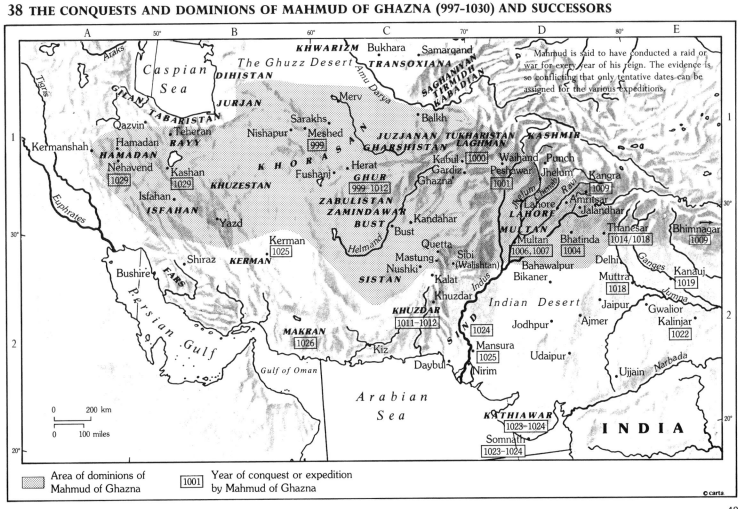

Mahmud is said to have conducted a raid or war for every year of his reign. The evidence is so conflicting that only tentative dates can be assigned for the various expeditions.

Area of dominions of Mahmud of Ghazna

1001 Year of conquest or expedition by Mahmud of Ghazna

© carta

39. LOS REYES DE TAIFAS OR PARTY KINGS IN SPAIN (C.1009-1286)

"In 1002," wrote a monk, "died Almanzor, and was buried in hell." During the rule of Hisham II (r. 976–1009), who succeeded the caliphate at age twelve, political power rested in his mother, Subh (Dawn), whose protégé, Muhammad ibn Abi-Amir, was royal chamberlain. He reduced the caliph to a nullity, shutting him up in the palace. For more than twenty years, up to his death in battle in 1002, he raided North Africa and the Christian kingdoms. In 997 he even raided Santiago de Compostela and robbed the church of its bells and doors.

Fragment by fragment the caliphate dissolved, as local leaders arose. In fact, the caliphate suffered a weakness inherent in all medieval (and some modern) Arab states: it never developed a written constitution or even an unwritten one, buttressed by law and convention. Even at its zenith it never developed beyond the loose organization of of an Arab tribe under a sheikh, chosen from a prominent family and ruling by skill, intrigue, and force.

Córdoba had rulers "whose interest in life," writes Ibn al-Idhari, "centered in sex and stomach, wine-bibbers, cowards and imposters." The Córdobans abolished the caliphate in 1027 in favor of a sort of republic, but they were absorbed by Seville in 1068. Berber families ruled Granada and Toledo; in Granada the real power rested in the hands of a Jewish vizier — similar pattern obtained throughout the peninsula.

The petty states were not without culture. The arts flourished. The failure to produce strong rulers benefited the Christian kingdoms of the north. It was an age par excellence of Christian chivalry, of which El Cid's conquest of Valencia was an example. The Muslim princes now made the fatal error of inviting the Almoravids to assist them, for the Almoravids swallowed the whole peninsula into their North African empire in 1090–1091.

40. THE ALMORAVIDS IN NORTH AFRICA AND SPAIN, 1056-1147

Like many of the petty dynasties that had called them into Spain, the Almoravids were Berbers. Originally they were a military religious brotherhood centered on a fortified monastery (Arabic, *ribat*) in lower Senegal. The founder of the dynasty in North Africa was Yusuf ibn Tashfin. In 1061 he assumed the title *amir al-Muslimin* (commander of the Faithful), thus acknowledging the suzerainty of the Abbasid caliph in Baghdad. His reign was character-ized by extreme zealotry and the persecution of liberal Muslims as well as Christians and Jews. Under the Umayyad caliphate, these minorities had enjoyed great toleration, and the Talmudic school of Córdoba was famous throughout the Mediterra-nean. In 1086 Yusuf crossed into Spain and defeated Alfonso VI so decisively at Zallaca that he is believed to have sent forty-thousand heads back as a trophy. Casualties among Christians were estima-ted at 300,000.

The new regime in Spain was essentially militaristic and soon succumbed to idleness. With no further foes to fight or conquer, the Berbers gave way to the vices of civilization. As a religion Islam had not penetrated deep into Spain, but Arab culture was paramount. In the Christian kingdoms the coinage had Arabic legends, and Peter I of Aragon (d. 1104) could write only in Arabic script. The Berber Almoravids thus faced a people who had already accommodated themselves to their conquerors' culture.

Cultural influences, however, flowed both ways. The Great Mosque of Tlemcen was modeled on the Great Mosque of Córdoba; and in many North African cities architectural traditions that Islamic Spain had derived from Syria and the Yemen engendered a new and elegant variant of Islamic art.

As a state the Almoravid dynasty was weak, and after the rise of the Almohads in the Atlas Mountains, it speedily collapsed (see map 45).

39 LOS REYES DE TAIFAS OR PARTY KINGS IN SPAIN (c. 1009-1286)

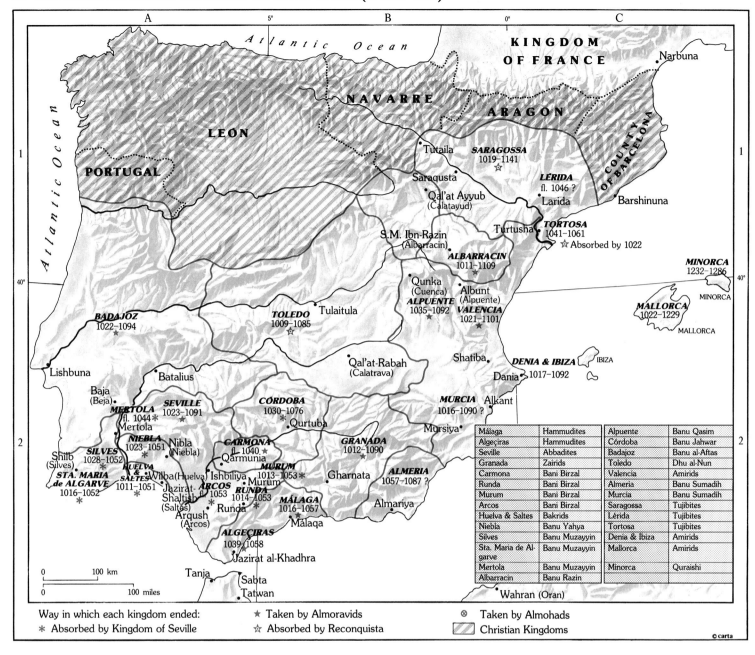

Málaga	Hammudites	Alpuente	Banu Qasim
Algeçiras	Hammudites	Córdoba	Banu Jahwar
Seville	Abbadites	Badajoz	Banu al-Aftas
Granada	Zairids	Toledo	Dhu al-Nun
Carmona	Bani Birzal	Valencia	Amirids
Runda	Bani Birzal	Almeria	Banu Sumadih
Murum	Bani Birzal	Murcia	Banu Sumadih
Arcos	Bani Birzal	Saragossa	Tujibites
Huelva & Saltes	Bakrids	Lérida	Tujibites
Niebla	Banu Yahya	Tortosa	Tujibites
Silves	Banu Muzayyin	Denia & Ibiza	Amirids
Sta. Maria de Al-garve	Banu Muzayyin	Mallorca	Amirids
Mertola	Banu Muzayyin	Minorca	Quraishi
Albarracin	Banu Razin		

Way in which each kingdom ended:

★ Taken by Almoravids   ⊗ Taken by Almohads

✴ Absorbed by Kingdom of Seville   ☆ Absorbed by Reconquista   ▨ Christian Kingdoms

© carta

40 THE ALMORAVIDS IN NORTH AFRICA AND SPAIN, 1056-1147

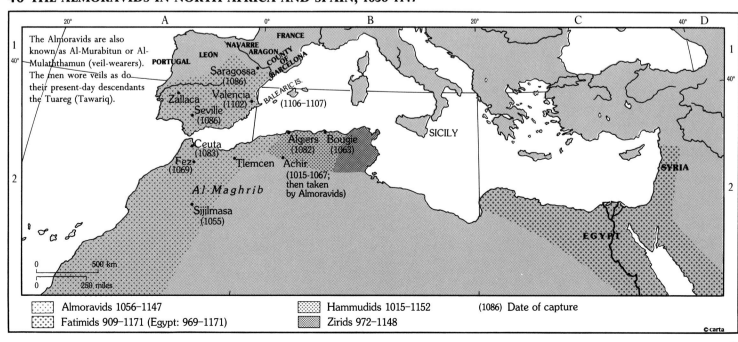

The Almoravids are also known as Al-Murabitun or Al-Mulaththamun (veil-wearers). The men wore veils as do their present-day descendants the Tuareg (Tawariq).

▨ Almoravids 1056-1147   ▨ Hammudids 1015-1152   (1086) Date of capture

▨ Fatimids 909-1171 (Egypt: 969-1171)   ▨ Zirids 972-1148

© carta

45

41. CHRISTIANITY AND ISLAM ON THE EVE OF THE FIRST CRUSADE, 1096

As the eleventh century drew to a close, Christians from the West and Seljuq Turks from western Asia converged in Syria, which was divided among many different chieftains, Arabs as well as Turks. The Seljuqs controlled the north and were encroaching upon eastern Asia Minor and the Byzantine dominions. In Lebanon the Ismailis — later to engender the Assassins, the Nusayris, and the Druzes — formed schismatic communities opposed to orthodox Islam. Christianity was no less divided among Armenians, Georgians, Greeks, and Maronites with a Syriac liturgy. In the south lay Shi'ite Fatimid Egypt, with important Coptic, Greek, and Jewish minorities. In the holy city of Jerusalem the Shi'ite Fatimids held the Haram al-Sharif, the Noble Sanctuary, where once the Jewish Temple had stood. Latin pilgrims had had a hostel and church adjacent to the Holy Sepulcher since the time of Charlemagne, and they, with Copts, Ethiopians, and others also celebrated at the Tomb of Christ.

A Seljuq sultanate had been established in Baghdad in 1055, and every city in Syria had either an Arab or a Seljuq ruler. The Byzantine frontier towns rapidly changed hands among the Seljuqs. In 1070 the Seljuq sultan Alp Arslan took Aleppo; at the same time his general Atziz entered Jerusalem. The Seljuqs soon took all Palestine from the Fatimids, conquering Damascus in 1075. In 1098 the Fatimids retook Jerusalem and the Levantine coastal towns, but this restoration of the former status quo had not been anticipated in the West.

The Byzantine emperor Alexius I Comnenus (r. 1081–1118) was a statesman of distinguished stature. He was also an experienced general, and not less expert in diplomacy. His treasury was empty, and he lived on a financial tightrope. In Europe he held the Balkan Peninsula, albeit precariously in Serbia and Dalmatia. His Danube frontier was continuously threatened by the Turkish Pechenegs. The Normans threatened him in south Italy and Sicily and finally defeated his forces by treachery in 1082. In the east he still held Antioch, but the Seljuqs had the greatest part of Asia Minor.

When the Norman military leader Robert Guiscard died in 1085, the Italian Normans were no longer troublesome to Alexius. By 1092 the Seljuqs had taken to quarreling, so negating their power. In the West a Christian concept of holy war had developed in response to the Islamic doctrine of jihad, which claimed that war against the infidels was justified in the eyes of God. Moreover, in such wars, Christian knights could retain the lands they conquered, along with the spiritual rewards their actions merited. In 1064 Pope Alexander II offered indulgences to all Christian campaigners — a doctrine that would flourish.

The patriarchs of Alexandria, Antioch, and Jerusalem were politically under the Muslim heel. Though the patriarch of Constantinople had the prestige of the imperial capital, Rome claimed supremacy, for had not Christ committed the power of the keys to Peter and to him alone?

Pope Urban II was forty-six years old when he was elected and in full vigor. He had had diplomatic experience as papal legate in France and Germany from 1082 to 1085. Rome itself was governed by the antipope Clement III, and Urban could not assume office until 1093. Careful diplomacy made him spiritual leader of Western Christendom by 1095. He was greatly concerned for Christian unity, and friendly relations among Christians were realized by 1090, when he convoked the council at Piacenza. The attending representatives laid emphasis, it seems, on the duty of Western Christians to sustain those of the East. Another council was held at Clermont in 1095, and there, on 27 November, Urban II called on Western Christendom to a crusade to regain Jerusalem and rescue the East from the infidels.

41 CHRISTIANITY AND ISLAM ON THE EVE OF THE FIRST CRUSADE, 1096

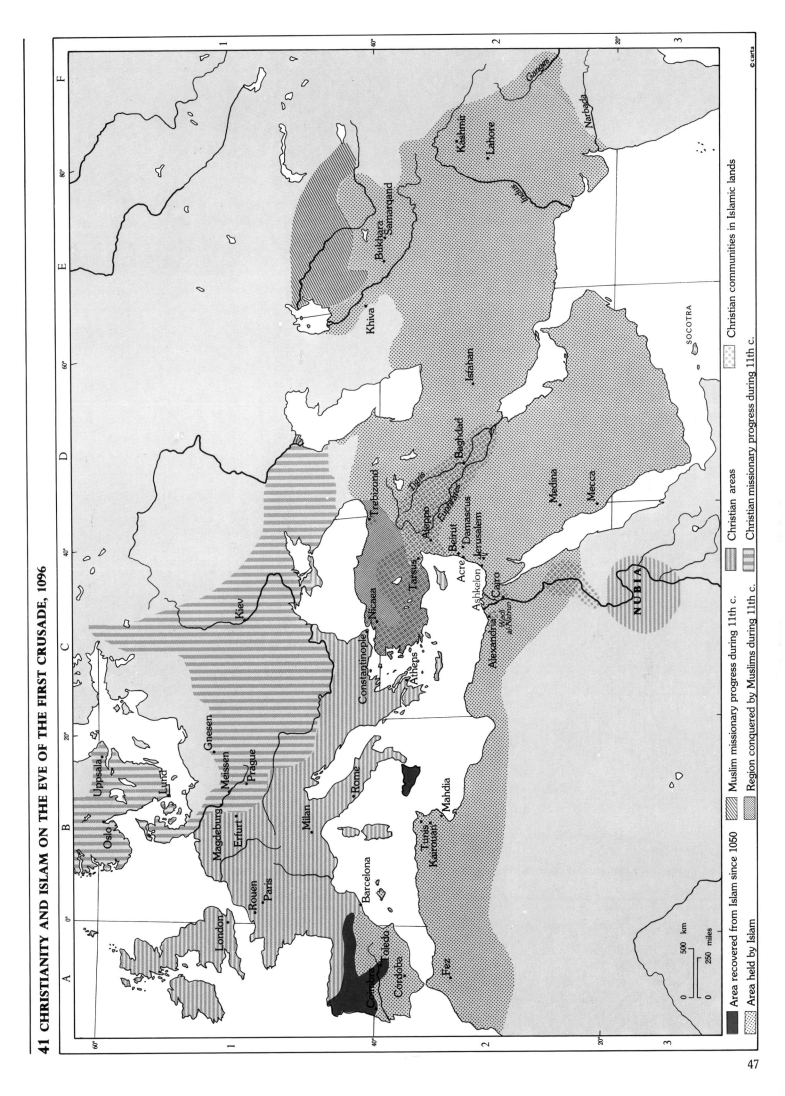

London • Rouen • Paris • Barcelona • Fez • Cordoba • Toledo • Coimbra • Milan • Rome • Tunis • Kairouan • Mahdia • Athens • Constantinople • Nicaea • Tarsus • Trebizond • Aleppo • Euphrates • Beirut • Damascus • Jerusalem • Acre • Ashkelon • Cairo • Alexandria • Wadi al-Natrun • Baghdad • Isfahan • Medina • Mecca • NUBIA • SOCOTRA • Khiva • Bukhara • Samarqand • Kashmir • Lahore • Ganges • Narbada • Indus • Oslo • Uppsala • Lund • Erfurt • Magdeburg • Meissen • Prague • Gnesen • Kiev

Area recovered from Islam since 1050

Area held by Islam

Muslim missionary progress during 11th c.

Region conquered by Muslims during 11th c.

Christian areas

Christian missionary progress during 11th c.

Christian communities in Islamic lands

© carta

500 km
250 miles

47

42. THE CRUSADES, 1095-1291

The immediate occasion of Pope Urban II's call to a crusade was a request by Emperor Alexius I Comnenus for assistance to recover Anatolia from the Seljuqs. By way of inducement, he suggested that the employed forces should continue on to liberate Jerusalem from the infidels. Urban II's response was the proclamation of a "holy war" and plenary indulgences — "the remission, that is, of all the punishment due to sin after sacramental absolution" — for all who took part.

Four separate armies converged in Constantinople in the winter of 1096–1097 from Lorraine; the Norman kingdom of Apulia; Brittany, Normandy, and Flanders; and Provence in France. In spite of quarrels among the leaders, Nicaea was taken in June 1097, and Dorylaeum on July 1. The armies then proceeded to Antioch, besieging it from 21 October 1097 until 3 June 1098. Al-Ruha was now conquered, and the first Latin state was founded as the kingdom of Armenia. The Norman crusader Tancred, from Apulia, took Cilicia. While this was occurring, the Fatimids retook Jerusalem from the Seljuq Turks.

Nevertheless the Crusaders, under the command of Raymond IV, continued down the Syrian coast. On 7 June 1099, Jerusalem was besieged, and Bethlehem shortly thereafter was taken. On 15 July Jerusalem fell to the Crusaders, who wept as they entered the Church of the Holy Sepulcher. Notwithstanding religious sentiment, they murdered every Muslim — men, women, and children alike — except for those who were fortunate enough to escape. The Jewish inhabitants had fled to their chief synagogue, where they were all burned alive.

The leaders now met and elected as king of Jerusalem Godfrey de Bouillon, the duke of Lower Lorraine. He declined the title, accepting only to be "Advocate of the Holy Sepulcher." Jerusalem was divided administratively into quarters, and the spoils of war were distributed among them. The Italian cities that had provided capital were now rewarded. A commercial agreement with Venice was concluded by Godfrey de Bouillon as he lay on his deathbed, and Pisa was given rights in Jaffa. In 1103 the crusader Tancred was finally awarded the regency of Antioch. By Any military danger from the Fatimids ended with Emperor Baldwin I's defeat of their army at Ramla.

The Crusaders seized territory that had formerly been within Byzantine provinces, to which Constantinople had juridical claim. Nevertheless, from 1104 until 1108 Bohemond I of Antioch campaigned against Byzantium. In 1109 Tripoli (Syria) was taken, and its territory made a county under Raymond I of Toulouse. Beirut and Sidon were added in 1110. In 1124 Tyre was taken, and in 1126 Baldwin II advanced as far as Damascus. The tide, however, was beginning to turn, and around 1140 the Assassins took the northern Syrian fortresses. Edessa fell in 1144, and it was this defeat that called forth the Second Crusade. Conrad III of Germany and Louis VII of France besieged Damascus inconclusively. Control of the frontier wavered among the Byzantines, Crusaders, and Muslims. Eventually the Muslim commander Saladin (see map 46) conquered Syria. There were no fresh attacks by the Seljuqs of Byzantine territory. On 3 to 4 July 1187, Saladin defeated Guy de Lusignan, king of Jerusalem, and took him prisoner.

In the Third Crusade (1189–1192), Barbarossa (Frederick I) of Germany, Philip Augustus of France, and Richard I of England responded. A peace was patched up in 1192 that left the Latins in possession of the coast. The Fourth Crusade (1202–1204) was diverted by the Venetians to Constantinople. They sacked the capital and established a Latin empire. Evicted in 1261, the Greeks have never forgotten — or forgiven. During the Fifth Crusade (1218–1221) the Crusaders attacked Egypt. It proved abortive. The Sixth Crusade (1228–1229) was led by the emperor Frederick II, who obtained a ten-year truce, which restored Jerusalem, except the Muslim holy places, to the Franks. Internal quarrels between Knights Templar and Knights Hospitaler so weakened the kingdom that it fell to the Khwarizm Turks in 1144. The Seventh Crusade (1248–1250), in which Louis IX of France attacked Cairo, cost him imprisonment. He ransomed himself, and he later was able to regain some lost ground and to rebuild Acre, Jaffa, Haifa, Caesarea, and Sidon. In 1260 a Mamluk general, Baybars I, halted the Mongol invasion of Syria. Shortly thereafter he captured all Palestine. In 1263 he destroyed the church at Nazareth; in 1266, in spite of an amnesty, he executed two-thousand Knights Templar. This slaughter marked the end of Latin rule, but not of Latin trade, for Venice, Pisa, Genoa, and other cities maintained a lucrative commerce. Trade, however, was hardly the original intention.

42 THE CRUSADES, 1095 – 1291

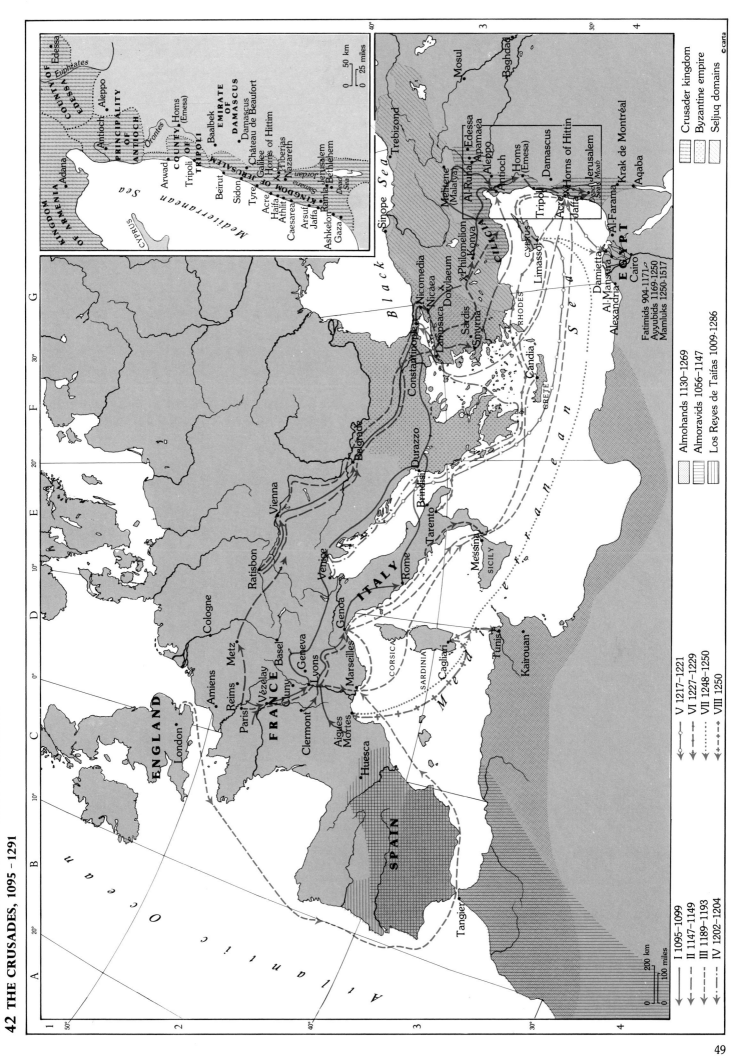

Inset map (upper left)

KINGDOM OF ARMENIA
Edessa
COUNTY OF EDESSA
Euphrates
Antioch · Aleppo
Adana
PRINCIPALITY OF ANTIOCH
Orontes
Homs (Emesa)
COUNTY OF Baalbek
TRIPOLI · Damascus
EMIRATE OF DAMASCUS
Arwad
Tripoli
Château de Beaufort
Beirut
Sidon
Tyre
Galilee
Horns of Hittin
Acre
Tiberias
Haifa
Nazareth
Athlit
Jordan
Caesarea · Samaria
Arsuf
Jaffa
Ramla · Jerusalem
Bethlehem
Ashkelon
Gaza
Dead Sea
KINGDOM OF JERUSALEM
CYPRUS
Mediterranean Sea
50 km
25 miles

Main map labels

Atlantic Ocean

ENGLAND
London

FRANCE
Amiens
Reims
Metz
Cologne
Paris
Vézelay
Cluny
Clermont
Vienna
Basel
Geneva
Lyons
Ratisbon
Aigues Mortes
Marseilles
Genoa
Venice

ITALY
Rome
Brindisi
Tarento
Messina
SICILY

SPAIN
Huesca
Tangier
Tunis
Kairouan
CORSICA
SARDINIA
Cagliari

Belgrade
Durazzo
Constantinople
Nicomedia
Nicaea
Lampsaca
Dorylaeum
Sardis
Smyrna
Philomelion
Konya
CILICIA
Methene (Malatya)
Al-Ruha
Edessa
Apamaea
Aleppo
Mosul
Baghdad
Antioch
Homs (Emesa)
Damascus
Tripoli
Acre
Jaffa
Horns of Hittin
Jerusalem
Krak de Montréal
Aqaba
Al-Farama
Damietta
Al-Mansura
Alexandria
Cairo
EGYPT

Trebizond
Sinope
Black Sea
RHODES
CYPRUS
Limassol
CRETE
Candia
Mediterranean Sea

Seas
Moab

Fatimids 904-1171
Ayyubids 1169-1250
Mamluks 1250-1517

Legend

I 1095–1099
II 1147–1149
III 1189–1193
IV 1202–1204
V 1217–1221
VI 1227–1229
VII 1248–1250
VIII 1250

Crusader kingdom
Byzantine empire
Seljuq domains

Almohands 1130–1269
Almoravids 1056–1147
Los Reyes de Taifas 1009-1286

© carta

200 km
100 miles

49

43. CRUSADER PRINCIPALITIES, 1098 TO 1291

The four Crusader principalities were the county of Edessa, founded in 1098; the Kingdom of Armenia, founded in the same year; the principality of Antioch, which had been founded in 1097; and the county of Tripoli, effecvtive from 1109, of which the kingdom of Jerusalem was the overlord.

The county of Tripoli had an unexpected ally in the Assassins, a Shi'ite sect that maintained itself by terrorism. For two-hundred years this unnatural alliance maintained a front against the Atabegs of Damascus, representing an extreme example of the process of social and economic adaptation that the Crusaders underwent. Their aristocracy intermarried freely with the Armenian royalty, the last of whom was to die in Paris. A series of castles guarded the flank of Tripoli and underwent twelve sieges between 1142 and 1271. While there are unmistakably European features, such as the twelfth-century citadel and walls of Cairo, which were built by Armenians from Edessa, the fundamental architectural concepts are to be found in the citadels of northern Syria.

The defense of these castles and the protection of pilgrims visiting Jerusalem were entrusted to the Knights: The Hospitalers originated as guardians of the hospice of St. John in Jerusalem; the Knights Templar were quartered in the Aqsa Mosque, and followed a military-cum-religious rule that had been composed by Bernard of Clairvaux in 1128; the Order of Teutonic Knights was confined to German citizens. All three had standing armies and were answerable to the pope as sovereign.

These Crusader principalities were feudal. During the twelfth century they steadily maintained and developed trading links with their countries of origin and with the East. For example, the Polo brothers made Acre the starting-off point for their journeys to China, but their connections extended to India and to eastern Africa. At Acre, too, Nicholas Tebaldi, served as papal legate when he was summoned to Rome to be elected pope as Gregory X (1270–1276). From here also, it was possible to outflank the Fatimid and Mamluk trade with the East in silks and spices.

44. THE SELJUQS, 1077-1307

The period from Tughril Beg's entry into Baghdad in 1055 through the reigns of his nephew and successor, Alp Arslan (1063–1072), and his son Malik-Shah (1072–1092) is one of Seljuq ascendancy over the Muslim East. In 1065 Alp Arslan took Ani, capital of Armenia, and in 1071 he defeated the emperor Romanus IV Diogenes at Manzikert, taking him prisoner. The Seljuq nomads were thus the first Muslims to bring Turkish culture to Asia Minor. In 1077 Sulayman ibn Qutlumish, a cousin of Alp Arslan, was made governor of the new province, establishing a dynasty that came to be known as the Seljuqs of Rum (Rome). The new capital was at Iznik (Nicaea). After 1084 the capital was transferred to Konya. In Syria, Tutush, a son of Alp Arslan, founded the Seljuq dynasty of Syria at Aleppo (1094–1117), from where the holy cities of Mecca and Medina were controlled. These cities functioned as provincial capitals, for Alp Arslan resided in Isfahan; only after 1091 did the Seljuq sultan reside in Baghdad, thereby maintaining a puppet caliph.

These sultans were not simply rulers. Roads, walls, mosques, canals, caravanserais, and khans, covered an empire that stretched from Transoxiana to Syria and Asia Minor. From 1065 to 1092, the vizier was the gifted Nizam al-Mulk, a cultured scholar and author of a treatise on the art of government. The revision of the calendar was entrusted to the poet Umar Khayyam, celebrated in his day as an astronomer and mathematician. In Baghdad the Nizamiyah academy was founded in 1065–1067, long anticipating the universities of the West. Nizam al-Mulk was murdered by a Persian Ismaili Assassin in 1092. In the East the Seljuq dynasty of Persia survived until 1157.

Although the Crusaders dominated much of this period, the caliphs and their sultans stood by as indifferent spectators.

43 CRUSADER PRINCIPALITIES, 1098 TO 1291

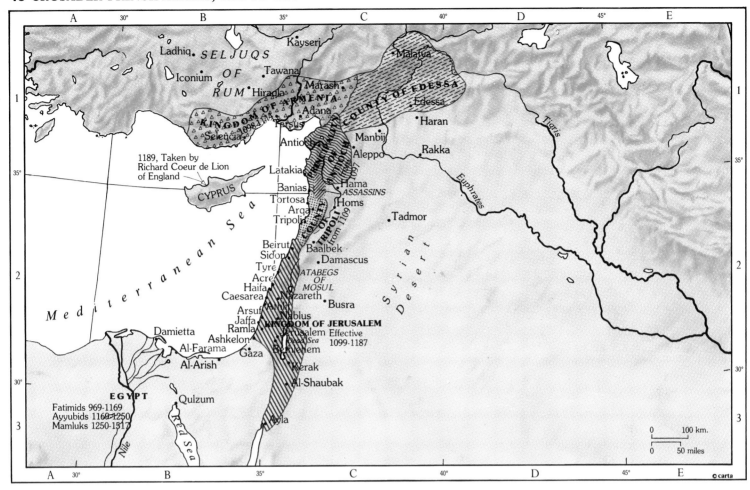

44 THE SELJUQS, 1077 TO 1307

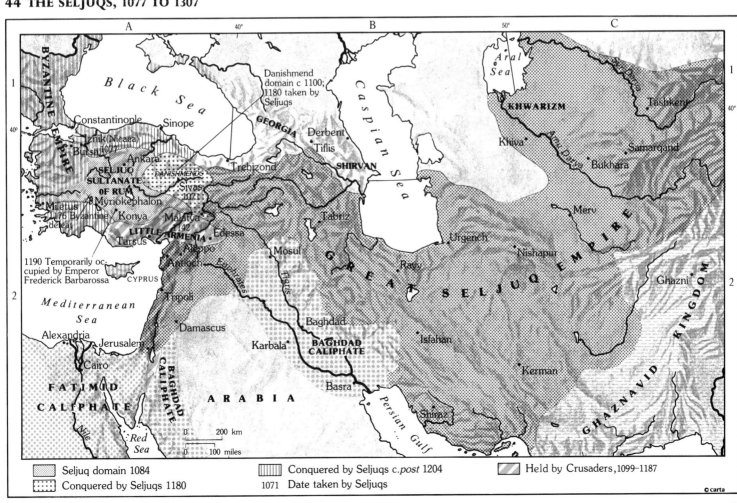

Seljuq domain 1084	Conquered by Seljuqs c.post 1204	Held by Crusaders, 1099–1187
Conquered by Seljuqs 1180	1071 Date taken by Seljuqs	

44. SALADIN AND THE AYYUBIDS, 1169-1250

With the accession of Zangi as governor of Mosul (r. 1127–1146), the tide began to turn in favor of Islam against the Crusaders. In Syria Zangi's son Nur al-Din (r. 1146–1174) recovered Damascus in 1154 and Antioch in 1164. In his campaign against Fatimid Egypt in 1164, the Kurdish general Ayyub took his nephew Saladin (Salah al-Din Yusuf) with him. A serious young man, Saladin sought to replace Fatimid Shi'ism with Sunni Islam and to wage a holy war against the Crusaders.

In 1174, following Nur's death, Saladin declared himself independent in Egypt, and in 1175 he was invested as sultan by the caliph, with full power over Egypt, the Maghreb, western Arabia, Palestine, central Syria, and Nubia. In 1176 he neutralized the Assassins, and then, on 1 July 1187, he defeated the Crusaders at the Horns of Hittin, near Megiddo. Jerusalem capitulated on 2 October, and only a small coastal fringe near Acre was left to the Crusaders.

Shortly thereafter, Saladin died. It was a life of extraordinary accomplishment. In Cairo he had built walls, *madrasas* (colleges for theological education), mosques, schools, canals, dykes, and the Citadel. He had patronized scholars, such as the Córdoban philosopher Musa ibn Maymun (Hebrew, Mosheh ben Maimon; Greek, Maimonides), his secretary and personal physician, but also an astronomer, theologian, and philosopher.

On Saladin's death members of the Ayyubid dynasty divided his sultanate among themselves, resulting in internal discord but favorable commercial relations with the Crusader colonies, especially the merchants of Venice and Pisa, who had consulates at Alexandria. The principal branch of the Ayyubids resided at Cairo, but in Syria and Yemen other branches proclaimed themselves independant of Cairo. They were eventually overthrown by the Mongols and then by the Mamluks.

45. THE ALMOHADS IN NORTH AFRICA AND SPAIN, 1130-1269

Like the Almoravids (map 40), the Almohads (Arabic, *al-Muwahhidun*) originated as a Berber politico-religious movement. Muhammad ibn Tumart proclaimed himself mahdi, the expected one who would come to foretell the Day of Judgment and to recall Muslims to the original purity of belief in *al-Wahid* (One God). He and his followers held that they were the only community of true believers. In 1147 Ibn Tumart's successor, Abd al-Mumin ibn Ali, seized all Morocco and extinguished Almoravid rule. By 1150 he had taken Spain, and then he advanced through North Africa, taking Algeria in 1152, Tunisia in 1158, and Tripoli and as far as the Egyptian border in 1160.

The capital of this huge empire was transferred to Seville in 1170. Here, in 1172, a great mosque was begun, of which the minaret with an atrium survives and is known as the Giralda Tower. In Morocco he built the city of Rabat, and in the city of Marrakesh he founded a hospital that was boasted to be unequaled in all the world.

In 1170 Abd al-Mumin's grandson, Abu Yusuf

Ya'qub al-Mansur, renewed the holy war against the Christians, but with little result. In 1184 his son Abu Yusuf succeeded. Crossing over the Andalusia, he made a five-year truce with the king of Castile and León. In 1195 he defeated Alfonso VIII of Castile at Alarcos. Although it was a great military victory, al-Mansur did not follow it up. This failure created a political stalemate. In 1212 an alliance of Aragon and Navarre, the Templars from Portugal, and French Crusaders was led by Alfonso VIII. At Las Navas de Tolosa this force annihilated the Almohad army; of 600,000 men it was claimed that only one thousand escaped death.

The Almohad regime in Spain now collapsed. Christian kingdoms and Muslim dynasties parceled out Spain. In North Africa the descendants of Abd al-Mumin reigned in Marrakesh until 1269, when the Banu Marins took the city. Once again, the failure to organize a stable, constitutional form of government that did not depend on the emergence of strong personalities proved the undoing of a dynasty.

45 THE ALMOHADS IN NORTH AFRICA AND SPAIN, 1130-1269

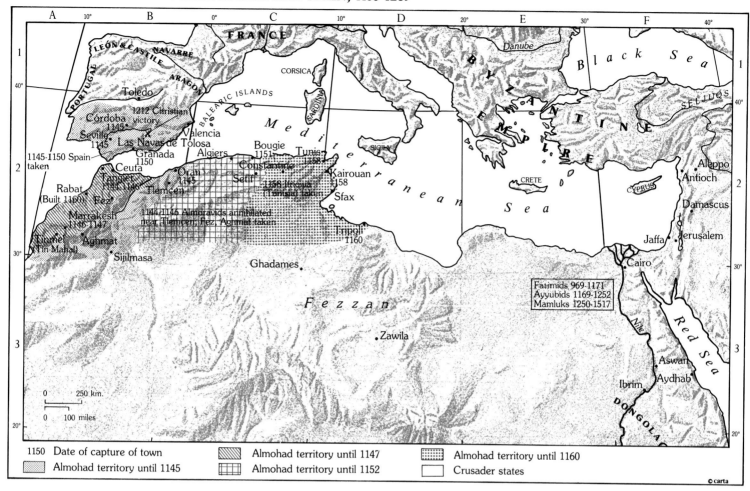

1150 Date of capture of town

▨ Almohad territory until 1147   ▦ Almohad territory until 1152   ▨ Almohad territory until 1160

▨ Almohad territory until 1145   ▦ Almohad territory until 1152   ☐ Crusader states

Fatimids 969-1171
Ayyubids 1169-1252
Mamluks 1250-1517

46 SALADIN AND THE AYYUBIDS, 1169 TO 1250

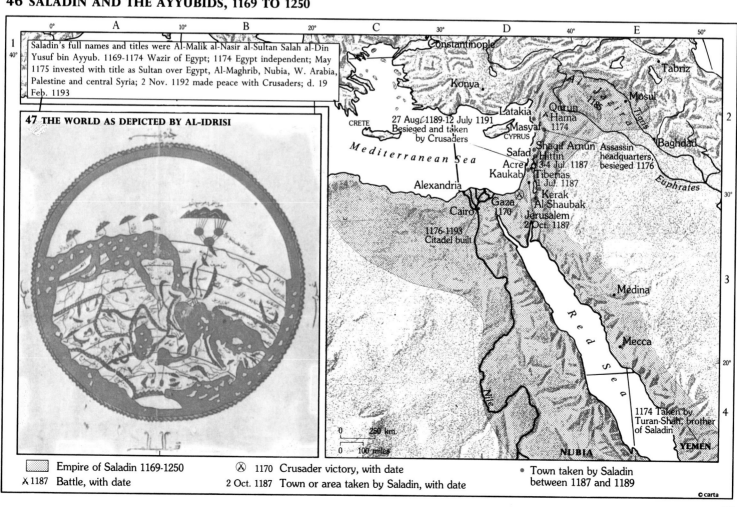

Saladin's full names and titles were Al-Malik al-Nasir al-Sultan Salah al-Din Yusuf bin Ayyub. 1169-1174 Wazir of Egypt; 1174 Egypt independent; May 1175 invested with title as Sultan over Egypt, Al-Maghrib, Nubia, W. Arabia, Palestine and central Syria; 2 Nov. 1192 made peace with Crusaders; d. 19 Feb. 1193

47 THE WORLD AS DEPICTED BY AL-IDRISI

▨ Empire of Saladin 1169-1250

⊗ 1170 Crusader victory, with date

✕ 1187 Battle, with date

2 Oct. 1187 Town or area taken by Saladin, with date

● Town taken by Saladin between 1187 and 1189

© carta

48. THE CITY OF CAIRO, FROM THE BEGINNING UNTIL 1517

The Historian Ibn Khaldun called Cairo the mother of cities. No city in the world, save perhaps Rome, contains so many monuments. By 1951 some five-hundred monuments were listed, but these did not include the Coptic churches nor some three-hundred buildings of the Ottoman period (1517–1804).

Cairo is located on the east bank of the Nile, opposite Memphis, which stretched between Giza and Saqqara. The pyramids and the Sphinx are all that remains of the pharaonic city. Modern Cairo — it was given the name al-Qahira in 969 — originated as a Roman fort, built in 27 B.C., that accommodated a legion stationed at the apex of the Delta. Beside the fort grew up the Greco-Coptic town of Babilyun (Babylon), where a Persian fort had been located in 500 B.C.. The Holy Family is believed to have sought refuge from Herod in its Jewish quarter, and the apostles Peter and Mark the Evangelist are reported to have preached here in A.D. 42. A synagogue and early churches still survive in what is known as Old Cairo.

When Amr ibn al-As took Egypt in 641 he built his garrison headquarters north and east of this site. A Friday mosque known by his name still stands, though it has been enlarged and rebuilt many times. This was the center of his buildings, around which other public buildings — a treasury, administrative offices, a post office for rapid communication with Medina, and courts — were built. The city of al-Fustat was divided into quarters, each with its own mosque and administration.

In 751 the Abbasids built a new headquarters at al-Askar, but this has wholly disappeared. In 868 the Egyptian governor, Ahmad ibn Tulun, knowing the weakness of the caliphate, declared Egypt independent. He seized all Syria as far as the Euphrates and Libya as far as Barca. In what is now the al-Qata'i quarter he built a splended mosque that still survives; the palace, barracks, offices, hospital, baths, markets, racecourse, and polo ground have long since disappeared.

After they conquered Egypt in 969, the Fatimids (see map 36) built a new palace city. On 5 August astrologers stood by to determine when the first sod should be turned. The city's boundaries had been marked with ropes, on which bells had been hung to give the signal to commence. A raven anticipated the astrologers by alighting on a rope. The moment was unlucky, for Mars (Arabic, *al-Qahira*) was in the ascendant, thus giving the city its name. Elaborate buildings now arose, of which the palace mosque, al-Azhar, was destined to become the intellectual center of the Islamic world.

The Fatimid dynasty collapsed in 1168. The next year Saladin (see map 46) became governor. His great monument, the Citadel, still stands. The surrounding walls, built by his Armenian commander, Badr al-Jamali, were never completed. He also built twenty *madrasas* (teaching colleges for religion), replacing Fatimid Shi'ism with Sunnite orthodoxy. Saladin also sought to organize an orderly administration. For this he trained Mamluks — slaves who received a full Islamic education and training in the arts of government and war. The early Mamluks, of largely Turkish origin until 1382 and thereafter chiefly of Circassian origin, dominated Egypt until it was seized by the Ottoman Turks in 1517.

On 8 August 1303, a massive earthquake devastated Cairo, destroying a majority of the buildings. The older part of central Cairo belongs chiefly to the Mamluk period between 1303 and 1517, for little other than domestic building can be attributed to the Ottoman Turks. To the Mamluks are owed the most splendid of the mosques, mausoleums, dervish monasteries, and hospitals, one of which still survives as an eye hospital. In the Citadel a new mosque and palace were built on a grand scale as were the rest of the buildings. Nor was it merely on a grand scale: under the Mamluks it was an age of taste and elegance for the whole city, which reached its apogee in the reign of Qayt Bay (1468–1495). This was made possible by the Mamluks' continuance of the trade policies that had been developed under the Fatimids. As the city slowly developed northward to take advantage of the prevailing north wind, the same wind inhibited sea traffic up the Red Sea. For most of the year, Cairo thus became a trading center for the caravan trade between east and west.

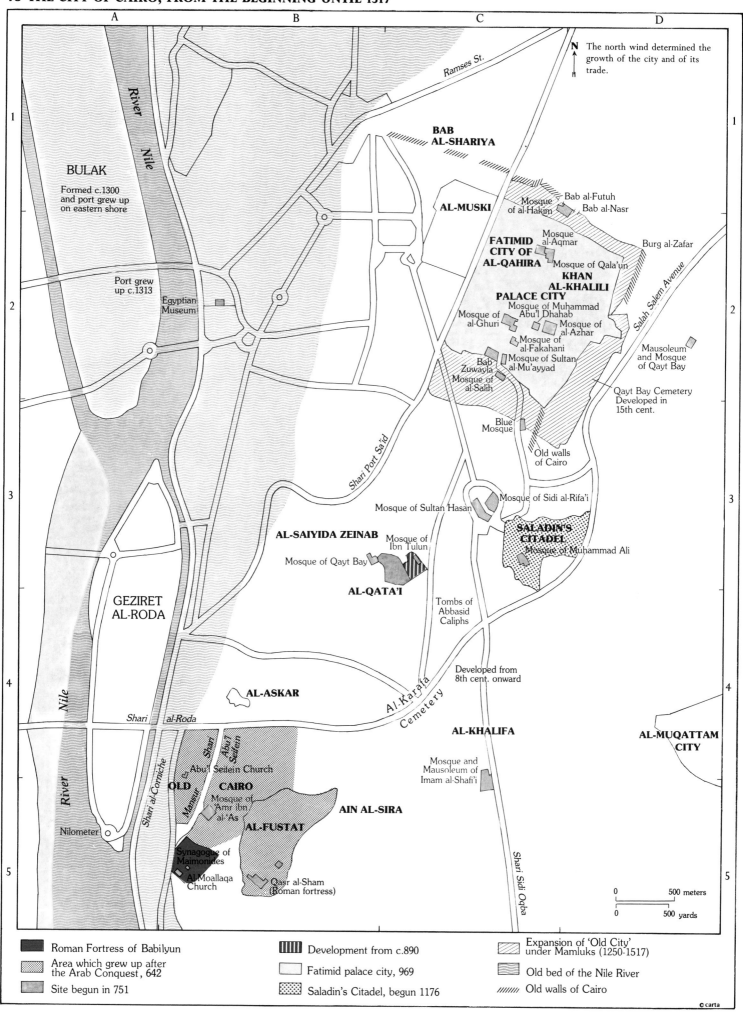

A   B   C   D

N

The north wind determined the growth of the city and of its trade.

BULAK
Formed c.1300 and port grew up on eastern shore

River Nile

Port grew up c.1313

Egyptian Museum

BAB AL-SHARIYA

AL-MUSKI

Mosque of al-Hakim
Bab al-Futuh
Bab al-Nasr

FATIMID CITY OF AL-QAHIRA
Mosque al-Aqmar
Mosque of Qala'un

Burg al-Zafar

KHAN AL-KHALILI
PALACE CITY

Mosque of Muhammad Abu'l Dhahab

Mosque of al-Ghuri
Mosque of al-Azhar
Mosque of al-Fakahani
Mosque of Sultan al-Mu'ayyad

Salah Salem Avenue

Bab Zuwayla
Mosque of al-Salih

Mausoleum and Mosque of Qayt Bay

Blue Mosque

Qayt Bay Cemetery Developed in 15th cent.

Old walls of Cairo

Shari Port Sa'id

Mosque of Sultan Hasan
Mosque of Sidi al-Rifa'i

SALADIN'S CITADEL
Mosque of Muhammad Ali

AL-SAIYIDA ZEINAB

Mosque of Ibn Tulun

Mosque of Qayt Bay

AL-QATA'I

GEZIRET AL-RODA

Tombs of Abbasid Caliphs

Al-Karafa Cemetery

Developed from 8th cent. onward

Nile

AL-ASKAR

Shari al-Roda

AL-KHALIFA

AL-MUQATTAM CITY

Mosque and Mausoleum of Imam al-Shafi'i

Shari al-Corniche

Shari Abu'l Seifein

Mansur

Abu'l Seifein Church

OLD CAIRO

Mosque of 'Amr ibn al-'As

AIN AL-SIRA

AL-FUSTAT

Nilometer

Synagogue of Maimonides

Al Moallaqa Church

Qasr al-Sham (Roman fortress)

Shari Sidi Oqba

0   500 meters
0   500 yards

■ Roman Fortress of Babilyun

▨ Area which grew up after the Arab Conquest, 642

▨ Site begun in 751

▥ Development from c.890

☐ Fatimid palace city, 969

▨ Saladin's Citadel, begun 1176

▨ Expansion of 'Old City' under Mamluks (1250-1517)

▨ Old bed of the Nile River

///// Old walls of Cairo

© carta

49. THE GHURIDS IN AFGHANISTAN AND NORTH INDIA, 1175-1206

Although Islam reached the Indus valley early (see map 19), it did not begin to expand across the subcontinent until the last quarter of the twelfth century. This expansion occurred almost accidentally. A successor of the sultan Mahmud of Ghazna had executed two princelings of Ghur, an obscure principality southeast of Herat. In response, the Ghurid Ala al-Din Husayn sacked Ghazna and laid it waste. Ghuzz Turkmans then attempted to seize the city, and it was from them that the Ghurids wrested it in 1173, when Muhammad Ghuri (Arabic, Muizzu al-Din Muhammad) emerged as a conqueror, moving steadily eastward. Following an unsuccessful attack on Gujarat in 1178, Muhammad Ghuri occupied the Punjab in addition to Sind.

Such aggression roused the Hindu rulers of northern India, who formed a confederacy under the ruler of Delhi, Rai Pithaura. At Tarain, which commands Delhi and the Ganges basin, Muhammad Ghuri was defeated. Once again, however, he was undeterred. In the following year, 1192, ten-thousand mounted archers utterly routed the Hindu confederacy — a defeat due largely to the toops' own immobility. Now the cities of India lay open to Muhammad Ghuri's general Qutb al-Din Aybak, a Mamluk slave from Turkestan, who advanced, taking Delhi, Kanauj, Gwalior, Anhilwara in Gujarat, and Ajmer. By 1199 or 1212, all Bengal was occupied — a defeat not only for Hinduism, but also for Buddhism, which had a greater hold in the eastern region.

Muhammad Ghuri died in 1206. Adopted as Muhammad Ghuri's son, Qutb al-Din now ascended the throne as sultan, the first sultan in Delhi. He ruled for little more than four years, dying in a polo accident. "Beneficent and victorious...his gifts were bestowed by hundreds of thousands, and his slaughters likewise by hundreds of thousands...." A new age had dawned in India.

50. SUCCESSOR STATES OF THE ALMOHADS IN NORTH AFRICA, 1200-1550

After the Battle of Las Navas de Tolosa, the Almohad empire gradually collapsed. In Ifriqiya (modern Tunisia), the Hafsid governor claimed independence in 1228. In 1235 the emir of Tlemcen, Yaghmorasan, proclaimed independence, giving his kingdom the title Zenata Kingdom of the Banu Abd al-Wad. He was of the Ziyanid tribe. In 1248 the Banu Marins, who already held Meknes, seized Fez from the Almohads; in 1269, they conquered Marrakesh. The latter was the final defeat of the Almohads.

These new kingdoms were primarily trading states, with long established connections with western Africa. The Hafsids had the recognition of Christian Mediterranean powers — Venice, Pisa, Genoa, and Sicily — and were in treaty relations with Spain and Egypt. At first, Tlemcen and Fez recognized Tunis as suzerain. Not only the Tunis economy, but also the quality of life was enhanced by immigrants — architects, artists, artisans, and writers — fleeing Christian Spain. The greatest of Islamic historians, Ibn Khaldun, was a descendant of such immigrants.

In the west the Marinids of Fez controlled the outlet of the shortest route to the gold-bearing lands of Mali as well as to supplies of salt and slaves. In Mali a fleet of canoes was sent out into the Atlantic in 1310 to ascertain whether there was land to the west. Shortly thereafter, its ruler, the fabled sultan Kankan Mansa Musa, made the pilgrimage to Mecca, with so splendid an entourage and so much in alms as to depreciate the value of gold in Cairo. Ibn Battuta's visit to Mali in 1352–1353 (see map 56) on behalf of the Marinid sultan was probably a commercial, diplomatic mission.

49 THE GHURIDS IN AFGHANISTAN AND NORTH INDIA, 1175-1206

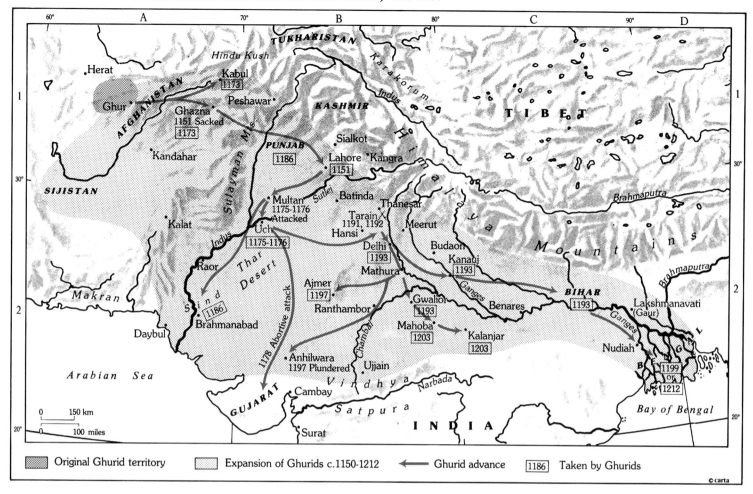

Original Ghurid territory
Expansion of Ghurids c.1150-1212
Ghurid advance
1186 Taken by Ghurids

© carta

50 SUCCESSOR STATES OF THE ALMOHADS IN NORTH AFRICA, 1200-1550

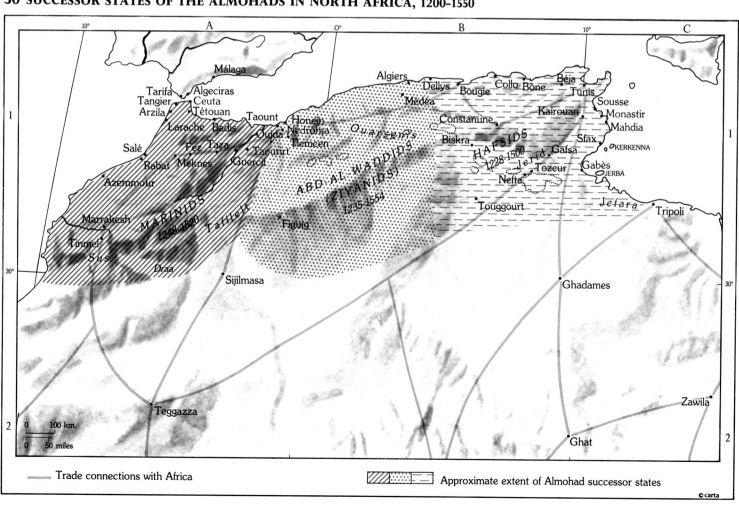

Trade connections with Africa
Approximate extent of Almohad successor states

© carta

51. THE MAMLUKS IN EGYPT, 1250 TO 1517

The Mamluks that Saladin introduced into Egypt were Turks or Greeks. Because they were quartered on Roda, an island in the Nile (Arabic, *Bahr al-Nil*), they were known as Bahri. Their successors after 1382 — known as Burgi because they were quartered in the Citadel (Arabic *Burg*) — were almost all Circassians from southeast Russia. *Mamluk* means "owned" or "slave," but, far from being a dishonorable status, capture in youth and training as a Mamluk could lead to the highest offices in the state. Strictly, they were not dynasties so much as military oligarchies based on regimental rather than family allegiance. Racially they kept themselves apart from the Egyptians, over whom they were the only dominant force from 1250 to 1517.

The Mamluk system was initiated by a woman, Shajar al-Durr ("tree of pearls"), who ruled for only eighty days before she was murdered. Successive commanders of the Bahri regiment followed, of whom the most distinguished was Baybars I, who ruled from 1260 until 1277. A remarkable general, he cleared Syria of the Mongols and remnants of the Crusaders and broke the power of the Assassins. His generals were sent westward to conquer the Berbers and southward to conquer the Christian kingdoms of Nubia.

Qalaun, a Kipchaq Turk (r. 1279–1290), was the only Bahri Mamluk who succeeded in founding a dynasty. He was succeeded by his second son, al-Nasir Muhammad (r. 1293–1294, 1298–1308, 1309–1340), who was succeeded by two sons, eight grandsons, two great-grandsons, and two great-great-grandsons. Al-Nasir is chiefly remembered as the restorer of Cairo after the earthquake of 1303 (see map 48). During this period a special characteristic of Cairene architecture developed — the ribbed carved stone dome over mausoleums. He and his successors used building as a form of publicity, endowing mosques, *madrasas*, dervish convents, hospitals, and public drinking fountains. Al-Nasir's palace set a new trend in *ablaq*, building in alternate courses of red and white stone. The grandest mosque of all, the *madrasa* and mausoleum of Sultan Hasan (r. 1347–

1351, 1354–1361), was built in 1354–1361: the sultan did not live to complete it nor was he buried in it. It provided lodgings for students and professors, up to five-hundred persons.

Under the Burgi Mamluks political power lay almost exclusively in the hands of their viziers, a highly unstable form of governing. Of twenty-three rulers, six reigned for a total of 103 years out of 134; the remaining seventeen rulers reigned for less than two years each.

Among these rulers one man was outstanding. Of very humble beginnings, Qayt Bay had been bought for the equivalent of fifty dollars. His strength of character took him through all the ranks of the army to commander-in-chief. He was as incorruptible as he was ruthless. He traveled incessantly, visiting Syria, Palestine, and the Hejaz again and again. Wherever he went during his long reign (1468–1496), he left roads, bridges, mosques, fortifications, schools, and other works. His *madrasa* in Cairo and his mosque and mausoleum in the Northern Cemetery are of incomparable elegance and beauty.

All this elegance and luxury, which was achieved by fostering trade at what was the crossroads between China and India on the one hand and the growing prosperity of Europe on the other, was, however, doomed. On 22 November 1497, Vasco da Gama rounded the Cape of Good Hope; on 7 April 1498, he was at Mombasa; on 20 May he anchored off Calicut in India. Portugal thus seized the carrying trade of the Indian Ocean. In 1508 an Egyptian fleet defeated the Portuguese of Chaul, but the fleet was annihilated the following year. Qayt Bay had kept a watchful eye on the growing power of the Ottomans (see map 63). Three years after the defeat of Chaul, Selim I, the Grim (r. 1512–1520), ascended the Ottoman throne. In 1514 the Persians were defeated by Selim at Chaldiran. In 1516 he defeated the Egyptian army at Marj Dabiq in Syria and took Jerusalem. In January 1517 he entered Cairo; for nearly three hundred years, until it revived under Muhammad Ali the Great (see maps 81 to 84), Egypt was a backwater.

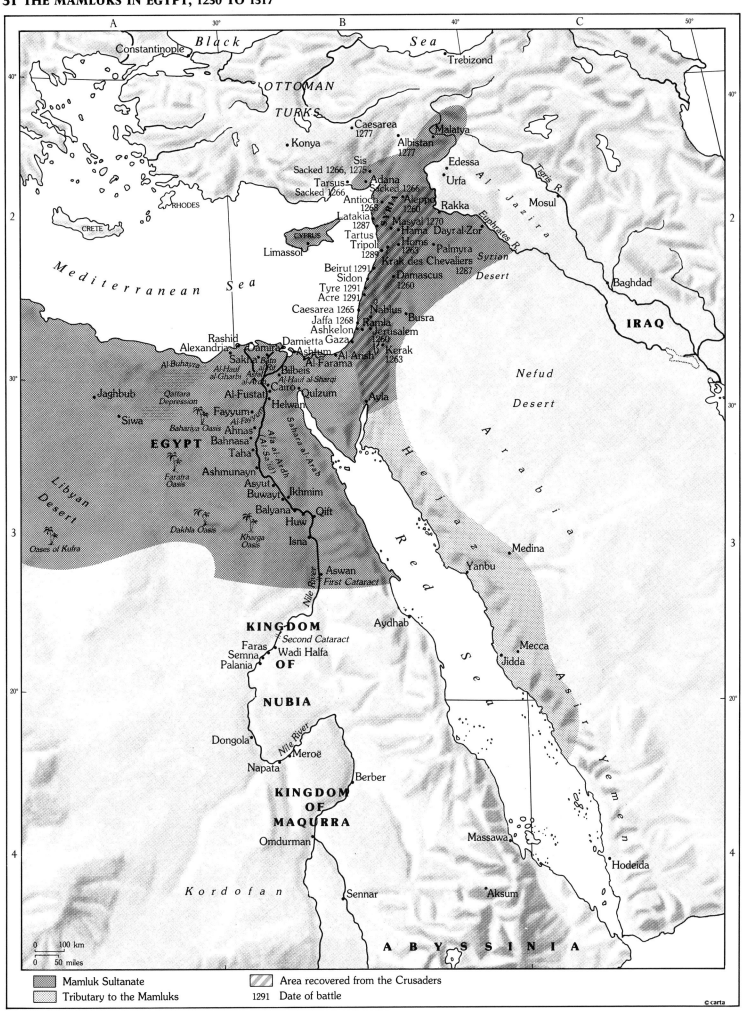

Mamluk Sultanate

Tributary to the Mamluks

Area recovered from the Crusaders

1291 Date of battle

52. THE CITY OF JERUSALEM

The present Jerusalem is a palimpsest of cities, superimposed one over the other, but with buildings from earlier layers protruding into later times. The layout of the Old City is that of the emperor Hadrian's Aelia Capitolina, built in A.D. 135; the walls were built by the Ottoman sultan Sulayman I, the Magnificent, in 1535–1538. Occupied by Jebusites until it was taken by David around 1,000 B.C., the earliest city was located on the ridge south of Mount Moriah, or Temple Mount, known also as the Haram al-Sharif, the Noble Sanctuary. The Tyropoeon valley divides it from the Upper City, Mount Zion and the two northern ridges. It was on Moriah Mount that Solomon built the first Temple, together with his palace and other buildings.

David's Jerusalem (map 52:1), which covered 10.87 acres, was sacked by Nebuchadnezzar in 587 B.C.. It was slowly restored after the return of the Jews from captivity in Babylon in 538 (map 52:2). This was the Jerusalem known to Jesus, together with extensions made under Herod I, the Great, to 140 acres. His grandson Herod Agrippa I, in four years of hectic building activity, increased it to 310 acres (map 52.2) between A.D. 40 and 44. This city was totally destroyed, the Temple included, by the future emperor Titus in A.D. 70. His arch in Rome commemorates the event. Jerusalem laid waste until 135, when the emperor Hadrian laid out the city anew as Aelia Capitolina, named after himself (map 52:3).

Hadrian's plan was somewhat modified after 326, when the emperor Constantine had the Basilica of the Holy Sepulcher built. Further additions were made by the emperor Justinian I (r. 527–565) in the southern part of the city, when his great church, the Nea, was built (map 53:4).

Under the Arabs, between 638 and 1099, no substantial changes took place. The caliph Abd al-Malik ibn Marwan (r. 865–705) added greatly to the beauty of the city by building the Dome of the Rock (al-Qubbat al-Sakhra), the rock on the Temple Mount from which the Prophet Muhammad is believed to have ascended in his mystical night journey to heaven. At the same time much of the Aqsa Mosque, which had undergone numerous modifications, was built on the site. It was believed that the caliph Umar I had built the first mosque when he visited Jerusalem in 640. The city had changed little when, in 1009, the mad Fatimid caliph al-Hakim ordered the destruction of all churches and had the Basilica of the Holy Sepulcher razed to the ground. By 1048 the Greeks had restored some of it, and under the Crusaders (1099–1187) the existing additions were completed.

Many of the monuments in the Haram al-Sharif and other parts of the city belong to the time when it fell under the Mamluk sultans of Egypt (1260–1517). In 1516 the Ottoman Turks took Syria and in 1517 Egypt. The city now became a backwater, and the area between the Basilica of the Holy Sepulcher and the Damascus Gate was a waste. The revival of the city began in the nineteenth century, partly as a result of Jewish immigration. Continuing up to the present time, the city has far outgrown its sixteenth-century walls (map 52:7). Following the British withdrawal in 1947, the city was divided between Israel and Jordan. In 1967, the Old City was captured by Israel (see map 102). Scientific excavations and restorations have greatly increased knowledge of the history of the Old City.

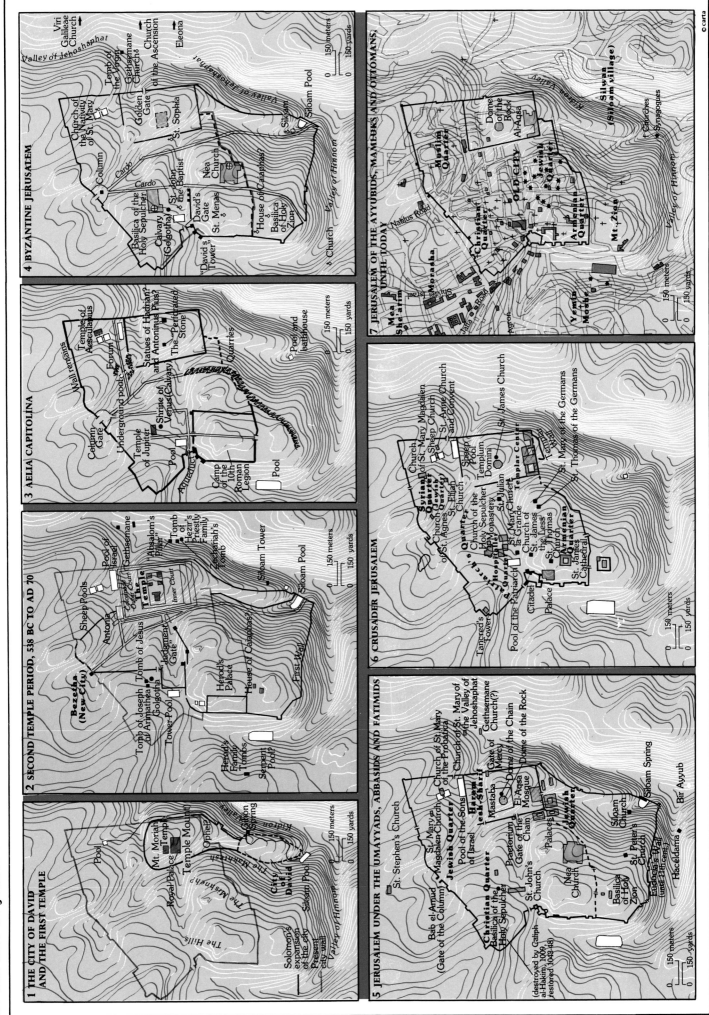

1 THE CITY OF DAVID AND THE FIRST TEMPLE

Pool
Mt. Moriah Temple
Royal Palace
Temple Mount
Ophel
The Mishneh?
The Makhtesh
City of David
Kidron Spring
Gihon Spring
The Hills
Solomon's expansion of the city
Present city wall
Valley of Hinnom
Siloam Pool
0 150 meters
0 150 yards

2 SECOND TEMPLE PERIOD, 538 BC TO AD 70

Pool of Israel
Sheep Pools
Gethsemane
Bezetha (New City)
Antonia
Colonnade Outer Court
Temple
Inner Court
"Absalom's Pillar"
Tomb of Hezir's Priestly Family
Zechariah's Tomb
Tomb of Joseph of Arimathea
Golgotha
Tomb of Jesus
Judgment Gate
Tower Pool
Herod's Palace
House of Caiaphas?
Herod's Family Tombs
Serpent Pool
First Wall
Siloam Tower
Siloam Pool
0 150 meters
0 150 yards

3 AELIA CAPITOLINA

Temple of Aesculapius
Wall remains
Temple of Hadrian? Statues of Hadrian and Antoninus Pius?
The "Perforated Stone"
Forum
Column Gate
Underground pool
Shrine of Venus (Calvary)
Temple of Jupiter
Pool
Aqueduct
Camp of the 10th Roman Legion
Quarries
Pool and bathhouse
Pool
0 150 meters
0 150 yards

4 BYZANTINE JERUSALEM

Viri Galileae Church
Tomb of the Virgin
Gethsemane Church
Church of the Ascension
Valley of Jehoshaphat
Church of the Nativity of St. Mary
Column
Golden Gate
Eleona
St. Sophia
Cardo
Cardo
Basilica of the Holy Sepulcher
Calvary (Golgotha)
St. John the Baptist
Nea Church
David's Gate
"David's Tower"
St. Menas
"House of Caiaphas"
Basilica of Holy Zion
Siloam
Siloam Pool
Church
Valley of Hinnom
0 150 meters
0 150 yards

5 JERUSALEM UNDER THE UMAYYADS, ABBASIDS AND FATIMIDS

St. Stephen's Church
St. Mary's Magdalen Church
Church of St. Mary of the Probatica
Church of St. Mary of the Valley of Jehoshaphat
Gethsemane Church(?)
Gate of Mercy
Bab el-Amud (Gate of the Column)
Christian Quarter
Basilica of the Holy Sepulcher
Jewish Quarter
Haram esh-Sharif
Mastaba
Pool of Israel
Dome of the Chain
Dome of the Rock
Praetorium?
Gate of the Chain
El-Aqsa Mosque
St. John's Church
Palaces
Jewish Quarter
Nea Church
Basilica of Holy Zion
Siloam Church
St. Peter's Church
Eudoxia's Wall (until 11th cent.)
Siloam Spring
Haceldama
Bir Ayyub
(destroyed by Caliph al-Hakim, 1009, restored 1048-48)
0 150 meters
0 150 yards

6 CRUSADER JERUSALEM

Church of St. Mary Magdalen
Sheep Church
St. Anne Church and Convent
Syrian Quarter
Jewish Quarter of St. Agnes Quarter
St. Elias Church
Church of the Holy Sepulcher
Templum Domini
St. James Church
Temple Wall
Patriarch's Quarter
Hospital Quarter
St. Mary la Grande
Monastery
St. Julian Church
St. Mary Church
St. James the Less
Templar Center
St. Mary of the Germans
St. Thomas of the Germans
Pool of the Patriarch
Citadel
Tancred's Tower
Palace
Armenian Quarter
St. Thomas Church
St. James Cathedral
0 150 meters
0 150 yards

7 JERUSALEM OF THE AYYUBIDS, MAMLUKS AND OTTOMANS, UNTIL TODAY

Mea She'arim
Muslim Quarter
Dome of the Rock
Al-Aqsa
Nablus Road
Christian Quarter
OLD CITY
Jewish Quarter
Meorasha
Jaffa Road
Armenian Quarter
Silwan (Siloam village)
Mt. Zion
Kidron Valley
Yemin Moshe
Agron
Valley of Hinnom
+ Churches
* Synagogues
0 150 meters
0 150 yards

© carta

53. THE CITY OF MECCA

Islam centers on the "Five Pillars": the profession of faith, prayer five times daily, almsgiving, fasting in Ramadan, and, once in a lifetime, the pilgrimage to Mecca. Some sects add a sixth pillar, jihad or holy war. Mecca thus has an unique importance to Muslims. The ceremonies incumbent on the pilgrim culminate with the *Id al-Adha*, the Festival of Sacrifice, which takes place on the tenth day of the month Dhu-al-Hijjah.

Pilgrimage is an ancient Semitic institution, to which references can be found in the Hebrew scriptures; local shrines likewise attracted pilgrimages. More than six-hundred Muslim shrines were recorded in Palestine in 1927. The pilgrimage to Mecca has had the effect of unifying the Islamic world, regardless of race or color, from Morocco and black Africa to Java and China.

Ancient Mecca was on the caravan route from the southern Arabian ports to both Egypt and Syria. It was already a pilgrimage center before Muhammad. The Ka'aba — built, according to Islamic tradition, by Abraham, Hagar, and Isma'il — was the principal shrine. It was this shrine that Muhammad purged of idols, making it the sole temple, or Holy House, of Allah. Although nominally subject to the Umayyad and Abbasid caliphates, Mecca had a somewhat independent existence. From 1269 it was under the Mamluk Egyptian sultans, and after 1517 it came under the Ottoman Turks. Sharifs, descendants of the Prophet Muhammad, ruled as governors. In 1925 it was seized by Ibn Sa'ud and incorporated into Saudi Arabia (see map 88).

The city centers upon the *Haram* (Sacred Enclosure) and the holy well of Zamzam. The enclosure has been greatly enlarged by the Saudis, thereby enabling it to accommodate 300,000 worshippers at one time. As many as a million persons attend the pilgrimage.

54. THE CITY OF MEDINA

In or around 620, some men from Yathrib met Muhammad and were impressed by what he had to say. In 622 a deputation from Yathrib invited him to make it his home — a welcome suggestion in light of the hostility in Mecca. The Prophet's arrival on 24 September 622 is known as the *hijrah* (migration). Yathrib, which was his mother's native city, became known as Medina (Arabic, *Madinat-al-Nabi*, the City of the Prophet).

This marked a turning point in Muhammad's mission. Prior to this migration, he had been simply a religious leader. Now he was not only a prophet, but also a lawgiver, chief judge, commander-in-chief of the army, and civil head of state. After his death in 632, his first four successors — Abu Bakr, Umar I, Uthman ibn Affan, and Ali (632–661) — ruled from Medina. They took the title *khalifah* (caliph, successor and vicar) in all but religious functions.

As capital of an ever-expanding Arab empire, Medina was far too off center and gave way first to Damascus under the Umayyads and then to Baghdad under the Abbasids (maps 22, 23, 27), becoming somewhat a backwater. Nevertheless, although at no time did a visit to Medina have the prestige of pilgrimage, it ranked second among Muslim holy cities because the tomb of the Prophet is located in the courtyard of the house where he had lived and which had served as the first mosque. Medina became a center of intellectual life, for law, the study of *hadith* (traditional sayings of the Prophet that have the force of law), and of the study and exegesis of the Koran.

When the followers of the Wahhabi movement obtained possession of Medina, King Ibn Sa'ud at first forbade pilgrims to visit it. He later relented and enlarged and rebuilt the sacred mosque.

53 THE CITY OF MECCA

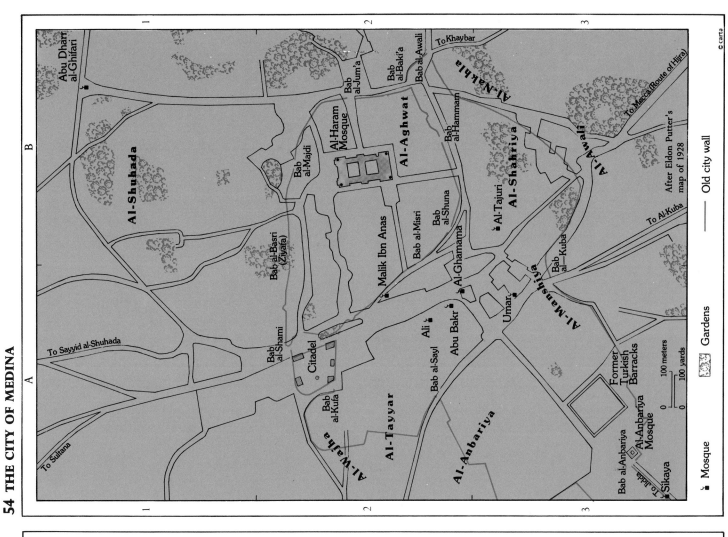

Former Turkish Barracks

To Jidda

To Wadi Fatima
Walled Garden
Hospital

Shaykh Mahmud

Jarwal

Jabal La'la

Jabal al-Fanna

Jabal Umar

Jabal Kaykan

Jabal Hindi

Jabal Hini

Kal'a Jabal Hindi

Graveyard

Harat al-Bab

Donkey Drover's Inn

Kal'a Jiyad

Jabal Jiyad

Jabal Kuda

Al-Halaka

Al-Falk

Al-Karara

Kal'a Filfil

Al-Jawdhariya

To Mina and Arafa

Al-Marwa

Al-Safa

Al-Haram

Masjid Bilal

Jabal Abi Kubays

Former Sharif's Palace

The Prophet's Birthplace

Shi'b Ali

After Eldon Putter's map of 1928

♪ Mosque   Gardens   Mountain   Jabal

0   100 meters
0   100 yards

---

54 THE CITY OF MEDINA

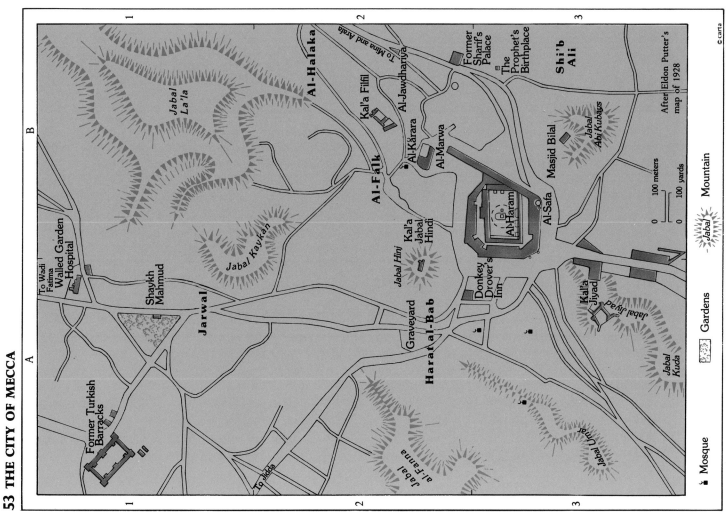

To Sultana

To Sayyid al-Shuhada

Abu Dharr al-Ghifari

Al-Shuhada

Bab al-Basri (Ziyafa)

Bab al-Shami

Citadel

Bab al-Kufa

Al-Wajha

Al-Tayyar

Al-Anbariya

Bab al-Sayl

Bab al-Majdi

Al-Haram Mosque

Malik Ibn Anas

Bab al-Misri

Bab al-Shuna

Al-Ghamama

Ali

Abu Bakr

Umar

Al-Manshiya

Bab al-Kuba

To Al-Kuba

Bab al-Jum'a

Bab al-Baki'a

Bab al-Awali

Al-Aghwat

Bab al-Hammam

Al-Nakhla

Al-Shahriya

Al-Tajuri

Al-Awali

To Khaybar

To Mecca (Route of Hijra)

After Eldon Putter's map of 1928

Former Turkish Barracks

Bab al-Anbariya

Al-Anbariya Mosque

To Jidda

Sikaya

♪ Mosque   Gardens   —— Old city wall

0   100 meters
0   100 yards

© carta

63

55. THE SPANISH RECONQUISTA, 13TH TO 15TH CENTURIES

The term *reconquista* refers to the recovery of the Iberian Peninsula from the Moors by Spanish Christian kings. This was a slow and drawn out process, partly because the Christian military was weak or merely inactive and slothful, partly because Spanish Christians had adopted Arabic culture and language, yet without changing their religion. Moreover, the finale of Moorish rule in Spain, the small kingdom of Granada (1235–1492), expressed a splendor of material culture, of which the Alhambra and its gardens is a permanent memorial.

Historians date the beginning of the Reconquista from the Christian victory at Covadonga in 718, when the Muslim advance was turned back at the Cantabrian Mountains. It was in fact a mere skirmish, but here the advance of Islam halted and the kingdom of the Asturias was born. By 797 Alfonso II had established a capital at Oviedo and ruled as far west as Galicia and eastward to Santander. During his reign (791–842), a body, believed to be that of the apostle James, was discovered. A national shrine, Santiago de Compostela, was built, to which pilgrims flocked from all Europe.

Louis I, the Pious, seized Barcelona in 801, the first territory to be reconquered. Thereafter it maintained absolute independence; in the Asturias, however, bribes — accepted as tribute — were paid to Muslim kingdoms. Out of the Asturias grew León and Castile, and then Navarre and Aragon. Their progress was marked in 1063 by the papal commendation that the Reconquista was a crusade, the forerunner of those to recover the Holy Land.

When the caliphate of Córdoba collapsed in 1031 the situation altered: al-Andalus (as the Arabs called all Spain) was divided into petty kingdoms (map 35). Saragossa, Toledo, Badajoz, and Seville became tributary to Castile. With the death of Ferdinand I in 1065, Castile, León, and Galicia were divided among his three sons, an act that weakened the Christian cause. Nevertheless Alfonso I of León (r. 1065–1109) and Castile (r. 1072–1109), after several raids, succeeded in capturing the ancient Visigothic capital of Toledo in 1085. A further major advance was made in 1143, when Portugal liberated itself, and Lisbon was made its capital with the help of English Crusaders in 1147. By 1179, Castile and Aragon recognized each other's boundaries in the treaty of Cazorla, which vertically divided Spain until the union of the crowns in the fifteenth century. Toledo now became a great cultural center. The masters of Arab, Hebrew, and ancient Greek culture — not simply belles-lettres, but also theology, law, science, astronomy, and medicine — were translated into Latin. Students flocked from England, France, and Germany.

In 1212 the united Christian forces defeated the Almohads at Las Navas de Tolosa. Muslim city after Muslim city fell to the Christians. The Great Mosque of Córdoba became a cathedral.

There now remained only Granada. Around 1231 an Arab of Medinese descent, Muhammad I al-Ghalib (r. 1231–1273), carved out a small kingdom around Jaén. In 1235, he made Granada his capital. The Nasrid dynasty encouraged commerce, particularly the silk trade, making Granada the richest city in Europe. The last Nasrid rulers had not the ability of the founder, and the city fell to Castile on 2 January 1492.

It was the end of Arab domination in the West. The eminent historian Stanley Lane-Poole wrote:
The Moors were banished; for a while Christian Spain shone, like the moon, with a borrowed light; then came the eclipse, and in that darkness Spain has grovelled ever since.

55 THE SPANISH RECONQUISTA, 13TH TO 15TH CENTURIES

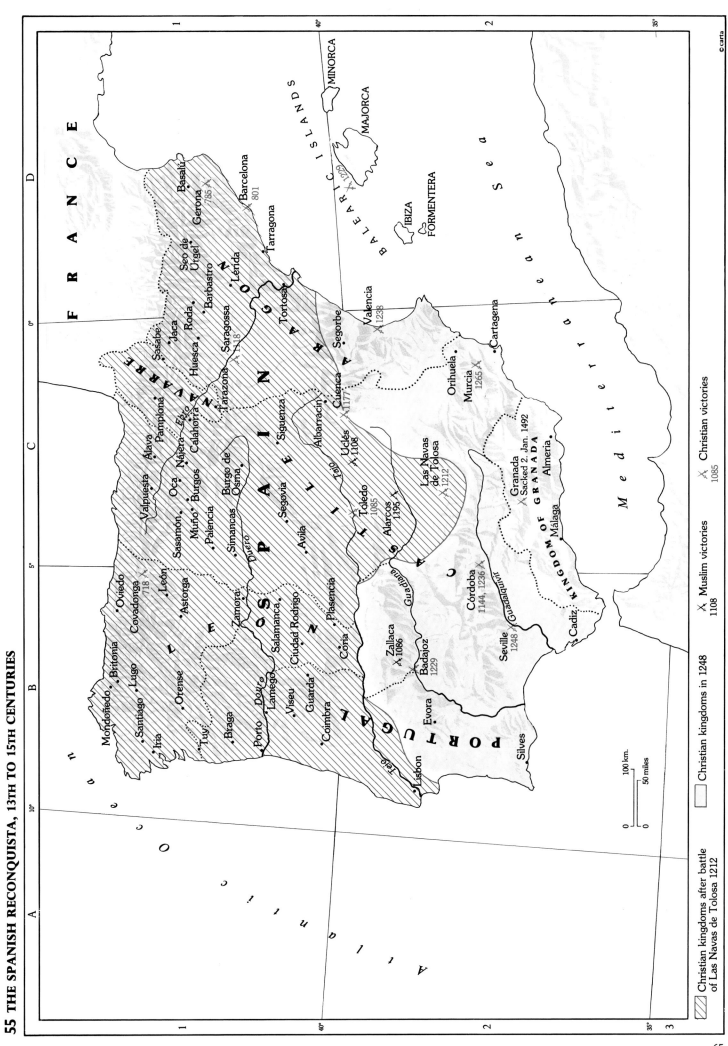

FRANCE

D

Basalú
Gerona 785 X
Barcelona 801 X
Tarragona
Seo de Urgel
Barbastro
Lérida
Tortosa
Jaca
Roda
Huesca
Saragossa
1118 X
Sasabe
Segorbe
Valencia 1238 X
Cartagena

C

NAVARRE
Pamplona
Alava
Ebro
Nájera
Calahorria
Tarazona
Siguenza
Cuenca 1177 X
Albarracin
Uclés 1108 X
Tajo
Orihuela
Murcia 1265 X
Valpuesta
Oca
Burgos
Muño
Sasamón
Burgo de Osma
Segovia
Avila
Palencia
Simancas
Duero
Toledo 1085
Alarcos 1195 X
Las Navas de Tolosa 1212 X
Granada Sacked 2. Jan. 1492 X
Almeria
Málaga

B

Mondoñedo
Britonia
Lugo
Oviedo
Covadonga 718 X
León
Astorga
Zamora
Salamanca
Ciudad Rodrigo
Plasencia
Coria
Guadiana
Cordoba 1144, 1236 X
Guadalquivir
Seville 1248 X
Cadiz
Santiago
Iria
Orense
Tuy
Braga
Porto
Douro
Lamego
Viseu
Guarda
Coimbra
Tejo
Evora
Lisbon
Silves
Zallaca 1086 X
Badajoz 1229 X

PORTUGAL

LEON

CASTILE

ARAGON

KINGDOM OF GRANADA

SPAIN

FRANCE

Mediterranean Sea

BALEARIC ISLANDS
MINORCA
MAJORCA 1229 X
IBIZA
FORMENTERA

Atlantic Ocean

A

100 km.
50 miles
0

Christian kingdoms after battle of Las Navas de Tolosa 1212

Christian kingdoms in 1248

X Muslim victories 1108

X Christian victories 1085

© carta

65

56. THE TRAVELS OF IBN BATTUTA, 1324-1348 AND 1352-1353

After al-Idrisi (map 47), no Arab geographer of importance emerged. In Granada geographical treatises were replaced by travel literature, among which was Ibn Jubayr's narrative describing his explorations of the East between 1183 and 1217. Ibn Jubayr traveled no further than Egypt, Iraq, and Mecca. Al-Mazini of Granada, however, reached Russia and described the trade of the Bulgars in the Volga region in fossil mammoth ivory, which was exported as far as Khwarizm.

Chief among these narrators was Ibn Battuta, who was born in Tangier in 1304, and died in Marrakesh in 1377. His uncle was *qadi* (religious judge) of Ronda, near Málaga. Living at a time when it was customary for well-to-do young men to travel as part of their education and to attend lectures in foreign centers of Islamic learning, Ibn Battuta's journeys extended throughout the Islamic world and beyond, into the Black Sea, and, via India, Ceylon, and the Maldives, to Bengal, Assam, Sumatra, and even China. His *rihla* (travels) thus went far beyond the traditional scope, which was generally confined to journeys to Mecca. As literature his Rihla became popular in Spain and Morocco.

Ibn Battuta's Rihla was transcribed at the command of the Marinid ruler of Fez, Abu Inan. The text was produced by the scholar Ibn Juzayy. Problems regarding the originality of certain passages as well as numerous editorial glosses and garnishes have plagued scholars. In many instances, the style is elaborate, in others it is succinct and irritatingly dry. It includes long and often tedious quotations from poetry. Nevertheless, having set out initially to educate himself, Ibn Battuta seems to have developed a passion for descriptive geography, for the movement of commerce, and for people — their migrations, their national habits, and, above all, their practice of religion. How his journeys were financed is not disclosed. In India and in the Maldives he served as *qadi*, a position he held in Marrakesh when he died. His journey to China was a diplomatic mission, and this would have been financed by Delhi. Despite his interest in commerce, he does not appear to have engaged in it.

Difficulties arise over the details of his journeys and their chronology, but it is possible to arrange them in a less than arbitrary fashion. In 1325 to 1326 he traveled from Tangier along North Africa to Egypt, Upper Egypt, and Syria, leaving Damascus for Mecca in September 1326. In 1326 to 1327 he visited Iraq, Khuzestan, Fars, Jibal, Tabriz, Baghdad, Samarra, and Mosul, before returning to Arabia. He remained in Arabia until 1330, making the Pilgrimage three times. In 1330 he set off for Yemen and traveled by sea to Zeila, Mogadishu, Mombasa, and Kilwa, returning via Oman and the Persian Gulf to make the Pilgrimage once again in 1332. He then traveled in Egypt, Syria, Asia Minor, Constantinople, Transoxiana, and Afghanistan, reaching Delhi in 1333 and remaining there as chief *qadi* until 1342. There followed a year and a half in the Maldives, followed by a voyage to Bengal, Assam, and Sumatra, and eventually China. It is disputed whether he actually reached Peking (Beijing). This journey and the return took until 1347, when, after passing up the Persian Gulf and visiting Iraq, Syria, and Egypt, he once again made the Pilgrimage.

Ibn Battuta was twenty-one years old when he set out; he was now forty-five. He returned home to Fez, via Tunis, Sardinia, and Algeria in 1349, making a visit to Granada and Ronda shortly after. In 1352 to 1353 he made what physically must have been the most difficult journey of all, to the kingdom of Mali, important to the ruler of Fez as a source of gold. His stories, especially of the Turkish lands, India, and China, must have seemed as incredible to his hearers as was James Bruce of Kinnaird's account of Ethiopia to his readers in London in the eighteenth century. Nevertheless, modern scholarship confirms Ibn Battuta's basic veracity.

56 THE TRAVELS OF IBN BATTUTA, 1324-1348 AND 1352-1353

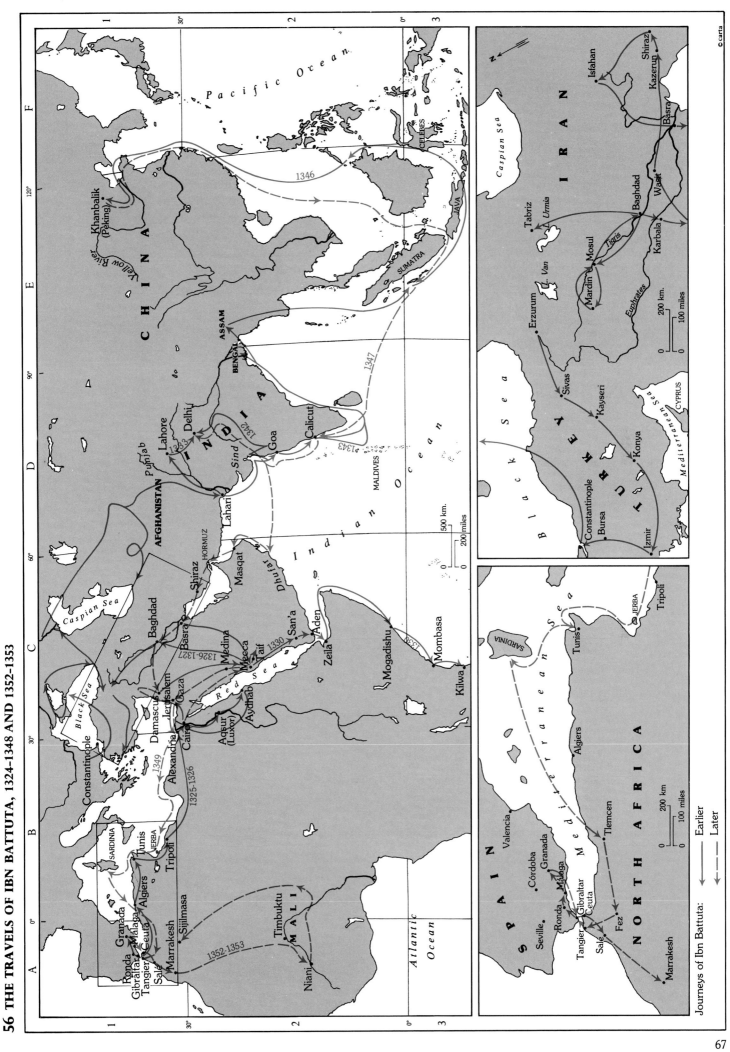

Journeys of Ibn Battuta: Earlier —— Later ----

57. CAMPAIGNS OF HULAGU KHAN AND HIS GENERALS, 1253-1260

In the first quarter of the thirteenth century the Mongols, under Chingis Khan, conquered the world from Korea to the Caspian Sea and The Himalayas. The once proud Baghdad caliphate had disintegrated into numerous petty dynasties. The unwieldy empire had had no cohesive administration, and Arabs, non-Arabs, Muslims, non-Muslims, Turks of differing tribes, and Persians inevitably drifted apart. In Islam, too, warring sects added to the degeneration of a society already weakened by slavery, eunuchs, harems, boy and girl slaves, and suffering from epidemics and, in Mesopotamia, disastrous floods.

In 1253, Chingis Khan's grandson, Hulagu, and his army set out from Mongolia with the intention of destroying the Assassins and then the caliphate itself. The caliph ignored Hulagu's request to join him against the Assassins, who by 1256 were largely annihilated. Hulagu then passed through Khorasan to Baghdad, which he invested. On 10 February 1258, he entered the capital. The caliph was put to death with three-hundred officials. The city was burned and plundered, and a majority of the population slaughtered without mercy.

In 1260 Hulagu marched into northern Syria, first against Aleppo, and then against Hama and Harim. Fifty-thousand persons were killed in Aleppo alone. An army was sent to besiege Damascus, while Hulagu returned to Persia on the news of the death of his brother Mangu Khan. This proved to be a turning point. At Ayn Jalut, near Nazareth, the Mongols were defeated by the Mamluk general Baybars, who was soon to be the Mamluk sultan. Hulagu returned later, but, having failed to make an alliance with the Crusaders to conquer Syria, he again returned to Persia, which was now to become the base of an empire (see map 64).

58. THE SPREAD OF ISLAM TO MALAYSIA AND INDONESIA, 13TH TO 17TH CENTURIES

A Chinese report exists of an Arab settlement in Sumatra in 671. According to al-Mas'udi (map 33), 120,000 Arab and Muslim traders were massacred in Canton in a peasant rebellion in 889. In consequence many fled to Kedah in Malaysia and Palembang in Sumatra. Malay chronicles, however, relate that Islam was brought to Sumatra by an Arab missionary in 1112; others claim that the sharif of Mecca sent a missionary in the mid-thirteenth century.

By the early fourteenth century Muslim burials are recorded on tombstones. In 1409 the ruler of Malacca Islamized, and made Malacca and Pasai centers of Sufi propaganda and Islamic learning. Ibn Battuta (see map 56) visited Pasai in 1346 and relates how the sultan was devoted to theological debate and zealous in propagating Islam. During the fifteenth century, Islam reached south Sumatra, south Borneo, Brunei, and the Moluccas; by the sixteenth century the whole area as far as Sumba and Ternate had been converted.

Various theories have been put forward to explain this surge eastward: more frequent trade contacts with Muslim traders; competition with Christian missionaries after the arrival of the Portuguese; political convenience and deference to sultans; and the influence of Sufism and its fraternities. Of these it may be said that, as later in Africa, the last, which would have been seen as an enrollment into a worldwide fellowship, was probably the most potent.

57 CAMPAIGNS OF HULAGU KHAN AND HIS GENERALS, 1253-1260

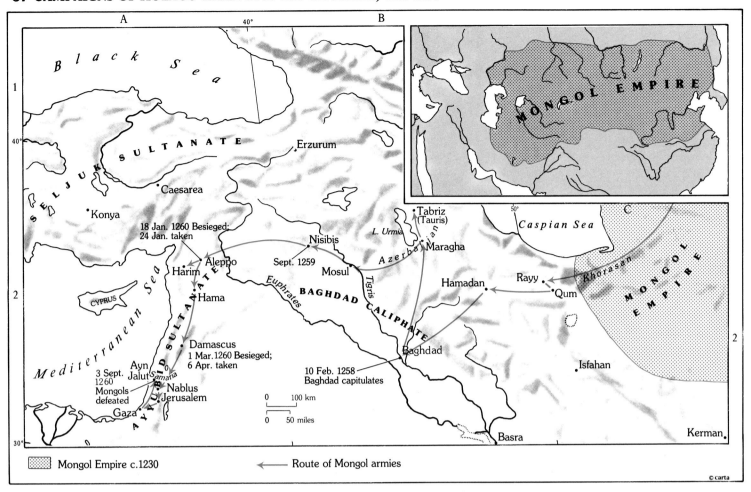

18 Jan. 1260 Besieged;
24 Jan. taken

Sept. 1259

10 Feb. 1258
Baghdad capitulates

3 Sept. 1260
Mongols defeated

Damascus
1 Mar.1260 Besieged;
6 Apr. taken

MONGOL EMPIRE

Black Sea

SELJUK SULTANATE

Erzurum

Caesarea

Konya

Aleppo
Harim
Hama

CYPRUS

Mediterranean Sea

AYYUBID SULTANATE

Ayn Jalut
Samaria
Nablus
Jerusalem
Gaza

Nisibis

Mosul

Euphrates

BAGHDAD CALIPHATE

Tigris

Tabriz (Tauris)

L. Urmia

Azerbaijan

Maragha

Hamadan

Baghdad

Isfahan

Basra

Caspian Sea

MONGOL EMPIRE

Rayy
Qum

Khorasan

Kerman

0   100 km
0   50 miles

▨ Mongol Empire c.1230   ← Route of Mongol armies

© carta

58 THE SPREAD OF ISLAM TO MALAYSIA AND INDONESIA, 13TH TO 14TH CENTURIES

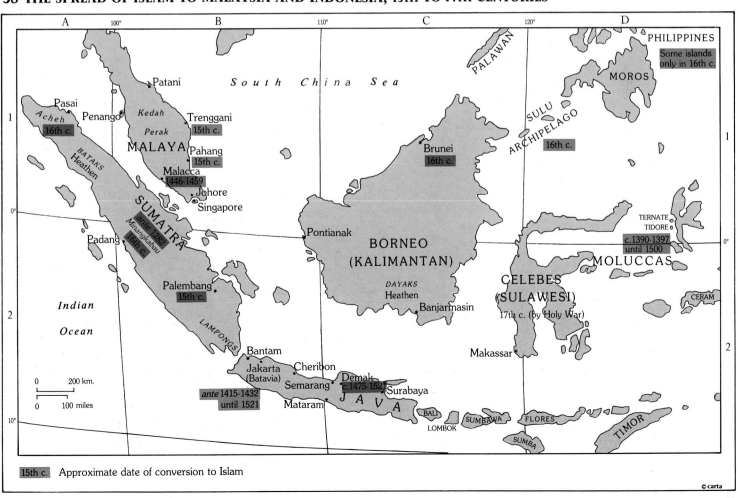

PHILIPPINES

Some islands only in 16th c.

PALAWAN

South China Sea

MOROS

SULU ARCHIPELAGO

16th c.

Patani

Pasai
Penango
Acheh
16th c.

BATAKS
Heathen

Kedah
Perak

MALAYA

Trenggani
15th c.

Pahang
15th c.

Malacca
1446-1459

Johore

Singapore

SUMATRA

Minangkabau
ante 1282
16th c.

Padang

Palembang
15th c.

Indian Ocean

LAMPONGS

Bantam

Jakarta (Batavia)

Cheribon

Semarang

Demak
c.1475-1521

Surabaya

ante 1415-1432
until 1521

Mataram

JAVA

BALI

LOMBOK

SUMBAWA

SUMBA

FLORES

TIMOR

Pontianak

BORNEO (KALIMANTAN)

DAYAKS
Heathen

Banjarmasin

Brunei
16th c.

CELEBES (SULAWESI)

17th c. (by Holy War)

Makassar

TERNATE
TIDORE
c.1390-1397
until 1500

MOLUCCAS

CERAM

0   200 km.
0   100 miles

▨ 15th c.   Approximate date of conversion to Islam

© carta

59. COMMERCE IN THE MIDDLE AGES

Located in the center of the market area of the older part of Cairo is the Khan al-Khalili (see map 48). It was founded in 1400 by Garkas al-Khalili, master of the horse to the sultan Barquq, and is a maze of lanes among a multitude of little streets. One can only enter it on foot and must beware of passing loaded donkeys. It is a microcosm of medieval markets from the Atlantic to China and from the Hanse towns to Zanzibar. Today one is still assailed by the rich scent of spices, the musk from central Asia, and civet from Ethiopia in the perfumers' booths and by the hammering of the coppersmiths, silversmiths, goldsmiths, and jewelers. Almost every conceivable commodity known to the medieval world can still be found.

Cairo was the trade center of the medieval world, the connecting link between Africa and Asia, of Europe with India and the Far East. Under the Bahri Mamluk sultan al-Nasir (r. 1293–1340, with some intermissions) embassies from Russia, Persia, Yemen, Ethiopia, western Africa, Constantinople, Bulgaria, India, Aragon, and France, and even to the Holy See were established. The goal of all these was commerce. After the disastrous earthquake of 1303, which destroyed most of Cairo, there was a period of unparalleled prosperity. Between 1303 and 1360 no less than forty-three mosques were built, a sure sign of a superfluity of wealth. The fourteenth century witnessed the development of a court culture, and Ibn Battuta (see map 56 remarks on how Mamluk court ceremonial was imitated in Yemen, India, and the petty courts of eastern and western Africa. There and in Malaysia and Indonesia the word *sultan* was used for the ruler. In the mid-fourteenth century the Chinese admiral Cheng Ho was sent on several voyages in the Indian Ocean, but these voyages appear to have been diplomatic rather than commercial. Trade with China was, however, long established, and even in the tenth century al-Mas'udi complained of the great quantity of ivory that was taken to China, creating a scarcity in Muslim lands. Trade throughout the Indian Ocean was primarily in the hands of Arab seamen, and it is not without significance that coins from eastern Africa with Arabic inscriptions have been found in northwest Australia, possibly from shipwreck.

All this was only one part of the commerce of Cairo and the Middle East. From the shores of the Levant and from the Black Sea radiated land routes to central Asia and onward to China. The Polo brothers made more than one journey and were acquainted with the whole commercial system of the Great Khan and his tributaries. The Khan was likewise aware of the Levantine world, and on their second journey, at his request, the Polo brothers brought him oil from the Holy Sepulcher in Jerusalem. In the aftermath of the first Crusade, consuls were established by Genoa, Pisa, Florence, and Venice in the Levant, Constantinople, Palestine, Syria, and Egypt. In 1251 French consuls were established at Alexandria and Tripoli; after 1268 Barcelona established consuls *in partibus ultramarinis* (in parts beyond the sea). These early consulates were the forerunners of the European consulates in the Ottoman Empire and throughout the Mediterranean. Though other Italian cities, such as Lucca, also participated in the oriental trade, Genoa and Venice were predominant. The object of these consulates was wholly commercial — the promotion of trade contacts and transactions from within their own boundaries, and from their posts with the whole commercial system of Europe.

59 COMMERCE IN THE MIDDLE AGES

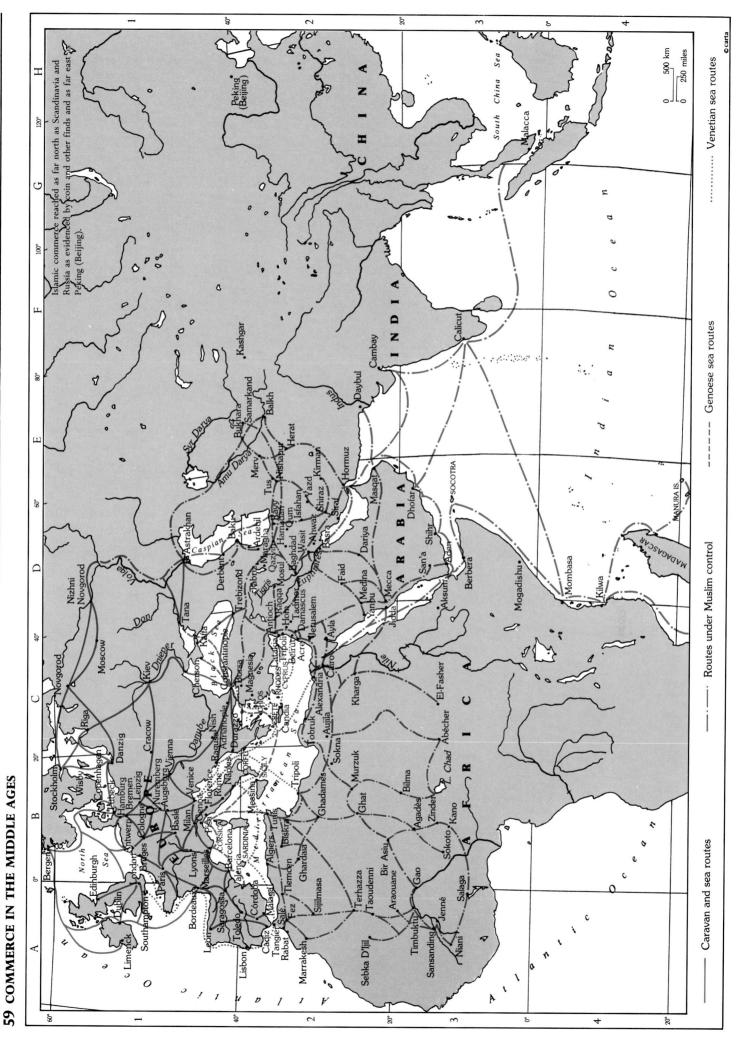

Islamic commerce reached as far north as Scandinavia and
Russia as evidenced by coin and other finds and as far east
as Peking (Beijing).

Key:

———— Caravan and sea routes

——— Routes under Muslim control

—·—·— Venetian sea routes

——————— Genoese sea routes

············· Routes under Muslim control

© carta

60. THE SPREAD OF THE BLACK DEATH, 1331-1368

In the mid-fourteenth century a devastating pandemic of plague swept the Middle East and Europe. The historian Ibn Khaldun, who lost his father, mother, and many of his teachers, wrote:

Civilization both in the East and the West was visited by a destructive plague which devastated nations and caused populations to vanish. It swallowed up many of the good things of civilization and wiped them out. It overtook dynasties at the time of their senility, when they had reached the limit of their duration. It lessened their power and curtailed their influence. It weakened their authority. Their situation approached the point of annihilation and dissolution. Civilization decreased with the decrease of mankind. Cities and buildings were laid waste, roads and way signs were obliterated, settlements and mansions became empty, dynasties and tribes became weak. The entire inhabited world changed. The East, it seems, was similarly visited, though in accordance with and in proportion to [its more affluent] civilization.

Long before the fourteenth century Middle Eastern people suffered from plague. Arab authors document it fairly well; however, they often do not distinguish the characteristic buboes, or swellings, in the thighs and armpits, so it is not certain whether a given epidemic was typhus, smallpox, cholera, or another contagious disease. From the sixth century on there are records of cases that can be attributed to rat-borne plague in Syria, Ethiopia (probably Nubia), the Sudan, Egypt, and Asia Minor as far west as Constantinople. In 639 it caused anxiety for the caliph Umar I, who suspended Arab operations in Syria. At the beginning of the Abbasid period, around 750, the plague was rife in Syria and Iraq, recurring in Kufa and Basra as often as every tenth year. It was not less endemic in Europe.

The Black Death of the mid-fourteenth century almost certainly originated in the Asiatic steppes. A permanent reservoir of infection still exists among wild rodents. Sources in both Latin and Arabic agree that the plague was preceded by violent ecological changes, such as earthquakes, flooding, and famines. This conjunction of events is equally clear in the Chinese annals. These disasters destroyed the natural habitats of the wild rodents and drove them into human settlements, where they infected domestic rats, mice, and other animals. The effective agent, however, was not the rodents, but the fleas in their fur. Thus the Black Death was carried into China and India, westward into southeastern Russia, along the trade routes into Syria and Egypt, then into the Mediterranean, and finally into northern Europe. Careful examination of the evidence does not support the older views that it was transmitted either from China and India along the routes to the Middle East — both by land and sea — or by the sea route from China through the Indian Ocean and the Red Sea to Egypt. There is no evidence of the plague in Iraq, Arabia, and Egypt before it had occurred in the Crimea or Mediterranean. When it did occur in Iraq, Arabia, and Egypt, the evidence suggests that it came from the north, and only after it had reached Egypt did it reach Yemen. The most potent source of dissemination appears to have been the Genoese trading agency at Kaffa (Feodosiya) in the Crimea.

It is difficult to estimate the number of deaths, but it is certain that in the towns of Egypt and Syria the population was greatly reduced, with serious economic consequences.

60 THE SPREAD OF THE BLACK DEATH, 1331–1368

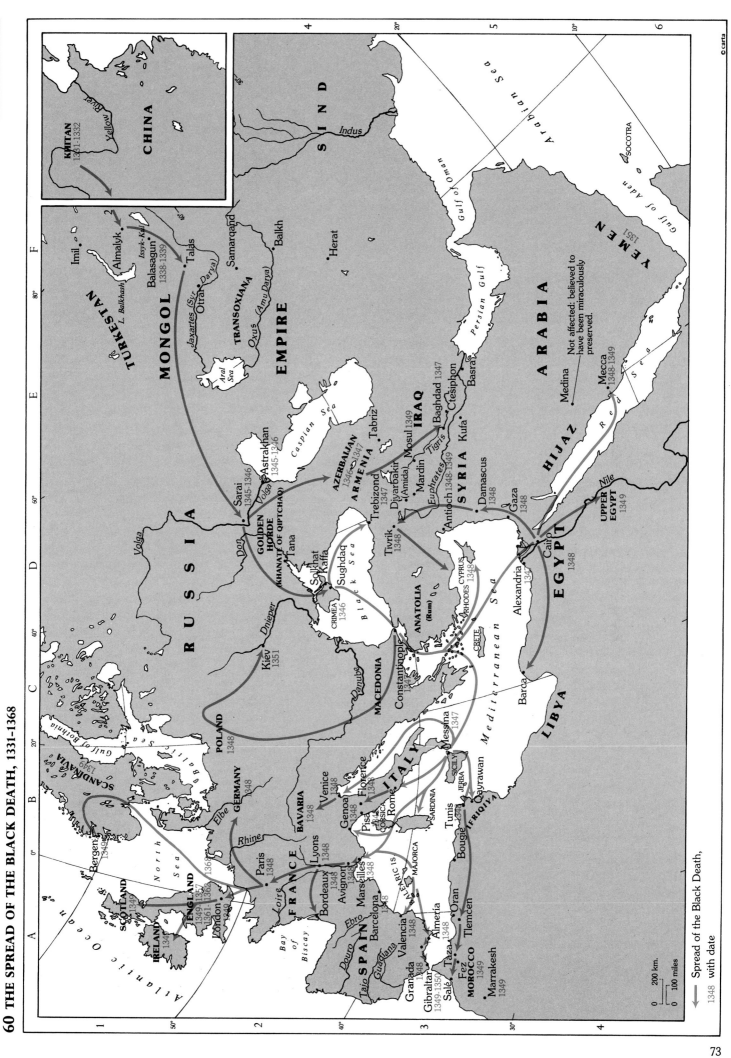

Spread of the Black Death,
1348 ← with date

61. THE DOMINIONS OF TIMUR-LENG (TAMERLANE), 1360–1405

Timur-Leng was born in 1336, allegedly the son of a shepherd. He claimed to be a descendant of Chingiz Khan. As a young man he showed distinction in battle, and in 1361 he was appointed vizier of Samarqand. Having defeated various opponents, he made himself ruler of Balkh in 1370; but it took until 1380, and nine expeditions, to make himself master of Jata and Khwarizm. On these expeditions as official protector of Islam, he was accompanied by Naqshbandiya Sufis, holy and learned men, as well as men of letters.

Now he began a far-ranging career of conquest in earnest, either in person or vicariously by his generals. In 1380–1381, Timur sent Toqtomish, the khan of Crimea, against Russia. Moscow was sacked. In 1391 Toqtomish turned against Timur, invading Transoxiana and threatening Samarqand. In 1380-1381 Timur invaded Khorasan, and in 1383 he seized Gurgan, Mazandaran and Seistan; in 1384 the city of Herat rebelled, whereon Timur suppressed its Kart dynasty. In 1384–1385 Mazandaran received similar treatment. In 1386–1387 Timur seized Fars, Iraq, Luristan, and Azerbaijan. He wintered at Tabriz, fining Isfahan for rebellion and killing seventy-thousand citizens, whose skulls were piled to form towers.

During the next five years he suppressed heretics in the Caspian region, eliminated the Muzaffarid dynasty in Fars, and campaigned in Mesopotamia. In Asia Minor he sacked Edessa, Takrit, Mardin, and Amida. He then conquered Georgia, and finally he occupied Moscow, where he remained for a year.

His attention was then drawn in another direction.

Contending that the Indian rulers were lax in imposing Islam on their subjects, he attacked India, taking Delhi in 1398. He plundered and destroyed the city, killing eighty-thousand citizens. Then he had to hurry westward, for Syria, Iraq, and Azerbaijan were in rebellion. The rebellions repressed, he ravaged Georgia and set out for Asia Minor in 1400, seizing Siwa and Malatya. He proceeded to Syria, taking Aleppo, Hama, Homs, Baalbek, Damascus and Baghdad, where some twenty-thousand to forty-thousand citizens were massacred. In the following year, 1402, he fought across Asia Minor, through Ankara to Bursa and Smyrna. There he received embassies from Constantinople and Egypt, recognizing his authority. He now retired to Samarqand, where he received further recognition, including that of Castile. Its ambassador left a lively account of the festivities celebrating the marriages of grandsons of Timur.

At the end of 1403 he set out to conquer China. On 17 January 1404, he died. His body was brought back to Samarqand and buried in the Gur-e Amir, a mausoleum that still exists. From 1370 until 1405 this extraordinary and restless character had dominated the Middle East. Yet he had created no permanent empire. He partitioned his vast domain among his sons and grandsons. Grave and serious in demeanor, he was wholly ruthless and without mercy to criminals and to those who displeased him. He had had little education, but he encouraged learning. Public works, administration, commerce, industry, the organization of the army, and, above all, the spread of Islam were his principal concern.

61 THE DOMINIONS OF TIMUR-LENG (TAMBERLANE), 1360–1405

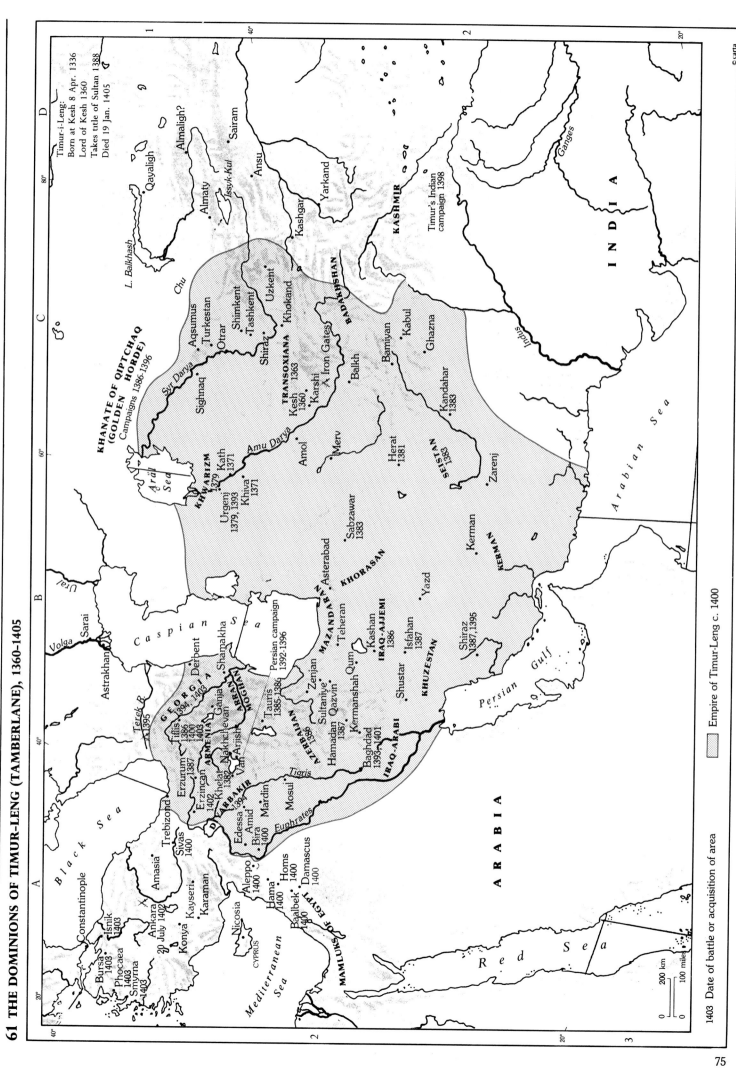

Timur-i-Leng:
Born at Kesh 8 Apr. 1336
Lord of Kesh 1360
Takes tutle of Sultan 1388
Died 19 Jan. 1405

KHANATE OF QIPTCHAQ
(GOLDEN HORDE)
Campaigns 1386-1396

Empire of Timur-Leng c. 1400

1403 Date of battle or acquisition of area

62. THE SULTANATE OF DELHI, 13TH CENTURY TO 1525

At the end of the twelfth century Muhammad Ghuri swept across India and established the seeds of Islam from Afghanistan to Bengal (map 49). His adopted son, Qutb al-Din Aybak, a Mamluk (cf. map 51), founded what is known as the "Slave Dynasty of Delhi" (1206–1290), of which the most eminent was his son-in-law Iltutmish. The inclusion of his domain within the eastern caliphate received formal recognition from Baghdad in 1232.

He was succeeded by his daughter, Rasiyyat al-Din (1236–1240), the first woman ruler recorded in Islam. The nobility deposed her, but the two feeble reigns that followed were no better. Another Mamluk, Ulugh Khan Balban, already vizier, took power and inaugurated a reign of terror (1246–1266). His successors are presented by Indian historians either as religious fanatics or as worthless debauchees. In 1290 the nobility again intervened and enthroned a Khalji Turk, Jalal al-Din Firuz Khalji. In 1292 he repelled a Mongol invasion successfully, only to be murdered by his nephew Ala al-Din (1296–1316). Although Ibn Battuta (map 56) describes him as "one of the best of sultans," an Indian contemporary speaks of his "crafty cruelty," his vicious conduct, and his lust for blood. His hatred was aimed primarily at Hindus, whose neighboring states were attacked in incessant wars. An infant succeeded him, but was murdered by Qutb al-Din Mubarak (r. 1316–1321), of whom the Indian historian wrote that "he attended to nothing but drinking, listening to music, debauchery, and pleasure, scattering gifts and gratifying his lusts."

In the struggle for power that ensued the ultimate victor was Muhammad ibn Tughluq (r. 1325–1351), to whom Ibn Battuta was chief *qadi* (judge) in Delhi for seven years. Both he, a Berber, and Barani, an Indian historian, condemn the sultan's inhuman tyranny, while praising his accomplishments, the elegance of his letters in Arabic and Persian, and his knowledge of logic, philosophy, mathematics, the physical sciences, and medicine. He prayed with regularity, abstained from wine, and was gallant in war. Both believed that absolute power perverted his judgment, and they suspected some degree of insanity. In such circumstances it is not surprising that his conquests were ephemeral. The quickly won empire began to fall apart, soon vast territories were lost. The empire was soon conquered by Timur-Leng in 1398.

Timur-Leng had no intention of remaining in India, and until 1450 chaos supervened with shifts of power among local rulers. Finally, in 1451 Buhlul Lodi, an Afghan of the Lodi tribe, was proclaimed sultan. This was the beginning of the Afghan dominance of northern India. He began the task of reunification, which was continued under his son Sikandar Lodi. Jaunpur and Bihar were regained, and his long reign (1489 until 1517) at last ended in natural death. Hostile to Hinduism, Buhlul Lodi took pains to foster the economy and to keep prices low for those with small means. Like his predecessors he took great interest in architecture and the erection of public buildings, which were greatly damaged by an earthquake in 1505. His son Ibrahim Lodi succeeded him, maintaining his father's economic policies. He was defeated and killed at Panipat by Babur in 1526 (map 72) — a defeat that signified the end of the Delhi sultanate.

Force had brought a new religion to India and with it a new outlook upon the world. Hindu armies had been shown to be inefficient. The Hindu caste system had been overthrown in vast areas. Not only a new architectural medium, combining Indian with Persian and Arab traditions, but a cosmopolitan culture and knowledge of the world from the Atlas Mountains to Afghanistan had been introduced. The Moroccan Ibn Battuta, chief *qadi* at Delhi, was the most apt symptom of an irrevocably changed world.

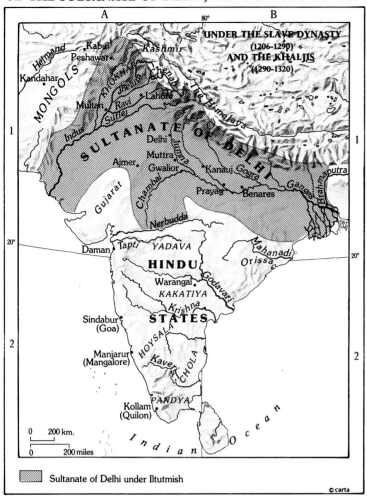

UNDER THE SLAVE DYNASTY
(1206-1290)
AND THE KHALJIS
(1290-1320)

Sultanate of Delhi under Iltutmish

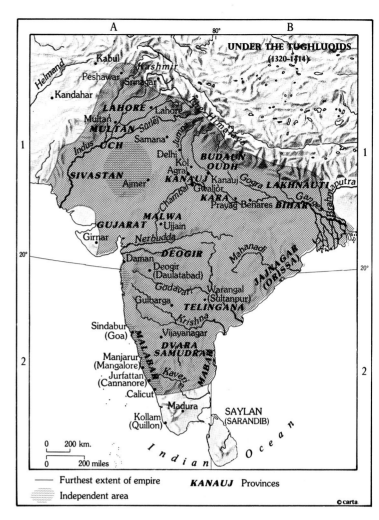

UNDER THE TUGHLUQIDS
(1320-1414)

— Furthest extent of empire   *KANAUJ* Provinces

~~~ Independent area

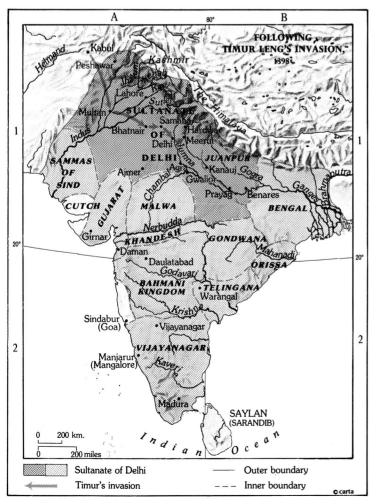

FOLLOWING
TIMUR LENG'S INVASION,
1398

Sultanate of Delhi   — Outer boundary

← Timur's invasion   --- Inner boundary

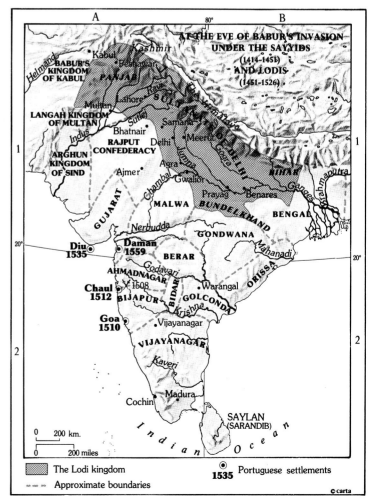

AT THE EVE OF BABUR'S INVASION
UNDER THE SAYYIDS
(1414-1451)
AND LODIS
(1451-1526)

The Lodi kingdom   ⊙ Portuguese settlements

--- Approximate boundaries   **1535**

63. THE EXPANSION OF THE OTTOMAN DOMINIONS, C. 1300–1520

Up to 1517 the history of the Ottoman Turks is characterized by almost continuous territorial expansion. The founder of the dynasty, Osman I, emerged as a minor chief in northwest Anatolia in 1293 and as leader of a band of *gazis* (fighters for the faith of Islam), against the Byzantines. By 1517 his descendants held Hungary, the Balkans, the Crimea, Asia Minor, Syria, Palestine, and Egypt. By mid-century North Africa, Mesopotamia, and the holy cities of Mecca and Medina had been added.

After a firm base with Bursa as capital was established in Asia Minor in 1324, the Ottomans by-passed Byzantium and crossed into Europe. The first major conquests in Europe provided a fruitful source of mercenaries. In 1361 Adrianople, the second city of the Byzantine empire, was seized and renamed the Ottoman capital Edirne. In 1364 Philippopolis fell. The Ottomans now controlled the principal Byzantine sources of grain and taxation. In 1371 Bulgaria, Hungary, and Serbia allied against the Ottoman advance. In the war that followed Bulgaria fell in 1382, Sofia in 1385, Nish in 1386, and Serbia in 1389. After crushing the allies in a battle at Kossovo the Ottoman conqueror Murad I was killed. His son Bayezid I could not follow up the victory because of a revolt in Anatolia. In a battle at Nicopolis in 1396 Bayezid I finally defeated the allies.

Timur-Leng (map 61) now felt threatened and campaigned against Bayezid throughout Asia Minor. Bayezid was defeated and taken prisoner at Ankara in 1402. The nascent empire was all but extinguished. Quarrels about the succession followed, and only in 1413 did Mehmed I emerge to control all the provinces. Under him and his son, Murad II (r. 1421–1451), the system of indirect rule, which had been earlier Ottoman policy, was restored. In 1422–1423 Murad besieged Byzantium and took huge amounts of gold in ransom. From 1423 to 1430 he challenged Venice's control of the Adriatic Sea. At the same time he freed himself from the jealousy of local Turkish nobles by instituting the Janissary corps — Christians recruited as slaves and instructed and trained as Muslims — the counterpart of the Egyptian Mamluks (map 51). This corps, owing allegiance to the sultan alone, enabled the completion of the conquest of the European provinces by 1451 (map 74).

The sole unconquered city, Constantinople, fell after a brief siege (6 April to 29 May 1453) to Mehmed II (r. 1451–1481). The Ottoman sultan had been transformed into a Byzantine emperor. Only slowly did the civil service become an Ottoman service, and for a long period Greeks, or Greek converts to Islam, remained dominant. While Islam was the state religion, the *millet* system, which gave each denomination, Christian and Jewish, internal self-government and the power to enforce its own laws, subject to payment of the poll tax, enabled a wide degree of freedom. The Sufi fraternities, and especially the Bektashis, of whose order the sultans were members, developed a syncretistic doctrine that was only nominally Sunni.

Under Bayezid II (r. 1481–1512) the empire was further extended with small additions in Europe north of the Danube. His successor, Selim I, the Grim (r. 1512–1520), inherited the aggressive spirit of his ancestors. In 1514 he attacked the Safavids in Persia (map 66), routing them at Chaldiran, and took Azerbaijan. No attempt was made to seize their empire. Instead Selim turned south and attacked the Mamluks, all of whose possessions in Syria and Egypt he took without difficulty in 1516–1517.

63 THE EXPANSION OF THE OTTOMAN DOMINIONS, C.1300–1520

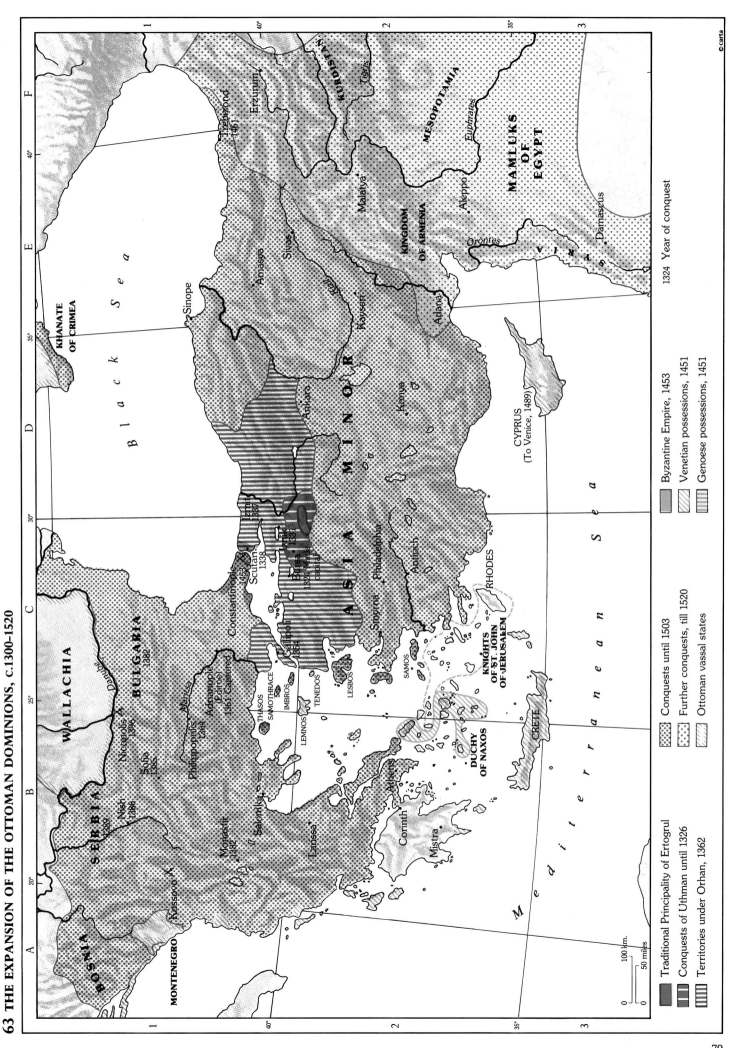

BOSNIA
MONTENEGRO
SERBIA
Kossovo ✗ 1389
Nish 1386
WALLACHIA
Danube
Nicopolis ✗ 1396
Sofia 1385
BULGARIA 1382
Monastir 1382
Salonika
Larissa
Athens
Corinth
Mistra
Philippopolis (Filibe) 1363 Conquered
Adrianople (Edirne) 1361
Maritsa
THASOS
SAMOTHRACE
IMBROS
LEMNOS
TENEDOS
LESBOS
SAMOS
DUCHY OF NAXOS
KNIGHTS OF ST. JOHN OF JERUSALEM
RHODES
CRETE
Constantinople 1453 ✗
Scutari 1338
Gallipoli 1354
Brusa 1326 (First capital)
Iznik 1337
Izmid 1337
ASIA MINOR
Philadelphia
Smyrna
Ankara
Abydoch
Konya
Kayseri
Adana
Sinope
Amasya
Sivas
Malatya
Trebizond 1461
Erzurum
KINGDOM OF ARMENIA
KURDISTAN
Tigris
MESOPOTAMIA
Euphrates
Aleppo
Orontes
SYRIA
Damascus
MAMLUKS OF EGYPT
KHANATE OF CRIMEA
Black Sea
Mediterranean Sea
M e d i t e r r a n e a n   S e a

CYPRUS
(To Venice, 1489)

0   100 km.
0   50 miles

1324 Year of conquest

▓ Traditional Principality of Ertogrul	▒ Byzantine Empire, 1453
▤ Conquests of Uthman until 1326	▨ Venetian possessions, 1451
▥ Territories under Orhan, 1362	▥ Genoese possessions, 1451
▒ Conquests until 1503	
░ Further conquests, till 1520	
▨ Ottoman vassal states	

© carta

79

64. THE IL-KHANIDS OF PERSIA, 1236-1353

Between 1218 and 1221, when the Mongols from central Asia advanced to the Middle East, they subjected only part of Khorasan. Around 1251 a further advance was determined. While Mangu Khan was fighting his brother Kubilai in China, their brother Hulagu was sent with 129,000 men to conquer Persia, Mesopotamia, and, if possible, Syria and Egypt (see map 57). It was this army that the Mamluk general Baybars, later sultan, utterly defeated at Ayn Jalut on 3 September 1260.

Baybars' victory now established a final boundary for the Mongol advance westward. They now held Armenia and the Seljuq possessions in Asia Minor, Mesopotamia, and much of Persia. They acquired Fars by marriage in 1284. Large parts of Persia were independent local dynasties. In 1295 the Persian Mongols adopted Islam and Persian culture and threw off allegiance to the Great Khan.

Some of the Mongols who invaded Persia were Nestorian Christians, but most were shamanists. When they adopted Islam, they were tolerant toward both Shi'ites and Christians, politically hostile toward the Sunni Mamluks in Egypt. Abaka (r. 1265–1282), himself a Buddhist, had diplomatic relations with the Holy See and Crusaders.

Despite its militaristic origin, the Il-Khanid period was one of great artistic activity. Far Eastern influences in textile, ceramics, and miniature painting permeated the Islamic world and, in part, transmuted Seljuq art, whose traditions were continued in the architecture of mosques, *madrasas*, mausoleums, shrines, *khanqas*, khans, and other buildings.

65. THE TIMURIDS, 1369–1506, AND SHAYBANIDS, 1506–1570

The term *Timurids* can include all Timur-Leng's descendants, but for practical purposes it is limited to those who ruled after him as princes. In the west his son Miranshah inherited Iraq, north Syria, Armenia, and Azerbaijan and, in turn, passed it on to his sons. In the east Shahrukh initially ruled only Khorasan. He soon added Transoxiana and eventually controlled most of the area his father had dominated. In contrast with that of his father, his long reign (1405–1447) was one of great tranquillity.

At first the emirs had wished to carry war into China, as Timur himself had desired, but this wish was frustrated when they fell out among themselves. Shahrukh's reign thus began with a series of risings, which lasted until 1429. To the last, peaceful period of his reign is owed his great library at Herat.

On the death of Shahrukh decline in the empire began. His sons quarreled among themselves. In Afghanistan the Uzbeks attacked from the north. The princes could not agree to unify, and the empire steadily disintegrated. The period, nevertheless, was remarkable for its culture. Shahrukh himself was devoted to history, and his son Ulugh Beg studied astronomy, poetry, theology, and another son, Baisonghor, calligraphy. Mystical poets, moralists, apologists, geographers, theologians, jurists, mathematicians, and physicians were numerous, and the arts of painting, bookbinding, calligraphy, ceramics, music, and, above all, architecture, flourished.

Of the later descendants one Babur established a great empire in India (see map 62), while in the north Shaybani's descendants ruled beyond the Syr Darya.

64 THE IL-KHANIDS IN PERSIA, 1236-1353

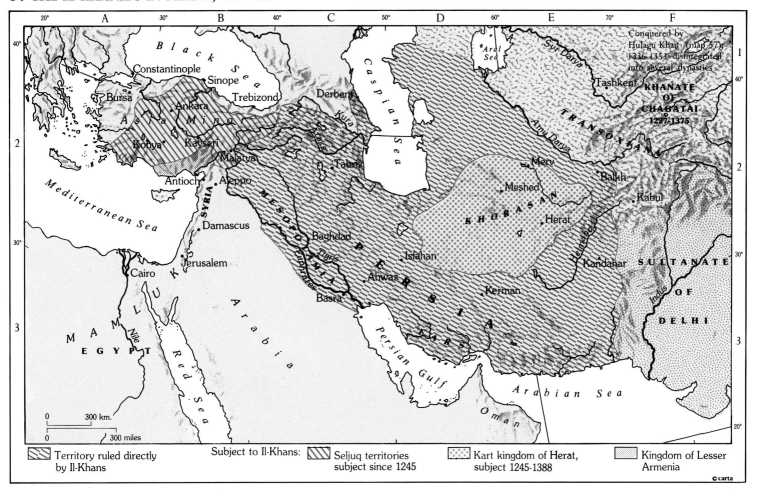

Conquered by Hulagu Khan (map 57) 1336-1353 disintegrated into several dynasties

KHANATE OF CHAGATAI 1227-1375

TRANSOXANA

| Territory ruled directly by Il-Khans | Subject to Il-Khans: Seljuq territories subject since 1245 | Kart kingdom of Herat, subject 1245-1388 | Kingdom of Lesser Armenia |

© carta

65 THE TIMURIDS, 1369-1506, AND SHAYBANIDS, 1506-1570

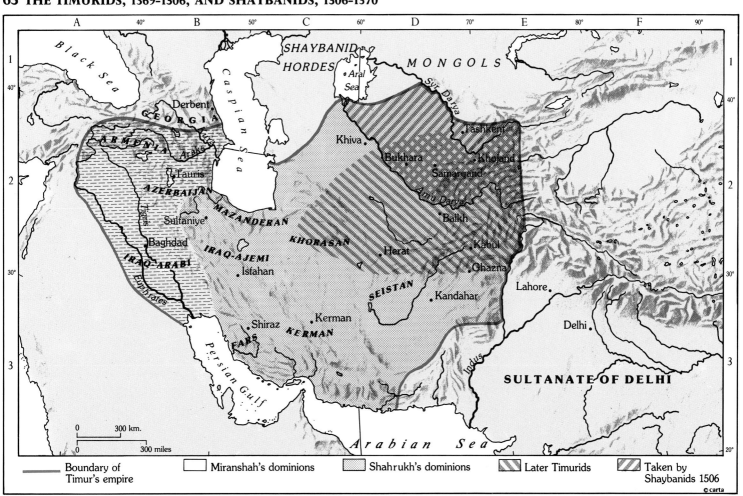

| Boundary of Timur's empire | Miranshah's dominions | Shahrukh's dominions | Later Timurids | Taken by Shaybanids 1506 |

© carta

66. THE SAFAVIDS IN PERSIA, 1501–1737

The Safavids are the most famous of the Persian Islamic dynasties. They left a permanent mark on the country by establishing Shi'ism as the state religion, thus giving the people of Persia what is now known as a sense of national unity, distinct from Arabs, Turks, and other peoples of the north and east.

The family of the founder, Isma'il I, had long been established in Ardabil and were hereditary teachers of religion. Thus backed by religious authority, the future shah Isma'il gradually extended political authority over Shirwan, Azerbaijan, Iraq, and finally the rest of Persia. Shi'ism which had long been popular in the region, was now a state religion; the Sunni faith was virtually wiped out.

Under Tahmasp I (r. 1524–1576), wars against the Uzbeks and the Ottoman Turks gave a further sense of unity, as did the shah's name and title, both derived from pre-Islamic Persia. His successor, Isma'il II (r.1576–1577), was a debauchee. His nephew, Shah Abbas was acclaimed in Nishapur in 989/1581; but only over all Persia at Isfahan in 996/1588, and ruled until 1628. He was the greatest of his line as a as a warrior against the Uzbeks and Ottomans, an organizer of commerce and international intercourse, and a patron of architecture. Under him Armenians were deported with abominable cruelty from Julfa to New Julfa, near Isfahan, to serve the needs of manufacturing and commerce.

After Abbas's death Kandahar was seized by Babur and Baghdad by the Ottomans. Kandahar was recovered by Abbas II, only to be lost finally in 1709, when a new state emerged in Afghanistan. Shah Sulayman I, also known as Safi IV, ruled Persia from 1666 to 1694 and not only had good relations with the Ottomans but also intercourse with the western powers, including Russia, which was important for the Armenian trade in furs. His son Shah Sultan Husayn was a weak ruler, controlled by the *mullah*s (doctors of the religious law), whose persecution of the Sunnites had angered the Afghans. The last of the line was Muhammad Shah, who was acclaimed in 1788, and lived in exile until 1794.

67. WARS BETWEEN TURKEY AND VENICE, 1423–1718

For a brief period, from 1204 until 1261, Venice had held Constantinople in fee, with parts of the Balkans and a strip of the Asiatic mainland. Primarily a sea power, Venice lost these lands in 1261 because the absence of the Venetian fleet enabled the Greeks to return. During the fourteenth century, in a series of wars, Venice wrested the trade monopoly in the eastern Mediterranean from Genoa, and in the early fifteenth century it acquired possessions on the Italian mainland, thus becoming both a commercial and political power.

It was inevitable that Venice should come into collision with Ottoman expansion (map 63). It could not expect, after the fall of Constantinople in 1453, to maintain a trade monopoly in the city or in the Levant. In the first Turkish war Venice lost Negropontus and parts of the Morea. The gain in 1488 of Cyprus was not at Ottoman expense, for it was abdicated by its queen and inheritor, Caterina Cornaro, who could not hold it unaided against the Ottomans. Then, in 1498, Vasco da Gama reached Calicut and established a new route from Europe to the East. The jugular vein of Venice was thus cut, and its commercial supremacy, shared with the Mamluks of Egypt (see map 59), lost.

It was thus as part of the Ottoman expansion into Europe that the wars with Venice are to be seen — an expansion that was finally reversed only before the walls of Vienna in 1683. In 1570 the Turks took Cyprus, only to have their fleet annihilated at Lepanto on 7 October 1571. The Venetians, however, failed to follow up their victory. The Turks reconstituted their fleet within six months, but they made no further serious advance until, after a long siege, they took Crete in 1669. In the final act the Venetians bombarded Athens in 1688, wrecking the Parthenon.

66 THE SAFAVIDS IN PERSIA, 1501–1737

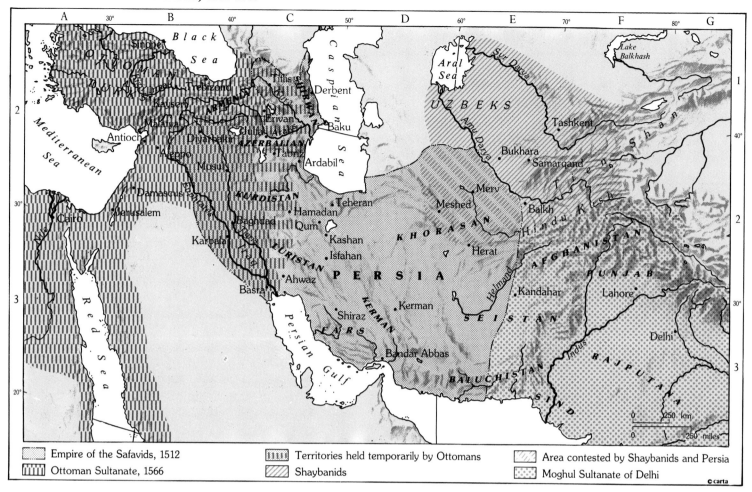

Empire of the Safavids, 1512

Ottoman Sultanate, 1566

Territories held temporarily by Ottomans

Shaybanids

Area contested by Shaybanids and Persia

Moghul Sultanate of Delhi

© carta

67 WARS BETWEEN TURKEY AND VENICE, 1423–1718

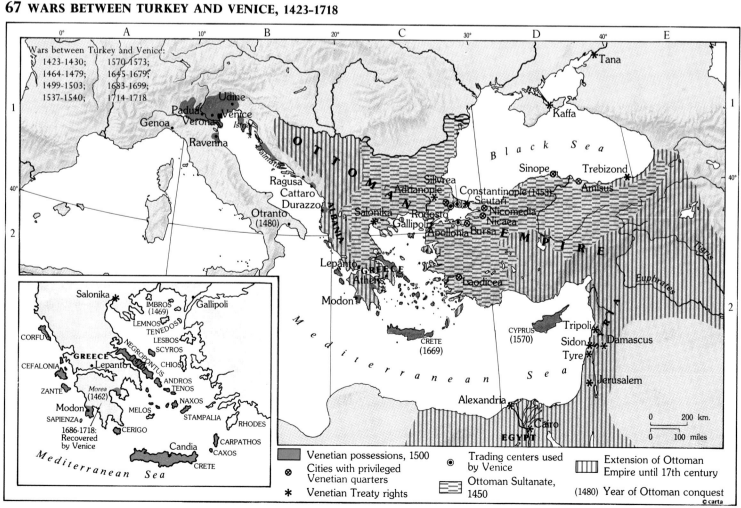

Wars between Turkey and Venice:
1423–1430; 1570–1573;
1464–1479; 1645–1679;
1499–1503; 1683–1699;
1537–1540; 1714–1718

Venetian possessions, 1500

Cities with privileged Venetian quarters

Venetian Treaty rights

Trading centers used by Venice

Ottoman Sultanate, 1450

Extension of Ottoman Empire until 17th century

(1480) Year of Ottoman conquest

© carta

68. ARAB TRADE IN THE INDIAN OCEAN, C. 1498

Both Arab and Portuguese sources give a very clear picture of Arab navigation and commerce in the Indian Ocean around 1498. Ahmad ibn Majid al-Najdi was the author of numerous navigational treatises, the earliest dated around 1462, and the last, 1512. Both father and grandfather had been Indian Ocean pilots, and, as a literary man, he regreted that few navigators left accounts of their knowledge and experience. It is improbable that he was the pilot who guided Vasco da Gama to India in 1498, for all the Portuguese writers who refer to the pilot's origins speak of him as an Indian from Guzerat. Ibn Majid himself claimed to be Arabian, and this is sustained by other Arab writers.

Ibn Majid's interests were strictly professional, and he related only navigational details of ports and distances. A broader view is found in Tomé Pires's *Suma Oriental* (c. 1515). An apothecary, Pires was sent to Goa and Malacca as an agent for drugs. In 1515, he was sent to China as the Portuguese ambassador. He thus had a unique opportunity to observe Arabian commerce in the Indian Ocean.

Cairo was the entrepôt for trade with Italy, Greece, and Syria, and their link with Aden, from which Indian Ocean trade as far as Malaysia was handled. Cambay was the main entrepôt in India, and Malacca was the trade center in Malaysia. Farthest east the entrepôt was the Banda Islands, in the Moluccas, dealing with China to the north. European exports via Cairo and Aden were gold, silver, quicksilver, copper, cloth, glass beads, and weapons. Westward from Malacca went spices of every description, brazil wood, pearls, musk, and silks, and porcelain from China. Cloth likewise was distributed to ports in southern Arabia and eastern Africa.

69. THE PORTUGUESE OFF SOUTH ARABIA, 1498–1698, AND THE ROUTE TO THE INDIES

The *descobrimento* (discovery) of the Indies, as the Portuguese term it, was in one sense the final act of the reconquista, outflanking Islam at perhaps its most sensitive point, the trade between Europe and the Far East. In 1498 the Ottomans controlled many of the land routes; Egypt still held the sea outlets of the caravan trade across Arabia from the Indian Ocean, over which Arabs, Indians, and Chinese had long had undisputed mastery. The discovery also marked a shift in sea power in Europe. Venice had long had a virtual monopoly on trade both with Cairo and Constantinople; the *descobrimento* broke this monopoly.

Between 1487 and 1498 Pero da Covilhã traveled from Cairo to Goa and along the eastern African coast thus supplying Vasco da Gama with vital information for his successful voyage from Lisbon to Calicut of 1497–1498. By 1505 *feitorias* (trading agencies) had been set up in Mozambique, Kilwa, Malindi, Socotra, Aden, and the key entrepôt of Hormuz. Forts were built on Mozambique, Kilwa, and Socotra, which paid tribute to Portugal; in all these places the trade that had enriched them was ruined. By 1512 the Portuguese were compelled to relax their control. Later in the century, Ottoman Turkish raids compelled the Portuguese to build a fort at Mombasa, principally to control the ivory trade. (Trade in gold, slaves and smaller commerce was of less importance.) During the seventeenth century Oman entered the Indian Ocean trade as a major competitor. The nobles of Mombasa sought deliverance by Oman from the Portuguese for the first time in 1652. In 1696 to 1698 the Omanis besieged Fort Jesus at Mombasa, and finally wrested it from Portugal. Although random and weak until the nineteenth century, Arab control of the eastern African coast was once again secured.

68 ARAB TRADE IN THE INDIAN OCEAN C. 1498

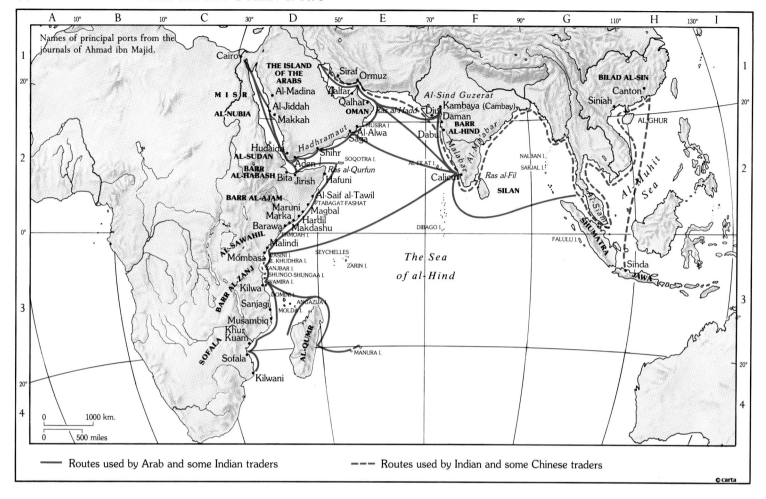

Names of principal ports from the journals of Ahmad ibn Majid.

Routes used by Arab and some Indian traders ——
Routes used by Indian and some Chinese traders ----

69 THE PORTUGUESE OFF SOUTH ARABIA, 1498-1698, AND THE ROUTE TO THE INDIES

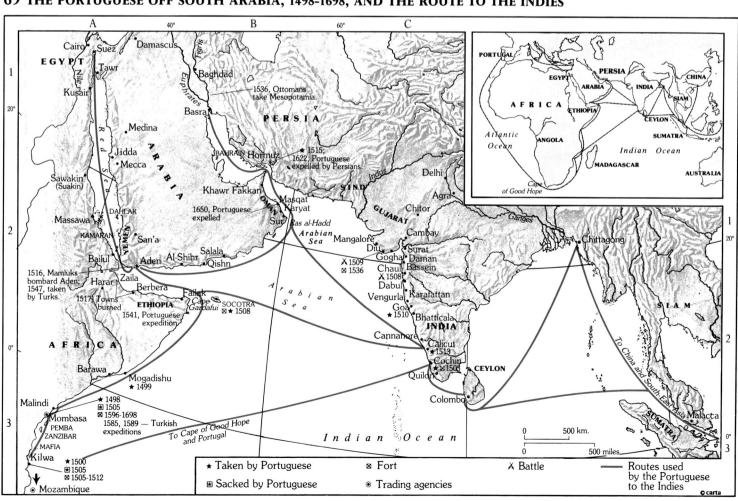

1536, Ottomans take Mesopotamia.

1515; 1622, Portuguese expelled by Persians.

1650, Portuguese expelled

1516, Mamluks bombard Aden; 1547, taken by Turks.

1517 Towns burned

1541, Portuguese expedition

★ 1498
⊞ 1505
⊠ 1596-1698
1585, 1589 — Turkish expeditions

★ 1500
⊞ 1505
⊠ 1505-1512

⊠ 1508

★ 1509
⊞ 1536

★ 1508
★ 1510

★ 1513

★ 1505

★ 1499

To Cape of Good Hope and Portugal

To China and South-East Asia

★ Taken by Portuguese   ⊠ Fort   ✕ Battle   —— Routes used by the Portuguese to the Indies

⊞ Sacked by Portuguese   ⊙ Trading agencies

70. THE BARBARY STATES, 1504–1574

At the turn of the sixteenth century Portugal occupied various ports in northern Morocco and on the Atlantic coast. Spain now made a vigorous drive to establish posts from Melilla eastward to Algiers. At times both the Abd al-Waddids and the Hafsids had to accept Spanish protection.

A band of five brothers — of whom Aruj and Khayr al-Din (commonly, Barbarossa) were two — were pirates based on the island of Lesbos. When they decided to transfer their activities to the western Mediterranean, the Hafsid sultan welcomed them and gave them Jerba island as a base. In 1516 Aruj established a stronghold in Algiers, and took Tlemcen from Spain, which promptly retaliated, retook Tlemcen, and killed Aruj.

Barbarossa now offered his services and possessions to the Ottoman sultan, Selim the Grim. He made Barbarossa *beylerbey* ("chief of the beys") over northern Africa, thus returning the region to the eastern caliphate after some 750 years. Barbarossa was given artillery and six-thousand janissaries, with whom he now expanded his possessions and made Algiers his capital. In 1534 he took Tunis, but lost it again to Charles V in 1535.

The sultan now made Barbarossa *kapudan pasha* (admiral of the fleet) in Istanbul. Until 1587 a succession of *beylerbeys* ruled from Algiers, after which three separate regencies were established in Algiers, Tunis, and Tripoli. Intermittent war on land and by sea, often misinterpreted as piracy, continued against Spain and Morocco. The *beylerbeylik* of Algiers was a military state, with a professionally trained army and cavalry (*sipahis*), who were recruited locally. After 1574 what had become known as the Barbary (from Berber) States acquired a different character.

71. THE HASANI SHARIFS OF MOROCCO, 1511–1659

The Hasani, or Sadi, sharifs of Morocco were a family that had settled in the Wadi Draa in the thirteenth century. Reaction to Portuguese and Spanish attacks on North-West Africa in the fifteenth century included a revival of religious sentiment among Muslims. Many refugees from the Reconquista in Spain had suffered for their faith, and Sufi teachings, imported from the East, were ready solace. Religious leaders arose, especially among the descendants of the Prophet's daughter Fatima. In response to the request of fellow Muslims Muhammad al-Mahdi from Taqmaddart became their leader, and waged war against the Portuguese. His sons followed him, and Marrakesh became the Hasani capital in 1554.

The final consolidation of Hasani power was the "Battle of the Kings" at Kasr al-Kabir in 1578, in which the Portuguese were utterly defeated. Twelve years later Ahmad al-Mansur sent a force across the Sahara to occupy Timbuktu and destroy the empire of Songhai. For half a century Morocco would be master of the western Sudan — the whole area from the Mediterranean to Senegal and Bornu — and its trade in gold, salt, hides, and slaves.

Modeled on the Sublime Porte in Istanbul, a splendid court was maintained at Marrakesh. A regular army of Christian renegades, Spanish Moors, and African slaves was trained by Turkish deserters and reinforced by Arab tribesmen, who were given land near Fez to secure their allegiance. The marabouts, or holy men, had initially supported the regime. Now, however, they turned against it in reaction to the luxury of the ruling class and found a leader in a branch of the sharifial family, Muhammad al-Hajj, whose son, al-Rashid, established a new dynasty (see map 75).

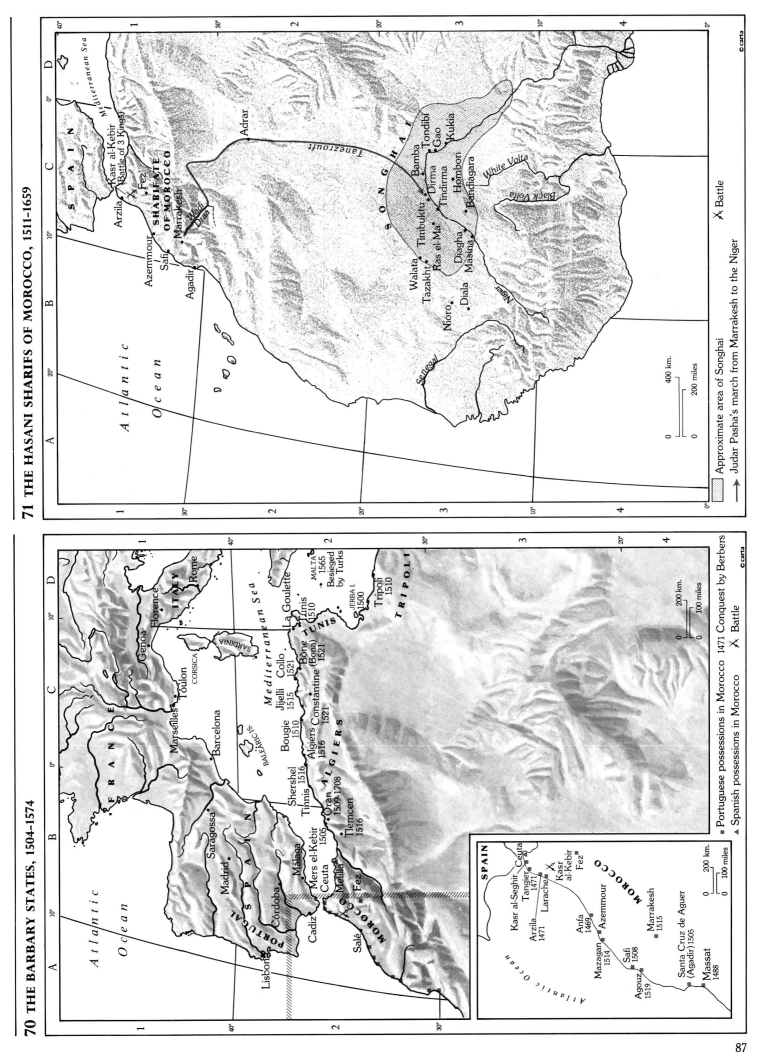

71 THE HASANI SHARIFS OF MOROCCO, 1511-1659

Mediterranean Sea

SPAIN

Kasr al-Kebir
Battle of 3 Kings
Fez
Arzila
SHARIFATE OF MOROCCO
Marrakesh
Wadi Draa
Azemmour
Safi
Agadir

Atlantic Ocean

Adrar

Tanezrouft

Walata
Tazakht
Timbuktu
Ras el-Ma
Nioro
Diala
Diagha
Masina

Bamba
Tondibi
Dirma
Gao
Kukia
Tindirma
Hombori
Bandiagara

White Volta

Black Volta

Niger

Senegal

SONGHAI

□ Approximate area of Songhai
→ Judar Pasha's march from Marrakesh to the Niger
✗ Battle

400 km.
200 miles

© carta

70 THE BARBARY STATES, 1504-1574

Atlantic Ocean

FRANCE
Marseilles
Toulon
Genoa
ITALY
Florence
Rome

SPAIN
Madrid
Saragossa
Barcelona
Córdoba
Málaga
Cádiz
Lisbon
PORTUGAL

CORSICA
SARDINIA
BALEARICS

Mediterranean Sea

Mers el-Kebir
Ceuta
Melilla
Fez
MOROCCO
Salé

Tlemcen 1516
Oran 1509-1708
Mers el-Kebir 1505
Tinnis
Shershel 1516
Bougie 1510
Jijelli 1515
Collo 1521
Algiers 1516
Constantine 1521
ALGIERS
Bône (Bona) 1521

TUNIS
Tunis 1510
La Goulette

MALTA
Besieged by Turks 1565
JERBA I. 1500

Tripoli 1510
TRIPOLI

© carta

■ Portuguese possessions in Morocco 1471 Conquest by Berbers
▲ Spanish possessions in Morocco ✗ Battle

200 km.
100 miles

SPAIN
Kasr al-Seghir
Ceuta
Tangier 1471
Arzila 1471
Larache
Kasr al-Kebir ✗
Fez
Anfa 1469
Azemmour
Mazagan 1514
Safi 1508
Agouz 1519
Santa Cruz de Aguer (Agadir) 1505
Massat 1488
MOROCCO
Marrakesh 1515

Atlantic Ocean

200 km.
100 miles

87

72. THE MUGHUL EMPERORS OF DELHI, 1526–1858

With the break up of Muhammad ibn Tughluq's empire a string of independent Muslim principalities emerged in Bengal, Malwa, Gujarat, Kashmir, the Deccan, Ahmadnagar, Berar, Bijapur, Bidar, Khandesh, and Golconda; in the south the Hindu kingdom of Vijayanagar (1336–1640), was established.

In the northwest, Babur (Zahir al-Din Muhammad), ruler of the petty princedom of Farghana, raided India in 1517 and 1519; in 1526 he defeated the sultan Ibrahim Lodi at Panipat and a battle in which Babur's twelve-thousand men overcame the sultan's 100,000 men. By 1530 he had conquered all northern India as far as Bengal.

A period of strife among Babur's sons and grandsons followed, which was ended only by his grandson Akbar, whose career of conquest began in 1564 with the ambition of conquering the whole subcontinent. This goal was only partly achieved when he died in 1605. With all the intellectual range of a polymath, Akbar was illiterate. He loved disputation, but he had no systematic learning. He repudiated Islam and attempted to unite Hindus and Muslims in a syncretic belief that also embraced Christianity. His rule was intensely personal, and it was only the impetus gained in his long reign (1556–1605) that enabled the empire to survive under the weak rule of his successor, Jahangir (r. 1605–1627). Akbar's most important achievement was a reform of the revenue system, which secured the needs of central government while giving security to the peasantry.

A war of succession followed in which Jahangir's elder son Shah Jahan was enthroned after killing all his male relatives. Between 1628 and 1658 he extended the empire southward, partly by treaties, partly by campaigns ably conducted by his son Aurangzeb (Almagir) as viceroy of the Deccan (r. 1636–1644). Then his attention turned westward, and between 1647 and 1653 Aurangzeb recovered most of the Afghan provinces. In 1656, Golconda was finally annexed. By then Shah Jahan had become incapacitated by age, and in 1658, after a struggle with his brothers, Aurangzeb seized absolute power. Another reign of unusual length (1658–1707) began, in which Mughul power in India was at its apogee. However, the conquest of the Deccan, which had a predominantly Hindu population, proved the Achilles' heel of Aurangzeb, who, unlike his predecessors, was bigotedly exclusive in his devotion to Islam. The hated poll tax, which Akbar had abolished, was again revived, and Hindus were actively persecuted. Further, the administration was weak and neglected, and the practice of farming the revenues led inevitably to corruption. The seeds of decline had now been firmly planted.

In the war of succession that followed none of the three claimants was a leader of any consequence. Civil wars dragged on, and slowly the Marathas and others carved out principalities for themselves. By the 1770s the once proud empire had dwindled to the size of a small province around Delhi. New factors in Indian politics contributed to the instability. Commercial rivalry between French and British traders led to wars, often with Indian allied participation, and, under the guise of the East India Company, a British India was growing steadily.

The Mughul empire was not, however, without a final heir. When, in 1947, the British finally withdrew, the once powerful Mughul state reemerged as Pakistan, a Muslim state that looked westward to Persia and the Middle East rather than its Hindu neighbor.

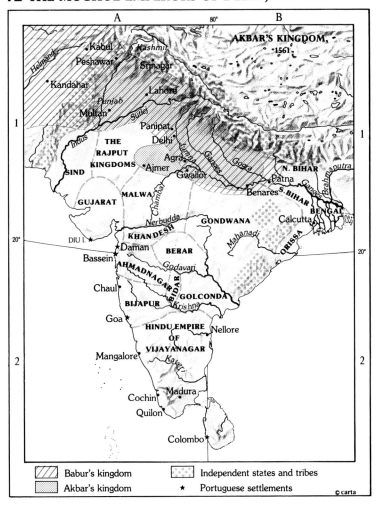

AKBAR'S KINGDOM, 1561

⊘ Babur's kingdom	⊙ Independent states and tribes
▦ Akbar's kingdom	★ Portuguese settlements

© carta

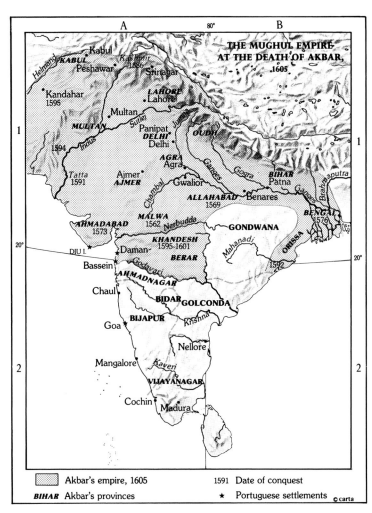

THE MUGHUL EMPIRE AT THE DEATH OF AKBAR, 1605

▦ Akbar's empire, 1605	1591 Date of conquest
BIHAR Akbar's provinces	★ Portuguese settlements

© carta

THE MUGHUL EMPIRE, END OF THE 17TH CENTURY

	European settlements:
▦ Approximate extent of Mughul empire	★ Portuguese ⊛ British ⊞ Danish
JATS Peoples in revolt	⊞ Dutch ⊠ French

© carta

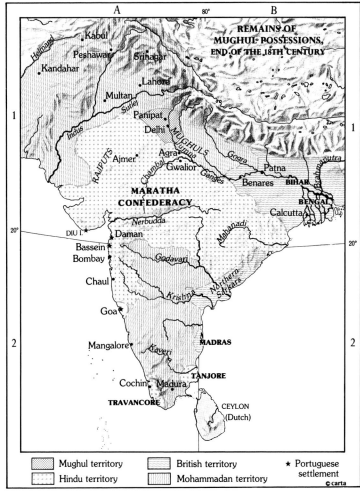

REMAINS OF MUGHUL POSSESSIONS, END OF THE 18TH CENTURY

▦ Mughul territory	▦ British territory	★ Portuguese settlement
Hindu territory	Mohammadan territory	

© carta

89

73. THE OTTOMAN EMPIRE AT ITS GREATEST EXTENT, 16TH TO 17TH CENTURIES

When Selim I the Grim succeeded (see map 63), he killed his brothers, seven of their sons, and four of his own sons. He left only Sulayman (r. 1520–1566), the ablest son. With the acquisition of Egypt he captured the commercial center and intellectual capital of Islam. Though the Portuguese had command of the sea trade with the East, Selim I still commanded the land routes of Egypt, Arabia, Syria, and Asia Minor. Eastern Europe, too, was firmly part of the Middle East (map 74). Under Sulayman the Magnificent, as Europeans called him, or the Lawgiver, as Turks called him, the empire fought the Habsburgs in a Europe weakened by Protestant dissidence. In spite of this fighting, in 1536, France was able to establish strong commercial ties with Istanbul. The favorable trade conditions granted by the Sublime Porte are known as the Capitulations. They gave France predominance in the Levant, with long-term effects that are still apparent.

During Sulayman's reign northern Africa was added to the empire (see map 70). He and his father were the first Ottoman sultans to pay attention to the Indian Ocean, and naval bases were built at Suez in 1517 and Basra in 1538. The Portuguese were not powerful enough to dominate the Indian Ocean completely, and to some extent the trading positions of Syria and the Middle East recovered from the shock of their initial incursion. Sulayman's reign marks the apogee of Ottoman power; under his successors decline set in. Selim II, the Sot (r. 1566–1574) and Murad III (r. 1574–1575) were weak, and the period between 1570 and 1578 is known as the "sultanate of women" because of the excessive influence of the harem on appointments. Thereafter, until 1625, power passed into the hands of the Janissaries.

In spite of the naval disaster at Lepanto (1570) (see map 67), the Ottomans retained command of the Mediterranean throughout most of the seventeenth century. Tunis was conquered by the Turks in 1574; Fez was seized from Portugal in 1578, and Crete from Venice in 1669. The military spirit of the original conquerors had declined, and the camp gave way to the boudoir. This decline was clear to all Europe during the Habsburg war (1593–1606). In the East the shah of Persia, Abbas I, (see map 66) was able to retake the Caucasus and Azerbaijan in 1603 and Iraq in 1624, though he lost Iraq again to Murad IV in 1638. Although finally victorious, the long sea war with Venice (1645–1669) was commercially debilitating for the Ottomans, who failed to destroy Venice.

The tide turned in 1683. From 14 July to 12 September, the Turks besieged Vienna, but at Kahlenberg, Parkau, and finally Stettin the Ottomans were routed. Although war continued with Austria, Poland, and Venice until 1698 — during which time their "Holy League" of 1684 was joined in 1686 by Russia — the Ottomans were never able to threaten Europe again. Nevertheless, between 1683 and 1792 there were forty-one years of war in which the Ottomans fought the Holy League. During the next century they fought Russia in 1710–1711; Austria and Venice in 1714–1718; and Russia and Austria together in 1734–1739, 1768–1774, and 1787–1792. The Ottomans lost Hungary, the Crimea, Croatia, Slavonia, and Transylvania.

These wars, which had begun with a Polish cavalry action of the greatest bravery at the siege of Vienna, was the beginning of a new era in eastern Europe. It not only brought Russia into the concert of Europe; it made Russia a participant in Middle Eastern affairs. It was also the beginning of the collapse of the inchoate, cumbrous Ottoman system, which was not completed until the end of World War I.

73 THE OTTOMAN EMPIRE AT ITS GREATEST EXTENT, 16TH TO 17TH CENTURIES

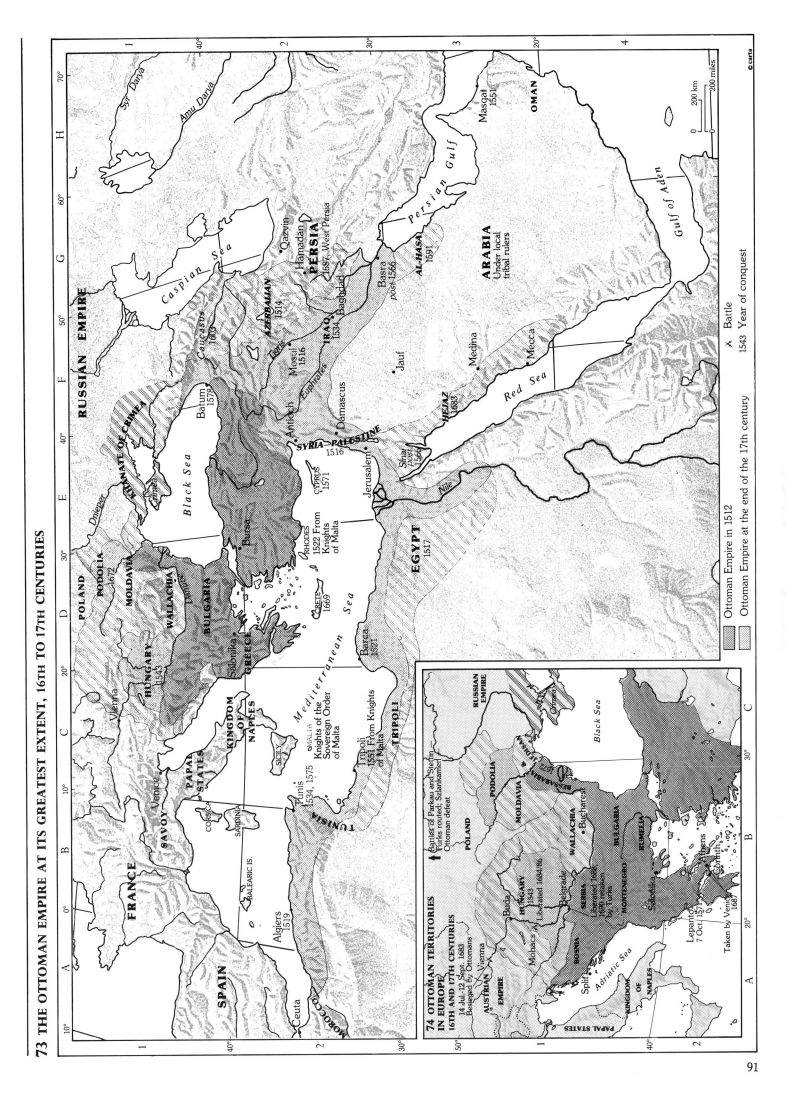

RUSSIAN EMPIRE

Syr Darya

Amu Darya

Caspian Sea

Qazvin •

Hamadan •
PERSIA
1587 *West Persia*

Caucasus
1603

AZERBAIJAN
1514

KHANATE OF CRIMEA

Crimea

Dnieper

Black Sea

Batum •
1578

Mosul •
1516
Tigris

IRAQ
1534

Baghdad •

Euphrates

Antioch •

Basra
post 1566

AL-HASA
1591

ARABIA
Under local
tribal rulers

Persian Gulf

Masqat
1551
OMAN

Gulf of Aden

POLAND

PODOLIA
1672

MOLDAVIA

Dniester

WALLACHIA

BULGARIA

Vienna •
HUNGARY
1543

Salonika •
GREECE

PAPAL
STATES

Venice •

SAVOY

KINGDOM
OF
NAPLES

CORSICA

SARDINIA

SICILY

Bursa •

RHODES
1522 From
Knights of Malta

CRETE
1669

CYPRUS
1571

Jerusalem •

Damascus •

SYRIA • PALESTINE
1516

Sinai
post
1566

Nile

EGYPT
1517

Jauf •

Medina •

Mecca •

HEJAZ
1683

Red Sea

FRANCE

SPAIN

Ceuta •

Algiers •
1519

MOROCCO

BALEARIC IS.

Tunis •
1534, 1575

TUNISIA

Mediterranean Sea

MALTA
Knights of the
Sovereign Order
of Malta

Tripoli
1551 From Knights
of Malta

TRIPOLI

Barca
1521

RUSSIAN EMPIRE

Ottoman Empire in 1512

Ottoman Empire at the end of the 17th century

× Battle

1543 Year of conquest

200 km
200 miles

© carta

74 OTTOMAN TERRITORIES IN EUROPE 16TH AND 17TH CENTURIES

14 Jul.–12 Sept. 1683
Besieged by Ottomans

Battles of Parkau and Stettin
Turks routed; Szlankamén
Ottoman defeat

AUSTRIAN
EMPIRE

Vienna •

POLAND

PODOLIA

Buda •
HUNGARY
1543

Mohacs ×

Belgrade •

BOSNIA

SERBIA
Liberated from
1596 retaken
by Turks

Split •
Adriatic Sea

KINGDOM
OF
NAPLES

PAPAL
STATES

MOLDAVIA

Bucharest

WALLACHIA

BULGARIA

MONTENEGRO

RUMELIA

Salonika •

Corinth •

Athens •

Lepanto
7 Oct. 1571

Taken by Venice
1687

BESSARABIA

RUSSIAN
EMPIRE

Crimea

Black Sea

91

75. THE FILALI SHARIFS OF MOROCCO, FROM 1631

When the last Hasani sharif was assassinated in 1653 the succession was disputed. One of the least conspicuous claimants was Muhammad al-Sharif, head of the Filali lineage of sharifs, who claimed descent from the Prophet's grandson Hasan. He had been expelled from the sultanate of Sijilmasa in 1646. By 1664 his son, Moulay al-Rashid, had laid the foundation for a monarchy that endures to this day. He took Fez in 1666 and Marrakesh in 1668 by creating an army of negroes, who were either bought or the descendants of slaves. Placed into the army at the age of eighteen; married to negro wives who had been trained in the royal palaces; given training for three years as muleteers and housebuilders and then for five years in archery, musketry, and fieldcraft; these men formed an army of 150,000 by 1686, dependent on the sultan alone. A new and splendid capital was built at Meknès.

The formidable army controlled the *blad al-makhzan* (the lands of the government) and the *blad al-siba* (lands of no authority, in which the sultanic writ did not run). Until a French protectorate was installed in 1912, these areas varied according to the ability and strength of the individual rulers. Among these rulers Moulay Ismail (r. 1672–1727) was the most remarkable. Under him the *blad al-siba* was virtually nonexistent. Of him and his successors Voltaire remarked that Moroccan veins contain vitriol, not blood. His passion for war was equalled only by his passion for women; the harem of Meknès contained five-hundred women; subsidiary harems were located at Fez and Marrakesh.

In the late nineteenth century Abd al-Aziz (r. 1894–1908) was too young, too impetuous, and too weak to carry out a consistent policy. This failure and that of his usurper and brother, Mulay Abd al-Hafid to maintain order, gave the French the opportunity to seize control. The French ruled until 1956, when the monarchy was restored as a kingdom.

76. THE DOMINIONS OF OMAN IN EAST AFRICA, 1698–1913

In the mid-seventeenth century Oman chafed under the declining Portuguese hegemony in the Indian Ocean. Around 1650 a delegation was sent from Mombasa to Oman, asking assistance to expel the Portuguese, but no serious response was made until 1696. Superficially, these events might look like the early emergence of nationalism; however, in reality these acts resulted from the ivory trade, in which Mombasa's rival, Pate, had a successful partnership with Masqat.

An Omani fleet was sent to besiege the Portuguese Fort Jesus in 1696 — a long, drawn-out, and inconclusive affair in which Swahilis from Pate played a major part. Disease overcame the defenders, and from 1698 the Omanis had nominal authority from Mogadishu to the Ruvuma River. In practice their control was little more than a series of custom posts, which, needless to say, the locals did all they could to evade. In Mombasa the governorship had become hereditary within the Mazrui family, which had made itself virtually independent. The real author of the new system was Sa'id ibn Sultan (r. 1806–1856), who visited Mombasa in 1827 and brought many eastern African ports under his control. In 1828 he visited Zanzibar, where he introduced clove production on confiscated property. From 1832 until 1840 he alternated residences between Masqat and Zanzibar, moving to Zanzibar in 1840. Zanzibar now became the leading commercial center in eastern Africa, trading in ivory, copal, slaves, hides, and other local products. Coastal cities shared in the growing prosperity, as caravans set out from the coast to the interior, seeking ivory and slaves, and thus reversing the age-old route by which Africans had brought products to the coast. Under Sa'id ibn Sultan's successors the British forced an end to the slave trade and established a protectorate, which was placed under the authority of the colonial office in 1913.

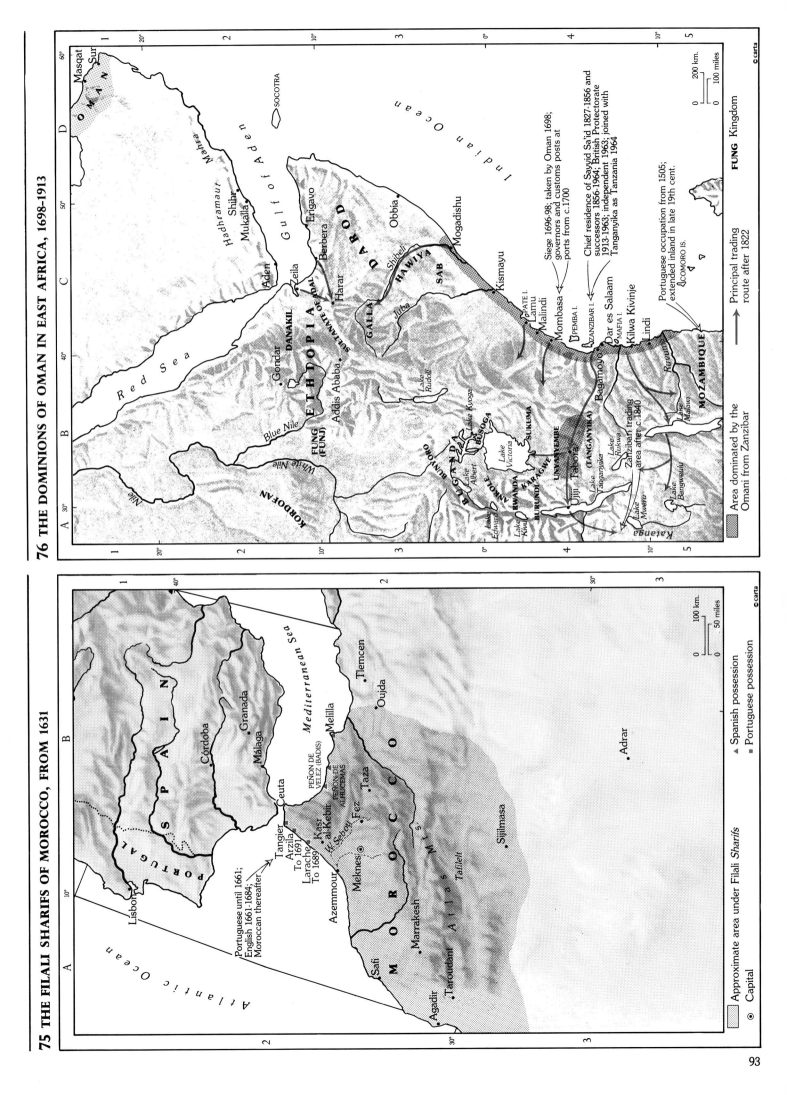

76 THE DOMINIONS OF OMAN IN EAST AFRICA, 1698–1913

Siege 1696-98; taken by Oman 1698; governors and customs posts at ports from c.1700

Chief residence of Sayyid Sa'id 1827-1856 and successors 1856-1964; British Protectorate 1913-1963; independent 1963; joined with Tanganyika as Tanzania 1964

Portuguese occupation from 1505; extended inland in late 19th cent.

→ Principal trading route after 1822

Area dominated by the Omani from Zanzibar

FUNG Kingdom

OMAN
Masqat
Sur
SOCOTRA
Mahra
Hadhramaut
Shihr
Mukalla
Aden
Gulf of Aden
Red Sea
Zeila
Berbera
Erigavo
DANAKIL
Gondar
ETHIOPIA
Blue Nile
White Nile
KORDOFAN
Nile
FUNG (FUNJ)
Addis Ababa
Harar
SULTANATE OF ADAL
Obbia
DAROD
Shibeli
HAWIYA
SAB
Juba
GALLA
Mogadishu
Kismayu
Lake Rudolf
Lake Kyoga
BUNYORO
BUGANDA
ANKOLE
RWANDA
BURUNDI
KARAGWE
BUSOGA
Lake Albert
Lake Edward
Lake Kivu
Lake Victoria
SUKUMA
UNYAMWEMBE
Tabora
Ujiji
Lake Tanganyika
Lake Rukwa
Lake Mweru
Lake Bangweulu
Lake Malawi
Katanga
(TANGANYIKA)
Zanzibar trading area after c.1840
Indian Ocean
PATE I.
Lamu
Malindi
Mombasa
PEMBA I.
ZANZIBAR I.
Dar es Salaam
MAFIA I.
Bagamoyo
Kilwa Kivinje
Lindi
Ruvuma
MOZAMBIQUE
COMORO IS.

Scale: 200 km. / 100 miles

75 THE FILALI SHARIFS OF MOROCCO, FROM 1631

Portuguese until 1661; English 1661-1684; Moroccan thereafter

SPAIN
PORTUGAL
Lisbon
Córdoba
Granada
Málaga
Mediterranean Sea
Tlemcen
Oujda
Ceuta
Melilla
PEÑON DE VELEZ (BADIS)
PEÑON DE ALHUCEMAS
Tangier
Arzila To 1691
Larache To 1689
Kasr al-Kebir
Wadi Sebou
Fez
Taza
MOROCCO
Meknes
Azemmour
Safi
Marrakesh
Agadir
Taroudant
Atlas Mts.
Tafilelt
Sijilmasa
Adrar
Atlantic Ocean

Approximate area under Filali *Sharifs*
◉ Capital
▲ Spanish possession
■ Portuguese possession

Scale: 100 km. / 50 miles

c carta

93

77. THE OTTOMAN EMPIRE IN DECLINE, 1699–1913

Except for the years 1710 and -1711, when some territory was recovered from Russia, the period between the Treaty of Carlowitz (1699) and the Treaty of Jassy (1792) were years of successive military disasters for the Ottoman Turks. To Russia they lost all their possessions north of the Black Sea — the Caucasus, Bessarabia, Podolia, and the Crimea — from which they had recruited a large proportion of their best fighting men. In the west they lost Hungary, Transylvania, Bukovina and the Banat of Temisvar causing them to retire to the frontier of 1512 on the Danube. In addition Austria and Russia intervened more and more in the affairs of the Christian subjects of the Porte, exercising an influence that reached a climax in the Crimean War.

In Anatolia, the Balkans, and Lebanon, local rulers established themselves in virtual independence, collecting their own taxes and making remissions to the treasury whose masters were too weak to restore a strong central government. Officialdom was wholly corrupt, from top to bottom. Thus in 1808, when, following a fire, restoration work was needed in the Holy Sepulcher in Jerusalem, a total expenditure of funds raised in Russia of 2.5 million roubles included no less than 1.5 million in bribes. Ottoman society was not only corrupt, it was supine. The Muslim population had no part in the industrial or commercial life of the empire, and took little interest in science or technology. These they left to Jews, Christians, Greeks, and Armenians, peoples they regarded as inferior, together with a small proportion of European merchants, many of them Italian. Having isolated itself, the Muslim population had little or no contact with the West. No books were printed in Turkish before 1727. The Tulip period (1717–1730) was exceptional in its positive passion for Westernization, expressed in the growing of tulips.

The strongest force within Ottoman Turkey during this period was inertia of the army and the navy, which was wholly destroyed by the Russians at Cesme in 1770. Most obstructive to change was the Janissary corps, once the finest military cadre in existence. Nevertheless, it was impossible to prevent the spread of ideas, and shock waves spread throughout the Ottoman system when Napoleon Bonaparte invaded Egypt (map 78). Shortly thereafter the Ottoman viceroy, Muhammad Ali Pasha, made Egypt an independent power in all but name (maps 81–84); in central Arabia the Wahhabi movement under Ibn Saud was wholly independent, as were the small shaykhdoms on the shores of the Persian Gulf; and Oman, long independent, was carving out a commercial empire in eastern and central Africa (map 76). In Europe the Balkan provinces dropped like ripe pears through the latter half of the nineteenth century and into the twentieth.

In the early nineteenth century a number of educational reforms were instituted, and in 1846 a plan for state education was drawn up. By 1914 there were 36,000 Ottoman schools. Less numerous, though not less important, were Greek and Armenian schools, as well as schools run by British, French, and United States missionary bodies. Among these, Robert College (1863) in Istanbul and the Syrian and Jesuit colleges in Beirut developed into universities. In these institutions pro-Western and antitraditionalist attitudes inevitably developed, with demands for reform. It was a tottering state that entered World War I under imperial Germany, because it was too weak to reform itself, and the war brought its final doom.

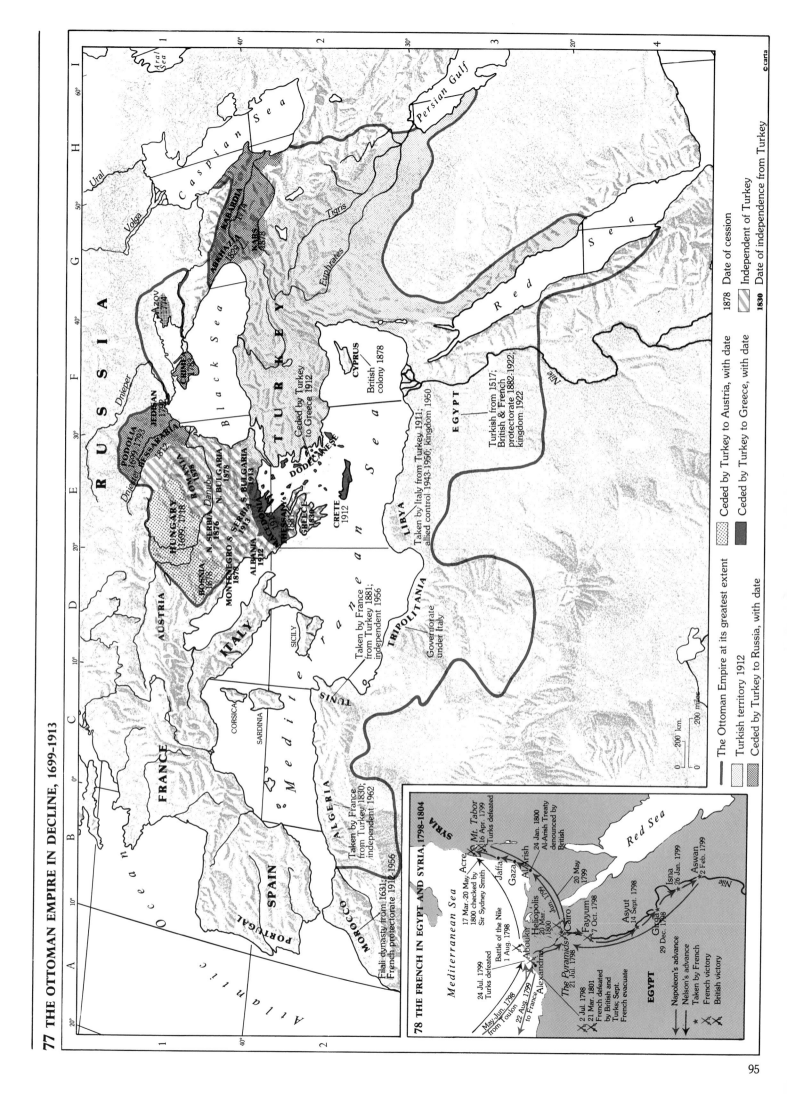

77 THE OTTOMAN EMPIRE IN DECLINE, 1699–1913

78 THE FRENCH IN EGYPT AND SYRIA, 1798–1804

Legend (map 77):

— The Ottoman Empire at its greatest extent

Turkish territory 1912

Ceded by Turkey to Russia, with date

Ceded by Turkey to Austria, with date

Ceded by Turkey to Greece, with date

1878 Date of cession

Independent of Turkey

1830 Date of independence from Turkey

Legend (map 78):

→ Napoleon's advance
→ Nelson's advance
★ Taken by French
✕ French victory
✕ British victory

95

79. THE BARBARY STATES, 17TH AND 18TH CENTURIES

The Ottoman Turks had no more interest in the development or prosperity of their North African provinces, so easily acquired, than they had in any of the others. They had come by sea, and, so long as taxes were paid, were content to look seaward. The seventeenth century was the golden age of piracy in the Mediterranean. Spain made several attempts to take Algiers, but it was not until after 1750 that English and French naval forces began to overcome piracy. It is estimated that in 1650 there were 35,000 Christian captives in Algiers and considerable numbers in Tripoli and Tunis. After 1750 the decline of Algiers was hastened by plague and famine.

In Tunis the family of a Corsican renegade, Murad, became hereditary beys from 1631 to 1702. Husayn ibn Ali, the son of a Cretan renegade, was an agha of Janissaries and treasurer to the bey. Proclaimed bey by the military he established a Husaynid dynasty, which ruled until 1957. In Tripoli the Qaramanli family ruled as hereditary pashas from 1714 until 1835, when the Ottomans imposed direct rule.

Piracy was not effectively suppressed until 1819. Following the Congress of Vienna, at which the suppression of piracy was a major concern, a combined Anglo-Dutch fleet attacked Algiers in 1816. The city, however, was so run down that only 1,200 Christian captives were found. In Tripoli the practice of paying tribute in return for freedom from piracy led to war between Tripoli and the United States (see map 80).

France established a protectorate over the Algerian coastline in 1830, but the occupation of the hinterland continued into the later nineteenth century. Taking advantage of national bankruptcy, a protectorate over Tunisia was added in 1881. Following war between Italy and Turkey, Italy acquired Tripoli and all Libya in 1911.

80. THE UNITED STATES' WAR WITH TRIPOLI, 1801–1815

Tripoli has a commanding position in the Gulf of Sidra, in the central Mediterranean. Under the caliphate it was generally subject to whomever was ruling Tunisia. In 1146 the Normans pillaged the city; from 1321 until 1401 it was ruled by the independent dynasty of Bani Ammar, with a short interval under Bani Makki from 1354 until 1369. It then returned to Tunisian suzerainty, until between 1528 and 1553 it was held by the Knights of St. John of Rhodes, when it was incorporated into the Ottoman Empire. The Turkish corsair Dragut is buried in one of the mosques.

In 1714 Ahmed Pasha Qaramanli, the Turkish governor, achieved virtual independence as an hereditary regent. Thereafter the regency sent "presents" to Istanbul, which were accepted as tribute. Its strategical position made it an admirable center for piracy, and during the eighteenth century payments were made by European nations to the regency for protection of their commerce.

Among these was the United States, which paid protection money from 1796. In 1801 the pasha demanded from the United States an increase in the tribute of $83,000. This was refused, and a naval force was sent to blockade Tripoli. During four inconclusive years the Americans lost the frigate *Philadelphia*, and the commander and crew were taken prisoners. A theatrical incident was provided by William Eaton, who marched five-hundred men across the desert from Alexandria in order to place the brother of the reigning pasha on the throne. With the aid of American vessels he succeeded in taking the small port of Derna. Shortly afterward the pasha relinquished his demands, but he obtained $60,000 as ransom for the prisoners.

Further outrages took place in 1815, and American vessels again blockaded Tripoli and forced the pasha to desist. The Ottomans reasserted their authority in 1835.

79 THE BARBARY STATES, 17TH AND 18TH CENTURIES

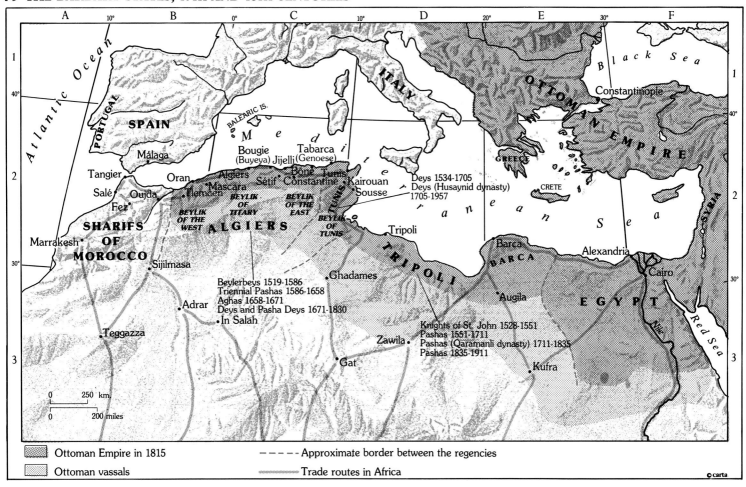

Deys 1534-1705
Deys (Husaynid dynasty) 1705-1957

Beylerbeys 1519-1586
Triennial Pashas 1586-1658
Aghas 1658-1671
Deys and Pasha Deys 1671-1830

Knights of St. John 1528-1551
Pashas 1551-1711
Pashas (Qaramanli dynasty) 1711-1835
Pashas 1835-1911

▨ Ottoman Empire in 1815   - - - - Approximate border between the regencies

▨ Ottoman vassals   ≈≈≈≈ Trade routes in Africa

© carta

80 THE UNITED STATES' WAR WITH TRIPOLI, 1801-1815

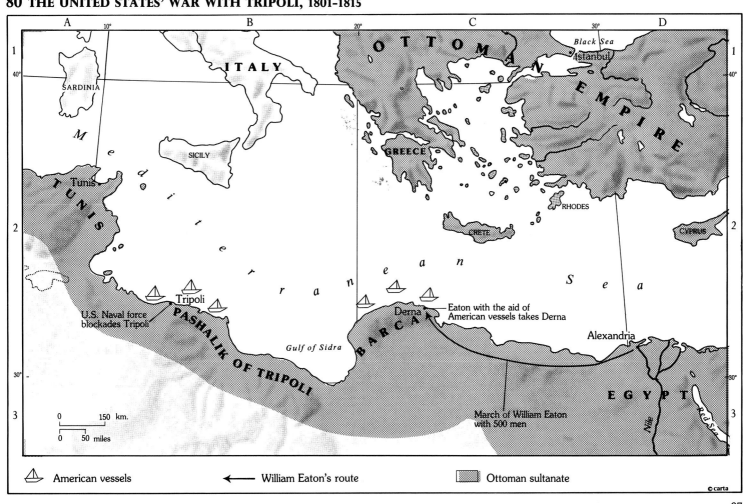

U.S. Naval force blockades Tripoli

Eaton with the aid of American vessels takes Derna

March of William Eaton with 500 men

⌂ American vessels   ← William Eaton's route   ▨ Ottoman sultanate

© carta

81. THE EGYPTIAN CAMPAIGN IN THE HEJAZ, 1812–1818

When the Muslim reformer Muhammad ibn Abd al-Wahhab died in 1792, his extreme puritanical doctrines, warmly supported by the chieftain Ibn Saud, had been established in most of Arabia. In 1801 Ibn Saud's son, Abd al-Aziz, seized Mecca, and, in 1804, Medina. After 1806 it was no longer possible for a non-Wahhabi to make the pilgrimage to Mecca.

From the point of view of the Ottoman Empire these events were a gross religious insult and an economic disaster that interrupted the normal channels of trade. To Muhammad Ali Pasha of Egypt, seeking to establish himself, these events presented an opportunity to achieve recognition and to rid himself of certain elements in his army. Muhammad Ali's first attempt to retake the holy cities, which was led by his son Toussoun, ended in a disaster; however, in 1812, with fresh troops, Yanbu and then the holy cities were taken. In 1813 Muhammad Ali made the pilgrimage in person. In the interior the Wahhabi rebels remained all-powerful. In 1815 Muhammad Ali mounted expeditions against Yemen and against the Wahhabi in Nejd. Toussoun was succeeded by his brother, Ibrahim Pasha, and the war took on a more aggressive character. In 1818, with an army of eleven-thousand men, Ibrahim laid siege to the Wahhabi villages and finally took their capital, Dariya. The successor to Abd al-Aziz, Abdullah, was sent to Istanbul, where he was executed in front of Hagia Sophia. Ibrahim ravaged the Wahhabi rebel's territory at leisure and then evacuated his army to Egypt.

82. THE EGYPTIAN CAMPAIGN IN THE SUDAN, 1820–1880

By 1820 Muhammad Ali was autonomous viceroy of Egypt, paying tribute only to the Porte. In 1811 he broke the power of the Mamluks in Egypt, but a remnant established itself in the petty Funj state of Dongola. Here they built a walled town, recruited slaves, and began to extend their power in the region. In 1812 Muhammad Ali sent an embassy to order the Funj ruler to expel the Mamluks, but the ruler lacked authority to do so. Two other factors weighed heavily with Muhammad Ali: Dongola was the center of a prosperous slave trade and, by repute, was rich in gold mines.

A further factor was unrest among Muhammad Ali's Albanian troops. In 1820 his third son, Isma'il Kamil Pasha, led six-thousand men on what was nominally an Ottoman expedition, but what in fact was a private venture of the viceroy. By 4 November the Shayqiyya were defeated at Kurti near Dongola, and thereafter there was no serious military resistance. In February 1821 Isma'il pressed southward, and by 13 June he had taken Sennar. Shortly thereafter the Kordofan province surrendered. At the end of 1821 Ibrahim Pasha (see map 81) took command, and occupied the gold-bearing region of Fazughli. A rebellion in his rear, protesting high taxation, was speedily suppressed.

Egyptian authority was now established over the Sudan, and a period of conciliation followed. Khartoum was founded as the capital, and commerce was encouraged by the protection of trade routes. Petty wars continued until 1838, when Egyptian borders reached Ethiopia. A long period of feeble and capricious rule followed, during which European traders penetrated the country. Under the khedive Isma'il Pasha (r. 1863–1879), Egyptian territories were considerably expanded. Under European pressure, a struggle began against the slave trade, which culminated in the Mahdist rebellion.

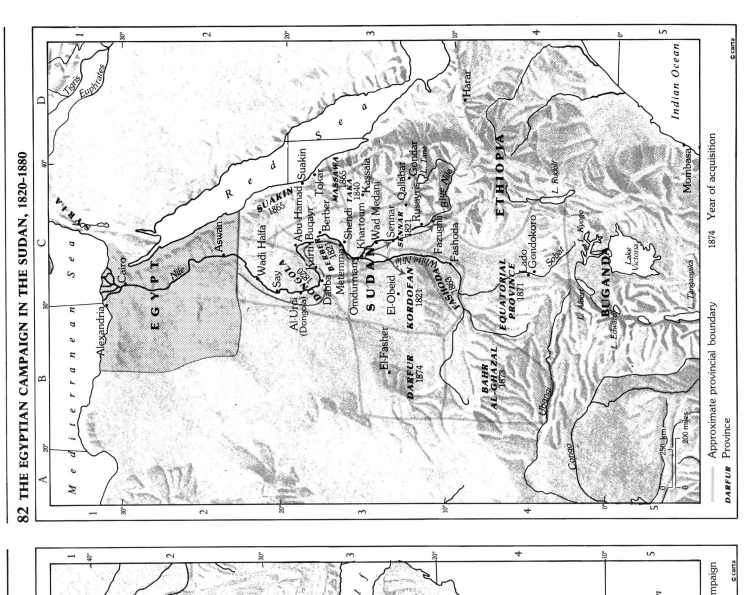

82 THE EGYPTIAN CAMPAIGN IN THE SUDAN, 1820–1880

Indian Ocean

1874 Year of acquisition

———— Approximate provincial boundary

DARFUR Province

Mediterranean Sea

E G Y P T

Alexandria

Cairo

Aswan

Wadi Halfa

Say

Al-Urdi (Dongola) 1820

DONGOLA

Dabba

BERBER 1820

Berber 1820

Kurti

Buqayr

Abu Hamad

Suakin

SUAKIN 1865

Tokar

MASSAWA 1865

Massawa

TAKA 1865

Kassala 1840

Shendi

Metemma

Ondurman

Khartoum

Wad Medani

SENNAR

Sennar

Qallabat

Rusayris

L. Tana

Gondar

Blue Nile

Harar

ETHIOPIA

SUDAN

KORDOFAN 1821

El-Obeid

FASHODA 1865

Fazughli

Fashoda

White Nile

EQUATORIAL PROVINCE 1871

Lado

Gondokoro

Sobat

L. Rudolf

El Fasher

DARFUR 1874

BAHR AL-GHAZAL 1873

Ubangi

Congo

BUGANDA

Lake Victoria

L. Edward

L. Albert

L. Kyoga

Tanganyika

Mombasa

0 250 km.

0 200 miles

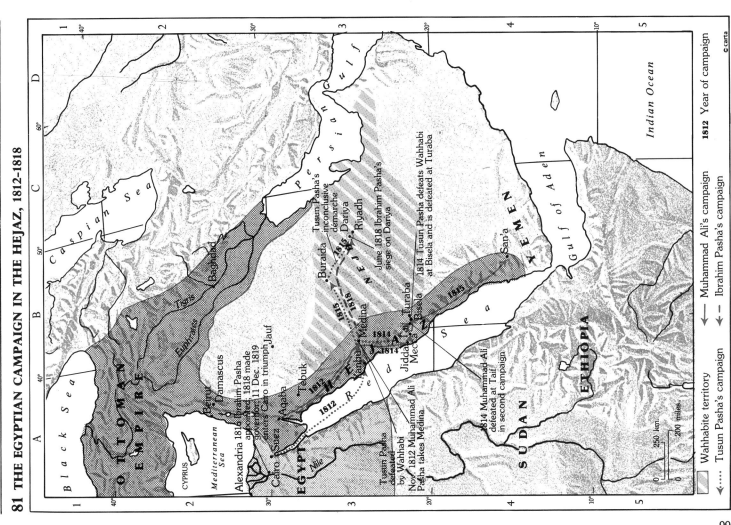

81 THE EGYPTIAN CAMPAIGN IN THE HEJAZ, 1812–1818

Black Sea

OTTOMAN EMPIRE

Caspian Sea

CYPRUS

Mediterranean Sea

Beirut

Damascus

Baghdad

Tigris

Euphrates

Alexandria 1816 Ibrahim Pasha appointed 1818 made governor; 11 Dec. 1819 enters Cairo in triumph

Cairo Suez

EGYPT

Nile

Aqaba

Tebuk

Jauf

Tusun Pasha defeated by Wahhabi Nov. 1812 Muhammad Ali Pasha takes Medina

H E J A Z

Medina

Yanbu

Jidda

Mecca

Taif

Turaba

Bisela

NEJD

Buraida

Riyadh

Dariya

1815

1818

Tusun Pasha's inconclusive demarche

June 1818 Ibrahim Pasha's siege on Dariya

1814 Tusun Pasha defeats Wahhabi at Bisela and is defeated at Turaba

1814 Muhammad Ali defeated at Taif in second campaign

Persian Gulf

Red Sea

1812

1815

San'a

YEMEN

SUDAN

ETHIOPIA

Gulf of Aden

Indian Ocean

Wahhabite territory

———→ Muhammad Ali's campaign

– –→ Ibrahim Pasha's campaign

······→ Tusun Pasha's campaign

1812 Year of campaign

0 250 km.

0 200 miles.

83. THE CAMPAIGN OF IBRAHIM PASHA IN GREECE, 1824–1833

When Ibrahim Pasha withdrew from the Sudan in 1822 a new opportunity arose for Muhammad Ali. On 13 January 1822 Greece proclaimed its independence of Turkey. Christian Europe, in which the governing classes had a classical tradition in education, expressed immediate sympathy for Greece. The sultan thus looked to Muhammad Ali as an ally rather than as a vassal.

In April 1823 an Egyptian army put down the rebellion in Crete. As a reward Muhammad Ali created the pasha of Acre, with instructions to reconquer Greece. After an unsuccessful start in 1823, Ibrahim Pasha, in command of a force of Albanians and Egyptians, disembarked in 1824. In 1825 the greater part of Morea was taken, and the city of Tripolitsa was entered. Ibrahim continued to Nauphlia, where an English squadron was stationed. In 1826 his army attacked Missolonghi, where the remainder of the insurrectionaries had assembled.

Assaults of 24 February and 6 April failed, but famine forced the heroic defenders to surrender. They were massacred without pity.

From 26 August until 2 June 1827, Ibrahim besieged Athens. An attempt by British naval commander Thomas Cochrane to set fire to the Egyptian fleet in Alexandria was foiled, and Muhammad Ali pursued him as far as Rhodes. By now all Europe was moved by the Greek losses, and Britain, France, and Russia combined to attack the Turco-Egyptian fleet at Navarino. On 26 October 1827, the Turco-Egyptian fleet was destroyed.

In Morea Ibrahim continued to resist, but his army had tired of war. The Egyptian troops were restless, and 2,700 Albanians deserted en bloc. In September 1828 a French expedition forced Ibrahim to surrender, and in the following year Greek independence was recognized by the Treaty of Adrianople.

84. THE EGYPTIAN CAMPAIGN IN SYRIA, 1831–1841

Between 1828 and 1829 Turkey was at war with Russia, and Ibrahim Pasha was ordered to take the fleet to the Dardanelles and to enter Syria with 28,000 men. So slow was Muhammad Ali in carrying out the order that the sultan showed his displeasure by nominating Ibrahim Pasha to be prince of Mecca, a rank higher than his father.

In 1830 Ibrahim besieged Acre with 35,000 men. Though the garrison of 25,000 defied Ibrahim for six months, Acre was taken on 27 April 1832. Ibrahim then marched north and took Damascus without resistance. The pasha of Aleppo unsuccessfully tried to stop his advance into Syria. On 26 July Ibrahim took Aleppo and cut off the Turkish forces.

Ibrahim now turned against the Ottomans, who raised an army of Albanians and Bosnians against him. He defeated them near Konya on 21 December 1832. He was received with enthusiasm in Asia Minor; on 28 February 1833, the port city of Smyrna

opened its gates to a single officer with four men. Ibrahim by then had reached Kutaya and threatened Bursa. Nothing stood between him and Istanbul.

The integrity of the tottering Ottoman Empire had long been a dogma of European foreign policy, and there was a general fear that it might collapse. The French ambassador intervened. Ibrahim was offered the lands of ancient Palestine, which he refused, demanding all Syria, part of Mesopotamia, and the Turkish province of Adana. Russia now intervened, and a squadron and twelve-thousand men effectively changed the situation. In 1833 a *hatti-sherif* (decree) ceded all Syria and Adana district to Muhammad Ali, while the secret treaty of Unkiar-Skelessi provided a Russian guarantee of the Ottoman domains. This decree marked the apogee of Egyptian expansion. It now held Syria, the holy cities, and the Sudan. There was, however, an Achilles' heel, for in November 1837 Britain took possession of the colony of Aden.

83 THE CAMPAIGNS OF IBRAHIM PASHA IN GREECE, 1824-1833

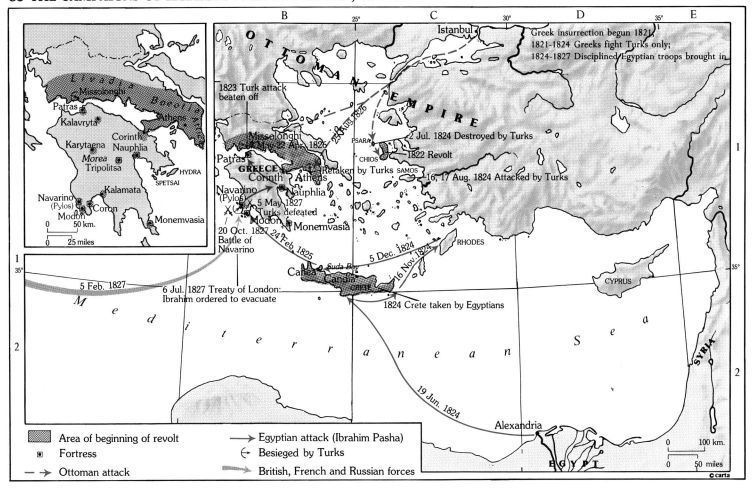

Greek insurrection begun 1821
1821-1824 Greeks fight Turks only;
1824-1827 Disciplined Egyptian troops brought in

1823 Turk attack beaten off

2 Jul. 1824 Destroyed by Turks

1822 Revolt

16, 17 Aug. 1824 Attacked by Turks

Missolonghi 24 May 22 Apr. 1826

Retaken by Turks

Navarino (Pylos)

5 May 1827 Turks defeated

20 Oct. 1827 Battle of Navarino

24 Feb 1825

5 Dec. 1824

16 Nov 1824

1824 Crete taken by Egyptians

5 Feb. 1827

6 Jul. 1827 Treaty of London: Ibrahim ordered to evacuate

19 Jun. 1824

	Area of beginning of revolt	→	Egyptian attack (Ibrahim Pasha)
⊡	Fortress	←	Besieged by Turks
— →	Ottoman attack	⟹	British, French and Russian forces

84 THE EGYPTIAN CAMPAIGN IN SYRIA, 1831-1841

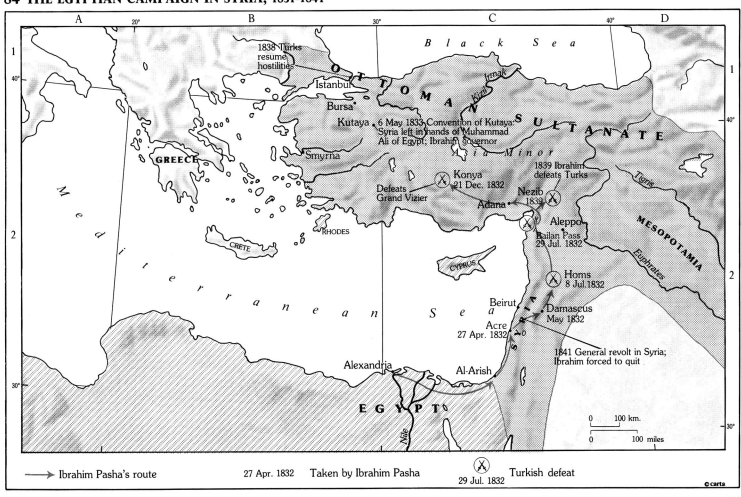

1838 Turks resume hostilities

6 May 1833 Convention of Kutaya: Syria left in hands of Muhammad Ali of Egypt; Ibrahim Governor

1839 Ibrahim defeats Turks

Konya 21 Dec. 1832

Defeats Grand Vizier

Nezib 1839

Bailan Pass 29 Jul. 1832

Aleppo

Homs 8 Jul. 1832

Damascus May 1832

Acre 27 Apr. 1832

1841 General revolt in Syria; Ibrahim forced to quit

Al-Arish

→	Ibrahim Pasha's route	27 Apr. 1832	Taken by Ibrahim Pasha	Ⓧ 29 Jul. 1832	Turkish defeat

85. THE SUEZ CANAL, 1869, AND WORLD TRADE

Only a narrow neck of land, 125 miles long, divides Africa from Asia, and the Mediterranean from the waters of the Red Sea. Trade eastward from the Mediterranean originally passed up the Nile and then overland to southern Egyptian ports. An inscription of Seti I at Karnak records a canal, dated 1380 B.C. that connected the Nile with the Great Bitter Lake. Its course is still traceable. In the sixth century B.C., Pharaoh Necho II chose a different route, which was completed in 520 B.C. by the Persian ruler Darius I. In 285 B.C., Ptolemy Philadelphus connected it to the Red Sea, but by 31 B.C. it had become unusable. The Roman emperor Trajan (r. 98-117) is said to have repaired and enlarged this canal in A.D. 98, joining it to the Nile at Babilyun, now Old Cairo, but some writers attribute this enlargement to Amr ibn al-As (see map 20). The canal was closed deliberately by the caliph al-Mansur in 770, when he feared attacks from pirates in the Red Sea. Nevertheless parts of it remained open until 1861, when it was used by French engineers to construct the fresh-water canal from Cairo to Suez between 1861 and 1863.

The caliph Harun al-Rashid (r. 786–809) is credited with a scheme to pierce the Isthmus of Suez. He abandoned it for fear the Byzantines might use it to attack him. The scheme was not raised again until after 1500, when the Venetians wished to construct a canal to outflank the Portuguese who had captured the spice trade by sailing round the Cape of Good Hope. The Ottoman conquest of Egypt put a stop to the project in 1517. Louis XIV of France toyed with the idea of an expedition to Egypt to build a canal in 1671, but nothing came of it, nor of the proposal of Ali Bey, Mamluk governor of Egypt, to do so in 1770. In 1798 Napoleon Bonaparte ordered a survey of the isthmus with a view to constructing a canal, but nothing more than debate took place until 1854, when the French engineer Ferdinand-Marie de Lesseps formed the Compagnie Universelle du Canal Maritime de Suez and subsequently obtained a concession from the khedive Said Pasha, granting a ninety-nine-year lease from 1856. Diplomatic opposition followed from England; other countries, including Russia and the United States, held aloof. England feared for her maritime interests. Despite difficulties regarding labor, finance, hot weather, and disease, the completion of the canal was celebrated in November 1869, when the empress Eugénie of France led a convoy of sixty-six vessels down the canal, leaving Port Said on 17 November and reaching Suez on 20 November.

From 1869 to 1870, there were 486 transits; by 1966-1967 the number recorded had reached 20,000. Following the beginning of commercial exploitation of Persian oil in 1907, the canal became the main artery of the oil trade. In 1913, 291,000 tons were carried through the canal; by 1966, the volume had reached 166 million tons.

At first, 52 percent of the shares of the canal company were held by France and 44 percent by the khedive. His extravagant habits forced him to sell his shares, which Benjamin Disraeli acquired for Britain. This acquisition secured the strategic route to India and led to British domination in Egypt until 1956. In that year, following British refusal to finance an additional dam above Aswan, Gamal Abdel Nasser nationalized the canal. France and Britain went to war, but were halted by U.S. financial intervention. Following war with Israel in 1967, the canal remained closed until 1975. Its importance has declined because of the growth of air transport, the virtual disappearance of the sea passenger trade, the development of oil tankers for which, when laden, the canal is too shallow.

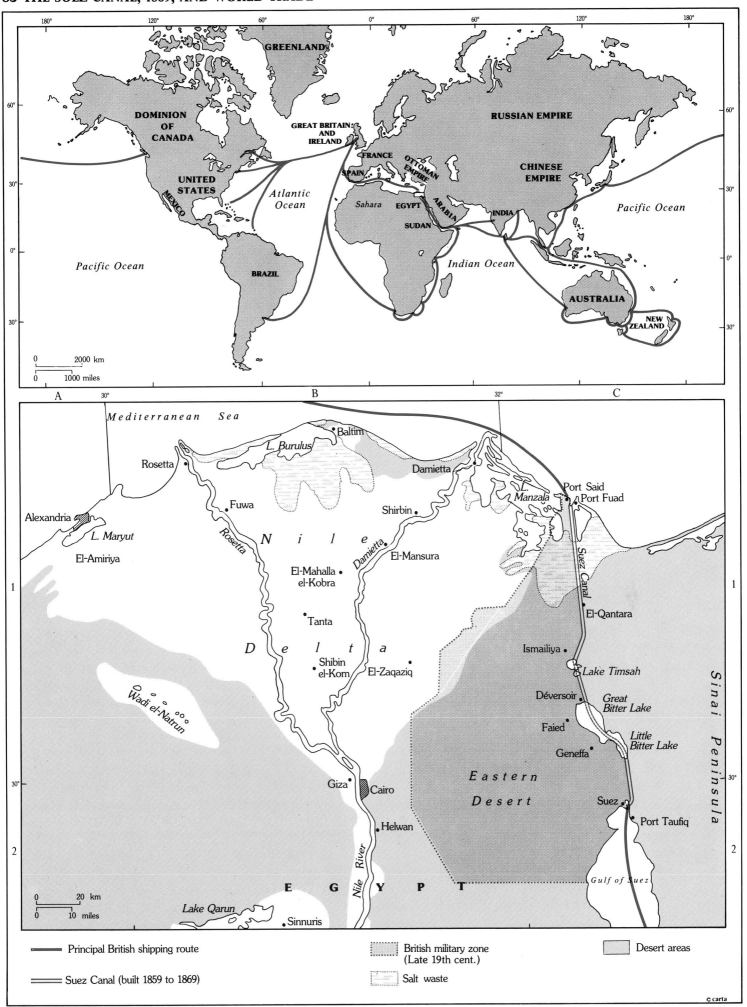

GREENLAND

DOMINION
OF
CANADA

RUSSIAN EMPIRE

GREAT BRITAIN
AND
IRELAND

FRANCE

UNITED
STATES

SPAIN

OTTOMAN
EMPIRE

CHINESE
EMPIRE

*Atlantic
Ocean*

Sahara

EGYPT

ARABIA

INDIA

Pacific Ocean

MEXICO

SUDAN

Pacific Ocean

BRAZIL

Indian Ocean

AUSTRALIA

NEW
ZEALAND

0   2000 km
0   1000 miles

Mediterranean   Sea

L. Burulus

Baltim

Rosetta

Damietta

L. Manzala

Port Said
Port Fuad

Fuwa

Shirbin

Alexandria

L. Maryut

Rosetta

N   i   l   e

El-Mansura

Suez Canal

El-Amiriya

Damietta

El-Mahalla
el-Kobra

El-Qantara

Tanta

Ismailiya

D   e   l   t   a

Lake Timsah

Wadi el-Natrun

Shibin
el-Kom

El-Zaqaziq

Déversoir

*Great
Bitter Lake*

Faied

*Little
Bitter Lake*

Geneffa

*E a s t e r n
D e s e r t*

Sinai   Peninsula

Giza

Cairo

Suez

Helwan

Port Taufiq

E   G   Y   P   T

Gulf of Suez

0   20 km
0   10 miles

Lake Qarun

Sinnuris

—————— Principal British shipping route

British military zone
(Late 19th cent.)

Desert areas

══════ Suez Canal (built 1859 to 1869)

Salt waste

© carta

86. ISLAM IN AFRICA, 19TH TO 20TH CENTURIES

Although the coastal territories of the Mediterranean were Islamized in the seventh and eighth centuries, Islam does not seem to have penetrated south of the Sahara much before the eleventh century. The coast of western Africa, however, is an exception. The earliest evidence of Islam in Africa, recently excavated at Shanga, off the Kenyan island of Lamu, is of a mosque that was rebuilt nine times between around 750 and 1450, the first construction being a simple enclosure of reeds. Possibly, Islam reached Madagascar during the early part of the period. In the Ethiopian lowlands inhabited by Somali herdsmen it is difficult to measure its progress, but by the thirteenth century there were stone-built mosques in trading towns along the coast to the south and the islands of Pemba, Zanzibar, and Mafia. Except in the Horn of Africa there is no evidence of the penetration of Islam inland before the nineteenth century.

In the west Islam seems to have reached southern Morocco and Mauritania in the eleventh century, but rulers of Mali were not converted until the thirteenth century. Though the first to make the pilgrimage to Mecca was Sakura in 1293–1294, that of his successor, Mansa Musa, in 1324 was rare enough to be sensational. Perhaps the most significant of his acts was his return with the architect Ishaq al-Saheli, who built the mosques of Gao and Timbuktu, from which learned men eagerly disseminated Islam. In spite of its proximity to Egypt, Nubia was not Islamized until the sixteenth century.

From the late twelfth century the intellectual hegemony of the university mosque of al-Azhar drew students from as far afield as western Africa and Indonesia. Among its dependencies were hostels for students from the Sudan, by which was meant the whole of Muslim "black Africa," as well as from Malaysia and beyond. *Awqaf* (charitable bequests) provided them with food, lodging, clothing, and pocket money. Returning home literate and with a knowledge of law, they were assured of a career.

At the beginning of the nineteenth century and up to midcentury a number of remarkable men appeared in Africa. In Egypt, following Napoleon's incursion (map 78), Muhammad Ali Pasha (r. 1806–1849) brought Egypt into the modern world as a power in its own right within the world community. Islam now penetrated equatorial Africa from Egypt. In the west this achievement was matched by Uthman dan Fodio, a religious reformer whose jihad, or holy war, was both military and spiritual. This was the basis of the empire of Sokoto in northern Nigeria, which embraced a number of earlier states, and it gave a Muslim character to the region that has become permanent. Similar movements arose under Ahmad Lobo in Massina and later in the century under Hajj Umar Tal in Segu, Kaarta, and Massina. In these movements the spiritual basis stemmed from Sufi religious fraternities, especially the Tijaniya, thus linking them with the outside world.

In the east the replacement of the Portuguese by the Arabs of Oman after the fall of Mombasa in 1698 (map 76) had no immediate effect. The first ruler of Oman to take a personal interest in eastern Africa was Sa'id ibn Sultan (r. 1806–1856), who first visited these Omani dominions in 1827. He finally moved to Zanzibar in 1840. Up to 1823 African traders brought their products to the coast. By 1844 this process was wholly reversed, and Arab and Zanzibari Swahili traders traveled inland, reaching the Congo (now Zaïre) by the end of the century. In their wake followed members of Sufi fraternities, who received ready acceptance in Uganda as well as Zaïre. Similarly the Mahdist state in the eastern Sudan of 1882 to 1896 and the Sanusi movement, which began in eastern Libya in 1837, derived initially from Sufis. These movements adapted to African ideas, and on the eastern African coast they established the "Mosque College" of Lamu, the principal center of Swahili culture and a center of popular pilgrimage even at the present time.

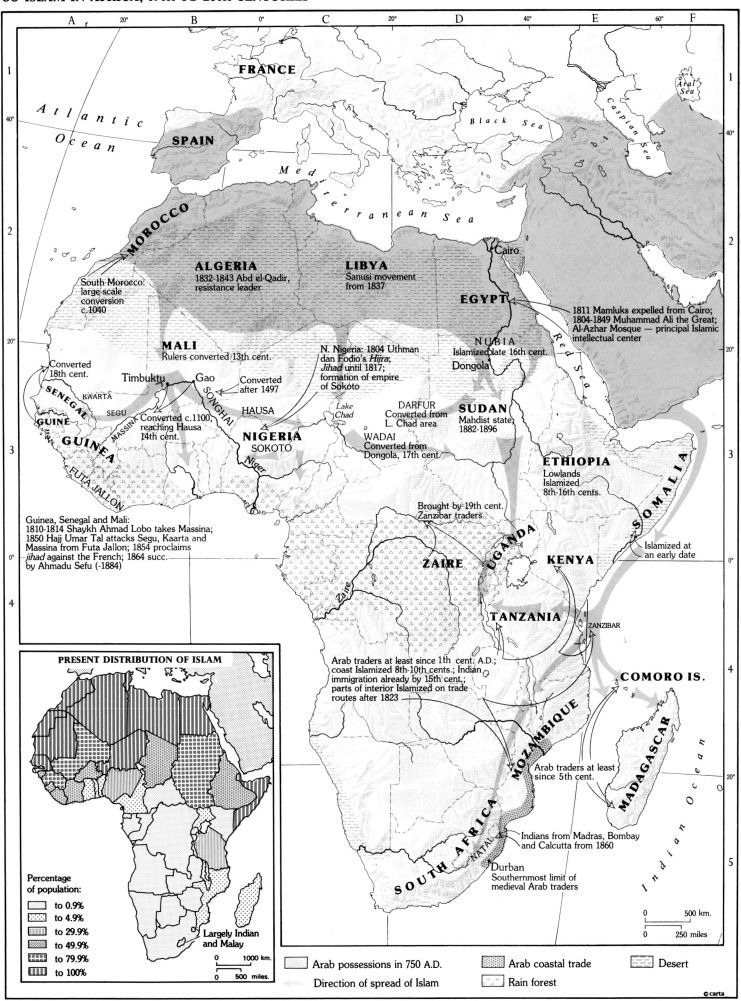

FRANCE

Atlantic Ocean

SPAIN

Med

terranean Sea

Black Sea

Aral Sea

Caspian Sea

MOROCCO

South Morocco:
large-scale
conversion
c.1040

ALGERIA
1832-1843 Abd el-Qadir,
resistance leader

LIBYA
Sanusi movement
from 1837

Cairo

EGYPT

1811 Mamluks expelled from Cairo;
1804-1849 Muhammad Ali the Great;
Al-Azhar Mosque — principal Islamic
intellectual center

MALI
Rulers converted 13th cent.

Converted
18th cent.

KAARTA

SENEGAL

GUINE

GUINEA

FUTA JALLON

SEGU

MASSINA

Timbuktu

Gao

Converted
after 1497

Converted c.1100,
reaching Hausa
14th cent.

SONGHAI

HAUSA

NIGERIA

SOKOTO

Niger

N. Nigeria: 1804 Uthman
dan Fodio's *Hijra*;
Jihad until 1817;
formation of empire
of Sokoto

Lake
Chad

NUBIA
Islamized late 16th cent.

Dongola

DARFUR
Converted from
L. Chad area

WADAI
Converted from
Dongola, 17th cent.

SUDAN
Mahdist state
1882-1896

Red Sea

ETHIOPIA
Lowlands
Islamized
8th-16th cents.

SOMALIA

Guinea, Senegal and Mali:
1810-1814 Shaykh Ahmad Lobo takes Massina;
1850 Hajj Umar Tal attacks Segu, Kaarta and
Massina from Futa Jallon; 1854 proclaims
jihad against the French; 1864 succ.
by Ahmadu Sefu (-1884)

Brought by 19th cent.
Zanzibar traders

ZAIRE

UGANDA

KENYA

Islamized at
an early date

Zaire

TANZANIA

ZANZIBAR

Arab traders at least since 1th cent. A.D.;
coast Islamized 8th-10th cents.; Indian
immigration already by 15th cent.;
parts of interior Islamized on trade
routes after 1823

COMORO IS.

MOZAMBIQUE

MADAGASCAR

Arab traders at least
since 5th cent.

SOUTH AFRICA

NATAL

Indians from Madras, Bombay
and Calcutta from 1860

Durban
Southernmost limit of
medieval Arab traders

Indian Ocean

0   500 km.
0   250 miles

PRESENT DISTRIBUTION OF ISLAM

Percentage
of population:

to 0.9%
to 4.9%
to 29.9%
to 49.9%
to 79.9%
to 100%

Largely Indian
and Malay

0   1000 km.
0   500 miles.

Arab possessions in 750 A.D.

Direction of spread of Islam

Arab coastal trade

Rain forest

Desert

©carta

87. NOTABLE EUROPEAN TRAVELERS IN THE MIDDLE EAST, 18TH TO 20TH CENTURIES

Apart from rare contacts with the Mongols, before the sixteenth century European contacts with the Middle East were confined almost entirely to Egypt and the Holy Land. Venice and other Italian cities had an almost exclusive trade with them. Pero da Covilhã, sent by the Portuguese Crown in 1497 to locate the coasts of Arabia, India, and East Africa, was an exception. The sixteenth century opened with the remarkable journey of Ludovico de Varthema, who was urged by the desire "to behold the various kingdoms of the world" and was the first known European to reach Mecca. Those whose object was largely curiosity were succeeded in the seventeenth century by men whose object was trade with India, China, and, occasionally, Persia, leaving Asia Minor, Syria, and Arabia virtually a complete blank.

It was not until 1766 that a Dane, Carsten Niebuhr, became the first scientific explorer to describe the Levant and Arabian coast, returning overland via Persepolis and Baghdad to Aleppo and Istanbul. Shortly thereafter war between Persia and Russia led to a complete exploration of Caucasia. Hydrographers and consular agents now joined journeys from Britain, Russia, and Germany, the most spectacular of which were the journeys of the Russian diplomat P. von Chihachev between 1842 and 1853.

The vast research on the Holy Land now became scientific. In 1798 to 1801 Palestine was mapped by Napoleon's surveyors who had recorded the Nile Delta, but the results were a state secret until 1817. By then U. I. Seetzen in 1805, François-Auguste-René de Châteaubriand in 1806, and Johann Ludwig Burckhardt in 1812 had traveled there. In the same year Lady Hester Lucy Stanhope became the first individual to conduct an excavation at Ashkelon, in the hope of finding buried treasure.

The true father of Palestinian exploration was the American scholar, Edward Robinson, who determined he could not teach biblical literature without visiting the country. His *Biblical Researches in Palestine, Mount Sinai, and Arabia Petraea* (1841)

consititutes a real landmark. A number of small expeditions added to the stock of topographical knowledge, until in 1864 a party of Royal Engineers was sent by Baroness Angela Georgina Burdett-Coutts to provide a water supply for Jerusalem. This led to the foundation of the Palestine Exploration Fund in 1865, and the Surveys of Western Palestine (1871–1877) and Eastern Palestine (1871–1882).

In the rest of Syria and in Mesopotamia things moved more slowly. Northern Syria was surveyed in the first half of the nineteeth century, but the real father of Syrian studies was Henry Creswicke Rawlinson. British political agent in Baghdad from 1843 until 1855, he made himself the foremost authority on the region in geography, history, and politics. During this time the English archaeologist Austen Henry Layard and French archaeologists were opening new windows into the history of Assyria and Babylon. Arabia now began to be explored, following the Egyptian expedition of 1812. Burckhardt reached Mecca in disguise in 1814 and gave a precise and scholarly description of the city. Oman was explored by James Wellsted in 1836. Richard Burton made the pilgrimage to Mecca disguised as an Afghan in 1877, and in 1885 the Dutch scholar Christiaan Snouck Hurgronje gave a detailed account of the social life of the city. Toward the end of the century Charles Montagu Doughty traveled in northern Arabia: his *Travels in Arabia Deserta* (1888) still stands as the greatest classic on Arabian travel and Bedouin life.

Doughty's work laid the foundation for works that arose as a result of World War I, among which were those by Gertrude Bell (just before the war), W. H. I. Shakespear, Harry St. John Bridger Philby, R. E. Cheesman, and T. E. Lawrence, known commonly as Lawrence of Arabia. Later in the twentieth century Philby carried out further journeys, chiefly in Nejd and Saudi Arabia. The last part of Arabia to be explored, the "empty quarter" in southeastern Arabia, was crossed finally, using different routes, by Philby, Bertram Thomas, and Wilfrid Thesiger.

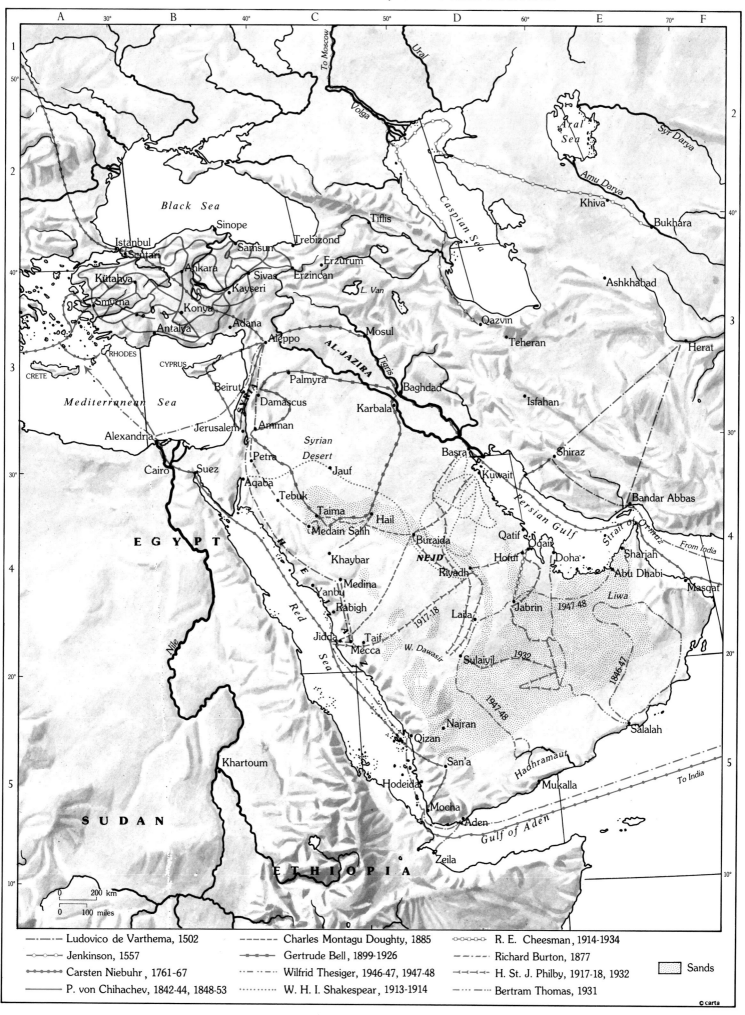

Ludovico de Varthema, 1502
Jenkinson, 1557
Carsten Niebuhr, 1761-67
P. von Chihachev, 1842-44, 1848-53

Charles Montagu Doughty, 1885
Gertrude Bell, 1899-1926
Wilfrid Thesiger, 1946-47, 1947-48
W. H. I. Shakespear, 1913-1914

R. E. Cheesman, 1914-1934
Richard Burton, 1877
H. St. J. Philby, 1917-18, 1932
Bertram Thomas, 1931

Sands

© carta

88. THE EXPANSION OF SAUDI ARABIA, 20TH CENTURY

The Saudi family ruled Dariya in Wadi Hanifa, in the province of Nejd in central Arabia, in the fifteenth century. It came to prominence in the eighteenth century when it accepted the puritanical Islamic revivalism of Muhammad Abd al-Wahhab, whose teachings were based on those of the jurist Ahmad ibn Hanbal (780–855). Under this inspiration, the Saudi family raided the Hejaz, Iraq, and Syria and captured Mecca in 1806. Because it caused a loss of revenue, these acts angered the Ottomans. They sent armies under Ibrahim Pasha from Egypt (see map 81) in a series of campaigns (1812–1818).

Although the family still possessed considerable territory, it fell into eclipse after 1865, when, after a civil war, the al-Rashid family displaced them.

Ibn Saud was born in Kuwait around 1880. He was determined to regain his patrimony. With only fifteen men, he seized Riyadh in 1902, killing the Rashidi governor. In 1913 he took al-Hasa on the Persian Gulf, and Asir in 1920–1926; Hail was taken in 1921 and the Hejaz, including the cities of Mecca and Medina, in 1924–1925. These territories formed what was proclaimed a kingdom in 1932.

Though it began as a poor kingdom, an oil concession awarded in 1933 and the first export of oil in 1938 brought riches. Even during 1990 new reserves of oil were identified in central Arabia, with the result that Saudi Arabia is not only the possessor of the greatest oil reserves in the world, but the richest of oil states. Nevertheless, although there have been certain concessions to modernity, Saudi Arabia remains the most puritanical of Arab states, forbidding the consumption of alcohol even to foreigners and making it illegal for women to drive cars or appear unveiled in public. A major problem is presented by the number of royal family members — in all more than seven-hundred persons — who enjoy every possible state preferment, privilege, and luxury, as opposed to the relative poverty of the majority of the people.

89. WORLD WAR I: THE TURKISH FRONTS IN THE CAUCASUS, SYRIA, MESOPOTAMIA, AND ARABIA

When war broke out in 1914 Bulgaria, Greece, Montenegro, and Serbia united against Turkey, where imperial Germany had long prepared a toe hold in the case of war. In November 1914 Britain and France declared war on Turkey. Their objective was twofold: to preserve vital British communication through Egypt with India as well as French interests in the Suez Canal and to relieve Russia from Turkish pressure in the Caucasus.

The Ottoman sultan proclaimed a jihad against the Allies, but, with the aid of British gold, this was declared invalid by the sharif of Mecca. At the end of 1914 a Turkish army from Syria attempted to cut the Suez Canal, but it was stopped on the canal's banks. Although ill-equipped, the Russians attacked Erzurum and repulsed the Turks at Kars and Ardahan in January 1915. A Russian offensive in 1916 took Erzurum, Trebizond, and Erzincan, but all these efforts were rendered vain by the collapse of Russia in 1917.

In 1915 the British and French had attacked Turkey in the Dardanelles, with the goal of taking Istanbul (see map 90). In spite of their failure, the flower of the Ottoman army was destroyed. The Turks at this time organized massacres of Armenians in Anatolia and especially in Istanbul, in which some 750,000 Armenians perished out of a total population of some two million. Many Armenians fled to Syria and Mesopotamia.

In Mesopotamia an expeditionary force, largely from India, took Basra in 1914, but it was not able to reach Baghdad until 1917. Encouraged by the British, the Arabs of Hejaz revolted in July 1916, serving the Allied cause by harassing the Turks in the peninsula during the advances in Mesopotamia and Syria. Baghdad fell to the Allies in March 1917, costing 92,500 casualties. From Egypt the British general Edmund Henry Hynman Allenby mounted an attack on Syria in 1917. Jaffa was taken on 17 November 1917, and Jerusalem on 9 December. Allenby continued, sweeping northward through Damascus to Aleppo. The Turkish army finally surrendered on 30 October 1918.

88 THE EXPANSION OF SAUDI ARABIA, 20TH CENTURY

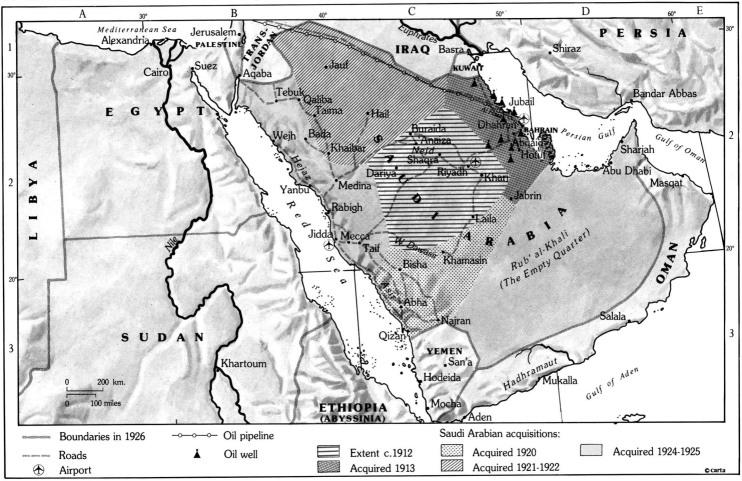

‒‒‒‒ Boundaries in 1926	‒∘‒∘‒ Oil pipeline
‒ ‒ ‒ Roads	▲ Oil well
✈ Airport	

Saudi Arabian acquisitions:

▤ Extent c.1912	▦ Acquired 1920	▨ Acquired 1924-1925
▨ Acquired 1913	▨ Acquired 1921-1922	

© carta

89 WORLD WAR I: THE TURKISH FRONTS IN THE CAUCASUS, SYRIA, MESOPOTAMIA AND ARABIA

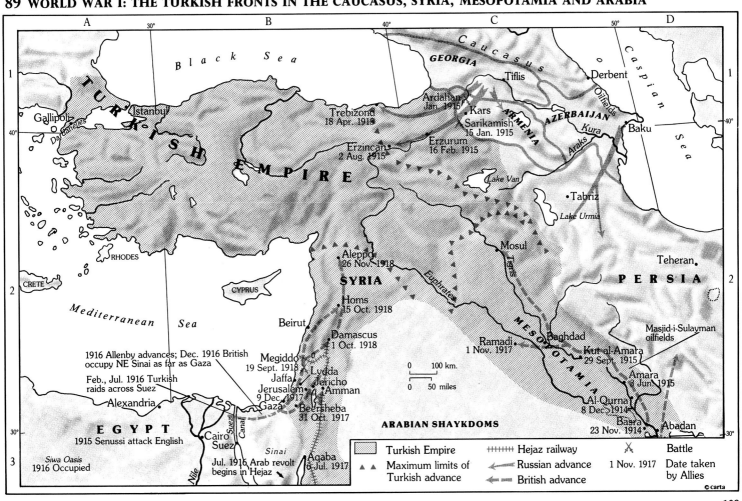

1916 Allenby advances; Dec. 1916 British occupy NE Sinai as far as Gaza

Feb., Jul. 1916 Turkish raids across Suez

1915 Senussi attack English

Siwa Oasis 1916 Occupied

Jul. 1916 Arab revolt begins in Hejaz

▨ Turkish Empire	┼┼┼┼ Hejaz railway	✕ Battle	
▲▲ Maximum limits of Turkish advance	⟵ Russian advance	1 Nov. 1917	Date taken by Allies
	⟵ British advance		

© carta

90. WORLD WAR I: GALLIPOLI, 1915–1916

The purpose of the campaign in the Dardanelles was to take Istanbul and thereby secure communications for the Allies with Russia from the Mediterranean to the Black Sea. The entry of the Turks into the war had, in fact, cut Russia off from sea communications for most of the year. In addition, Germany had closed the Baltic to the Russian navy.

A joint British and French fleet was assembled, but a series of naval bombardments proved ineffective. Accordingly a heterogeneous army was assembled, and French and British troops, including those from Australia, New Zealand and the United Kingdom landed on 25 April and several following days. By midyear the Allies had gained very little ground. On 6 August an offensive began, with heavy losses on both sides and little or no progress being made. The Allies, moreover, suffered greatly from heat, for which they were unprepared, and from disease. By 15 August the British commander was asking for 95,000 reinforcements, a figure based on an estimate of the Turkish force.

By mid-September the French government regarded the campaign as futile. From an Ottoman point of view, the troops were holding down Allied divisions that could have been employed against them elsewhere, and they were content to offer no more than a passive defense. Moreover, they occupied the higher ground. Slower to reach a conclusion than the French, the British eventually determined on evacuation, which began on 19 December, the Allies having 130,000 men killed, wounded, and missing. It had been an ill thought-out exercise of utter futility.

91. THE MIDDLE EAST FOLLOWING THE TREATY OF VERSAILLES

When the Conference of Paris met in 1919 the principal problem in the Middle East was the dismemberment of the Ottoman Empire. Britain and France were already bound to one another by the Sykes-Picot Agreement of 1916. It provided for French control of coastal Syria, Lebanon, Cilicia in Asia Minor, and northern Iraq and for British control in central Iraq and Basra and northern Palestine. Southern Palestine was to be placed under international administration, with Arab states to be recognized in the remaining Arab territories. Britain was further committed to the Zionist movement by the Balfour Declaration of 1917 to further the establishment of a "Jewish national home" in Palestine. The precise meaning of this expression, however, was never clearly defined in terms of institutions or territorial boundaries.

After some argument and adjustment, Britain obtained League of Nations mandates over Palestine, Transjordan, and Iraq; France obtained mandates over Lebanon and Syria. Egypt, under British occupation since 1882, became a kingdom in 1922 and had the former Ottoman province of Sinai attached to it.

Some adjustments followed. Remembering that Asia Minor, Syria, Palestine, and Egypt had once been Byzantine provinces, Greece tried to establish itself in Smyrna and its environs in 1920. The Turks drove the Greeks out in 1922. Cyprus, ethnically Greek and Turkish, remained in British possession.

The mandated territories in the Middle East, Africa, and the Far East were committed to the mandatory powers for administration, welfare, and local development until the local population was deemed ready for self-government. The French mandates were terminated in 1943, the British mandate over Iraq was terminated in 1927, Jordan in 1946, and the remainder of Palestine in 1948.

90 WORLD WAR I: GALLIPOLI, 1915-1916

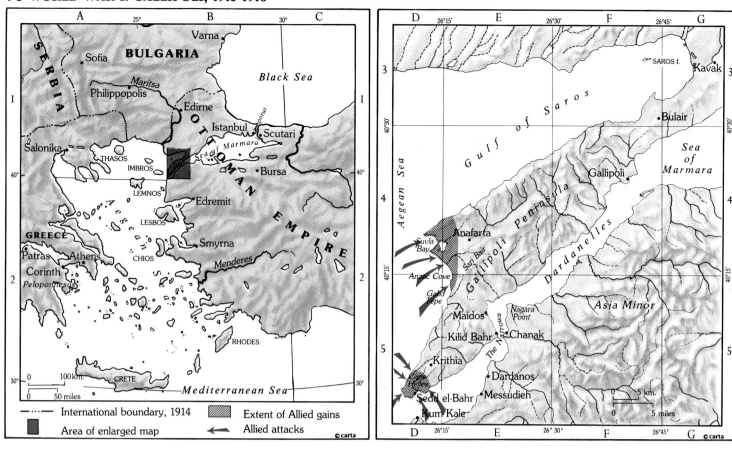

Legend:
- – – – International boundary, 1914
- ▨ Area of enlarged map
- ▨ Extent of Allied gains
- ← Allied attacks

© carta

91 THE MIDDLE EAST FOLLOWING THE TREATY OF VERSAILLES

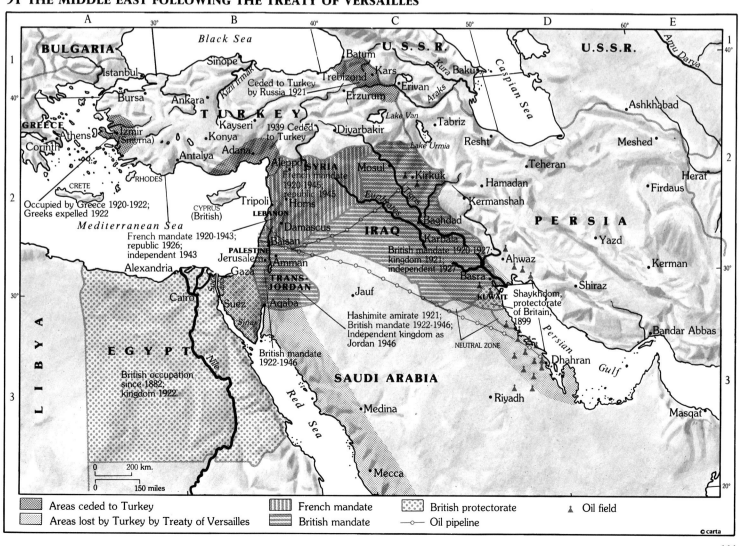

Legend:
- ▨ Areas ceded to Turkey
- ▨ Areas lost by Turkey by Treaty of Versailles
- ▥ French mandate
- ▤ British mandate
- ▨ British protectorate
- ○—○ Oil pipeline
- ▲ Oil field

© carta

92. THE JEWISH DIASPORA, 1920s TO 1930s

In 1650 Jews numbered about one million and were concentrated chiefly in eastern Europe and the Ottoman Empire. Toward the end of the nineteenth century there were some 7.5 million Jews in eastern Europe, or 70 to 75 percent of the world's Jewish population. This number was due primarily to a natural increase, which Jews shared with other Europeans. During the nineteenth century Jews in western Europe, except for Spain, enjoyed almost full civil liberty. In Russia, however, massacres occurred between 1886 and 1906. Pogroms accelerated an existing migratory movement after the 1870s, establishing new Jewish communities in the U.S.A., Canada, Argentina and other Latin American countries, South Africa and many western European countries. This movement was also part of a general movement throughout Europe from the Old World to the New World, or to establish colonies in Africa and Australia.

The modern Zionist movement, first organized in the 1880s, eventuated in the creation of the State of Israel in 1948. From A.D. 70 the Diaspora had never lost its sense of nationhood nor its historical link with Palestine. Anti-Semitism, as narrowly defined not to include other Semites, fostered this sense. The idea of a continued Jewish existence among non-Jewish societies was rejected by some Jewish groups. Theodor Herzl's *The Jewish State* (1896) crystallized these ideas, as did the First Zionist Congress he convened in Basle in 1897. After 1901 the congress met biennially.

The return of the Jews to Palestine began only as a trickle. When Britain took Palestine in 1917 the Balfour Declaration (2 Nov. 1917) promised the Jews a "national home," without defining what the term should or could mean. Nevertheless the declaration provided an impetus in an atmosphere rendered politically favorable by the mandate of Palestine, conferred by the League of Nations in July 1922. The Jewish population was now about 85,000, or approximately 11 percent of a total population of some 750,000 persons, chiefly Arabs. The Arabs were excluded from the discussion, with the result that friction ensued from what was a valid complaint.

During the 1920s and 1930s a small but steady stream of immigrants brought the Jewish population of Palestine to 581,000 in 1939, as the Jewish world population reached its demographic high point of 16,651,000. Of these 56% lived in Europe, 29% in North America, 1.05% in central and South America, 7.6% in Africa, and 0.2% in Australasia.

An unique feature of Jewish migration was the extent to which Jews were urbanized. Nearly one-third of all Jews lived in twenty-two communities of more than 100,000 Jewish inhabitants. The two largest communities were New York and Warsaw, but even so they were minorities in those cities. Outside the U.S. community of 4.5 million, the largest Jewish communities were in Poland (3.5 m.) and Russia (2.8 m.). Though prominent in public life, the actual number of Jews was so small as scarcely to be noticeable in the majority of European countries. This partly explains why reports of persecution as a preamble to the Holocaust were regarded in Britain with scepticism. It was only when the number of refugees reached considerable proportions that the real facts began to be believed.

92 THE JEWISH DIASPORA, 1920s TO 1930s

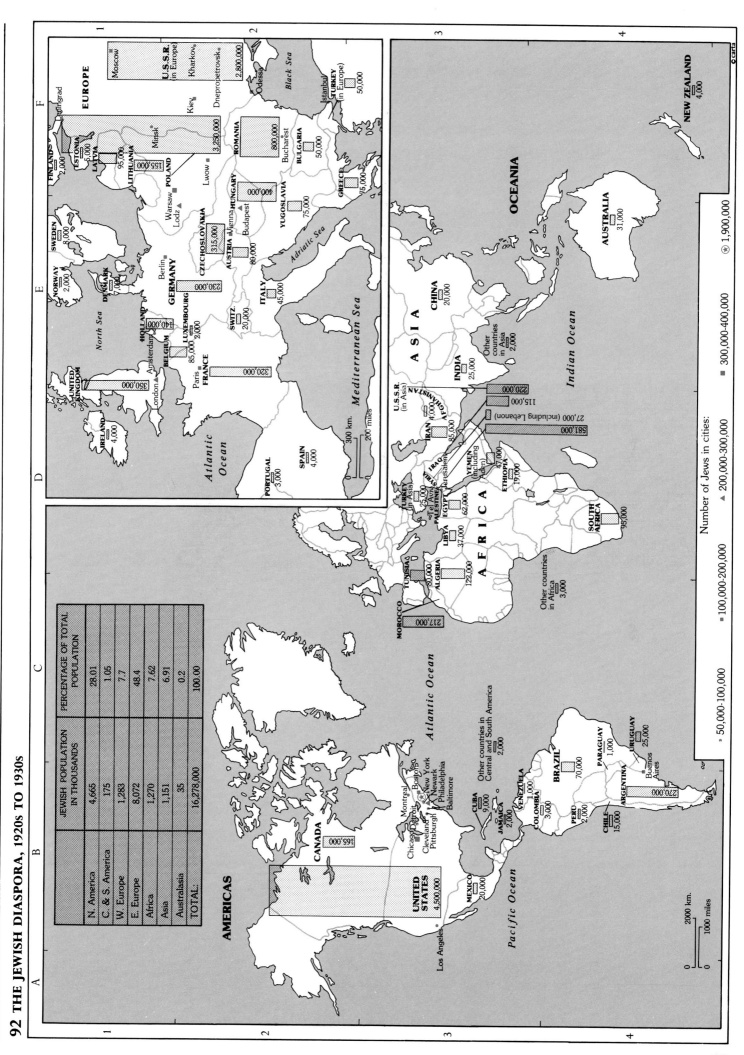

	JEWISH POPULATION IN THOUSANDS	PERCENTAGE OF TOTAL POPULATION
N. America	4,665	28.01
C. & S. America	175	1.05
W. Europe	1,283	7.7
E. Europe	8,072	48.4
Africa	1,270	7.62
Asia	1,151	6.91
Australasia	35	0.2
TOTAL:	16,278,000	100.00

EUROPE

U.S.S.R. (in Europe)

AMERICAS

ASIA

AFRICA

OCEANIA

Number of Jews in cities:
■ 50,000–100,000
■ 100,000–200,000
■ 200,000–300,000
▲ 300,000–400,000
⊛ 1,900,000

© carta

113

93. PALESTINE FROM THE PEEL COMMISSION TO THE WAR OF INDEPENDENCE, 1937–1949

Although President Woodrow Wilson's principle of the right to political self-determination was accepted at the Peace Conference in 1919, it was applied unevenly in the Middle East. The claims of Armenians and Kurds were disregarded, and Arab lands were partitioned between Britain and France. The mandate over Palestine disregarded the views of Zionists and Palestinian Arabs.

In 1921 Britain enabled Faysal I's brother Abdullah to seize what is now Jordan. Though included in the mandate over Palestine, it was excluded from designated Palestine.

Winston Churchill's Memorandum of June 1922, while reaffirming the Balfour Declaration, nevertheless recognized a "double obligation" to Arab and to Jew. The concept of a simple unitary or federal state was acceptable to neither party and was rejected. During the 1920s the British temporized, but in 1929 Arab and Jewish nationalisms boiled over into riots. A commission of inquiry found that the main cause of the violence was Arab antagonism to a Jewish "national home"; another report concluded that further Jewish immigration was unacceptable. In 1930 a white paper reinforced views unfavorable to Jewish hopes, but it was modified in 1931.

In January 1933 following the establishment of Nazi Germany, Jews in Europe faced a major crisis. Jewish immigration at once increased. Many of the immigrants were educated, giving a new character to a largely agricultural society. Almost immediately a "national home" became a concern for survival.

The influx of Jews, even though it might mean greater prosperity for Arabs, was regarded by Arabs as an obstacle to national independence. The Arabs had a high rate of natural increase, far outweighing any possibility that the Jews might reach equality of numbers. A manifesto of the Arab Executive Committee in March 1933 declared that "the general tendency of the Jews to take possession of the lands of this holy country and their streaming into it by hundreds and thousands through legal and illegal means had terrified the country." The document regarded the Jewish immigrants "as the true enemy whom they must get rid of through every legal means." In 1936, and lasting until 1939, violence erupted.

In these circumstances Earl Peel reported the belief of the Palestine Royal Commission that partition was the only possible solution. A United Nations decision of 29 November 1947 recommended partition on lines similar to the Peel Report.

94. WORLD WAR II: EGYPT AND NORTH AFRICA, 1940–1941

The jackal Mussolini, as Churchill called him, declared war on the Allies on 3 June 1940, following the British retreat at Dunkirk. He took Nice and Savoy; on 4 July he invaded the Sudan from Ethiopia (see map 95); in August he took British Somaliland. Now before his eyes arose the glittering prospect of an Italian empire stretching from Tripolitania to Egypt and Iraq, and south through the Sudan to Uganda and Kenya. The whole of this vast area, including Cyprus and Greece, was within the area of the British Middle East command based in Cairo. Through its center passed the Suez Canal and the Red Sea, the life line of communication with India and the East. No less important was the Persian Gulf, which was to become the life line to Russia.

By 7 February 1941, the British had driven the Italians out of Cyrenaica. While Mussolini's eyes were set on territorial aggrandizement, the Italian people had no stomach for war, nor had they regarded the British with hostility. Two British divisions destroyed ten Italian divisions, and took 130,000 prisoners.

The German high command saw things differently and sent Erwin Rommel to take command of German forces in Africa on 12 February 1941. On 31 March he launched his attack, which covered over fifteen hundred miles of desert. A highly confused battle followed throughout the year, which exhausted both sides. Rommel could not follow up his limited success and retreated. This was fortunate for the British, for British and Australian units had been withdrawn to face the Japanese in the Far East, while other British units were committed in Kenya and the Sudan. As things were, it was a stalemate.

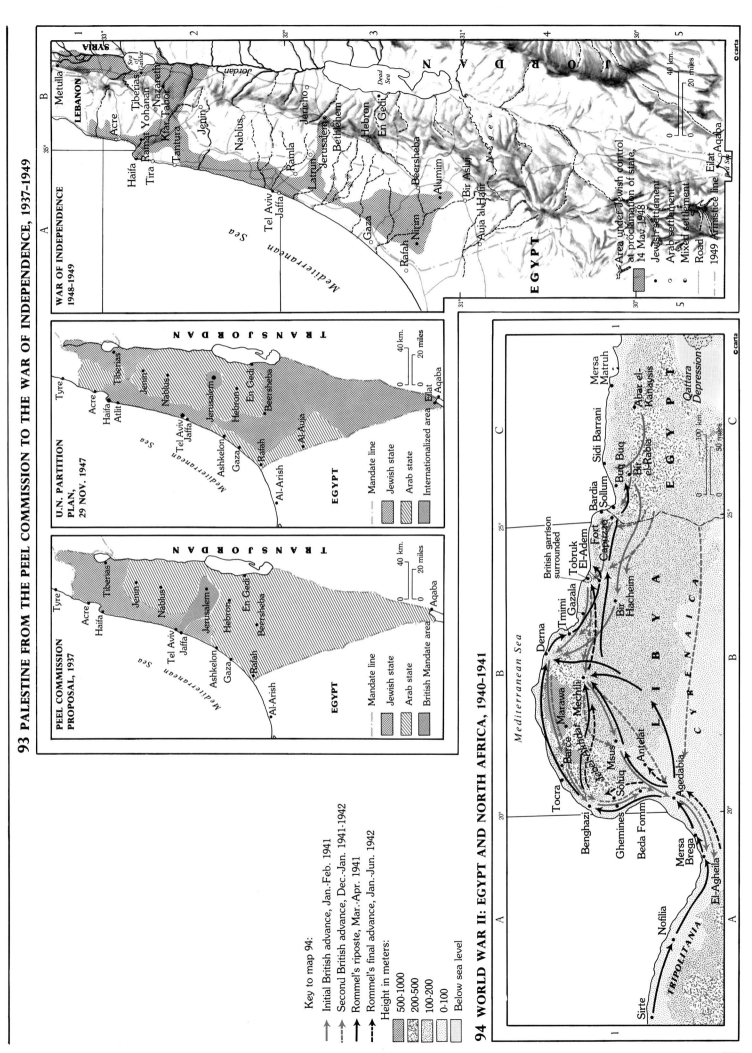

93 PALESTINE FROM THE PEEL COMMISSION TO THE WAR OF INDEPENDENCE, 1937-1949

94 WORLD WAR II: EGYPT AND NORTH AFRICA, 1940-1941

95. WORLD WAR II: SUDAN, ETHIOPIA, AND SOMALIA, 1941

Following Italy's entry into the war in 1940, Italian forces in Ethiopia seized Kassala from the British and overran British and French Somaliland. These territories were of strategic importance to Middle Eastern command in Cairo because from these locations one could control the Red Sea, the passage to the Far East, and the French naval installation at Djibouti.

In 1940 the British already had a working partnership with Ethiopian guerrillas. An offensive was mounted on 19 January 1941, which drove the Italians out of Kassala. This column, under General Platt, was held up at Keren until 1 April, when the Italian forces collapsed. The British were able to enter Asmara on the following day.

Supported by Ethiopian guerrillas, the unit known as the Gideon Force, under Major Orde Wingate, and eight-hundred Sudanese troops entered Ethiopia south of Gallabat. Frequent raids, rather than a frontal attack, gave the Italians the illusion that they were being attacked by a vastly superior force. The

Ethiopian emperor Haile Selassie accompanied the Allies. On 16 May General William Platt encircled the Italian forces at Amba Alagi, and with their surrender, Italian resistance collapsed.

In British Somaliland, with the support of the South African air force, Nigerian and South African brigades took Mogadishu on 25 February. After a brilliant march across the Ogaden desert they took Jijiga on 17 March, Diredawa on 29 March, and they reached Addis Ababa on 6 April. The success of all three columns was assured by the Royal Air Force, based in the Sudan and Aden, which attacked the Italian air force and protected Red Sea convoys, while the South African air force supported the southern column.

At the Ethiopian emperor's personal request British advisers now assisted the restoration of orderly government. The recovery of Ethiopia and Somaliland had effectively taken no more than ten weeks.

96. WORLD WAR II: IRAQ AND IRAN, 1941

Following World War I (see map 91) the League of Nations made Iraq a mandated territory under Great Britain. After local consultations with a council of state in 1920, Faysal I, second son of the sharif of Mecca, was made king as a constitutional monarch. The country was considered stable enough to govern itself in 1930 and was recognized as fully independent.

This proved optimistic. After Faysal I's death in 1933, he was succeeded by the weak king Ghazi I. A series of coups, none of them successful, followed. Anti-British, nationalist feeling and unrest, fermented by Axis powers and hatred of British policy in Palestine, resulted in the emergence of a pro-Nazi party. It was led by Rashid Ali al-Gaylani, who seized power in May 1941. This gave the Axis a toe hold in the Middle East and cut off Iran, now essential to the Allies as a supply route to Russia. Crossing the desert in August 1941, the British-led Arab Legion took

Baghdad with a squadron of armored cars, deposed Rashid Ali, and restored constitutional rule.

In 1921 Reza Khan, commander of a Cossack brigade, overthrew the Qajar dynasty in Iran and made himself shah in 1925. His rule was essentially military, and, from 1932, following the rise of Hitler, he leaned more and more toward Nazi Germany. His army consumed one third of the budget. By 1941 a German fifth column was firmly established in Iran, and in 1941 Britain and Russia presented a joint ultimatum demanding the immediate expulsion of German technicians, cultural officials, and tourists. Reza Shah refused. On 25 August Britain and the U.S.S.R. jointly invaded Iran. On 16 September Reza Shah abdicated. He was succeeded by his son Muhammad Reza, whose compliance insured a line of communications for Allied supplies to beleaguered Russia.

95 WORLD WAR II: SUDAN, ETHIOPIA AND SOMALIA, 1941

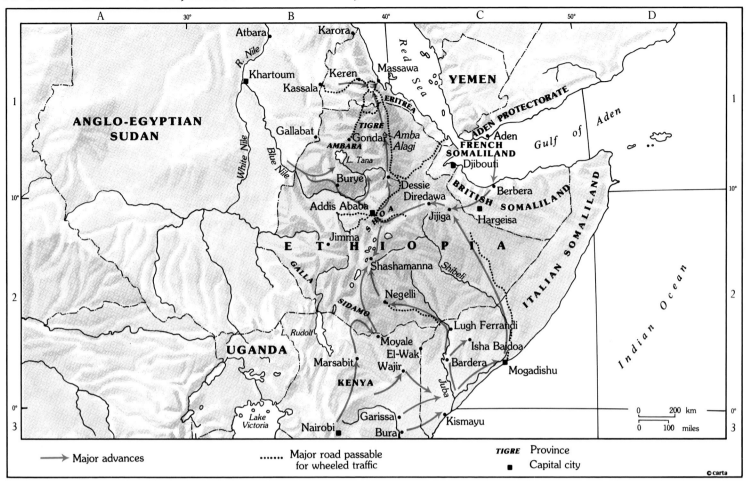

Major advances ——▶

Major road passable for wheeled traffic ·······

TIGRE Province

■ Capital city

© carta

96 WORLD WAR II: IRAQ AND IRAN, 1941

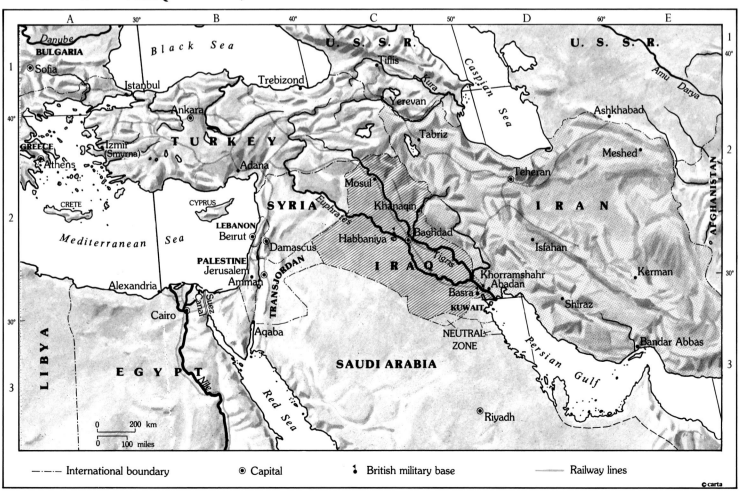

—·—·— International boundary   ◉ Capital   ♪ British military base   —— Railway lines

© carta

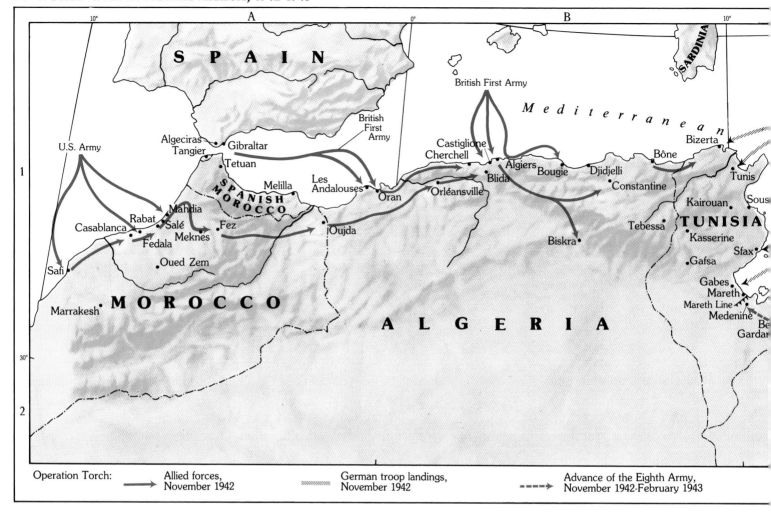

Operation Torch: ⟶ Allied forces, November 1942 ▨▨▨ German troop landings, November 1942 ---▶ Advance of the Eighth Army, November 1942-February 1943

97. WORLD WAR II: NORTH AFRICA, 1942-1943

When Rommel withdrew to recoup the strength of his forces in 1941, the British troops in North Africa were dispirited and there was friction between senior tank and infantry commanders. The pause enabled Rommel to build a superior force. His rear was secured by Algeria, which was controlled by Vichy France, and, behind it, Spanish Morocco, neutral, but obligated to Germany for assistance during the Spanish Civil War.

Rommel's attack began on 21 January 1942. By 26 June he had taken Tobruk. On 6 July he was near the Egyptian village of El-Alamein and within fifty miles of Alexandria. There was panic in Egypt, and the whole Middle East seemed open to the German forces.

Rommel had traveled more than 1,500 miles from his base. He had suffered heavy casualties in tanks and men. Gas supplies were so lacking that he was dependent upon what he had captured from the British. This too he had to waste in support of weak Italian units that the British were able to harass. Rommel was thus forced to retreat. The British commander Claude John Eyre Auchinleck was sacked by Winston Churchill for failing to attack the Germans decisively.

With General Harold R. L. G. Alexander in command of Middle Eastern forces, Auchinleck was now replaced in the field by Bernard Montgomery. A flamboyant and charismatic character, he was able to restore the morale of the troops. In spite of parliamentary criticism that he was slow, he made meticulous preparation for attack, amassing equipment and men. On 23 October a massive artillery barrage opened the Battle of El-Alamein, for which Montgomery is famous. By 2 November Rommel had only thirty-five tanks left and was compelled to retreat, although Hitler had forbidden him. The British troops were equally exhausted and could not

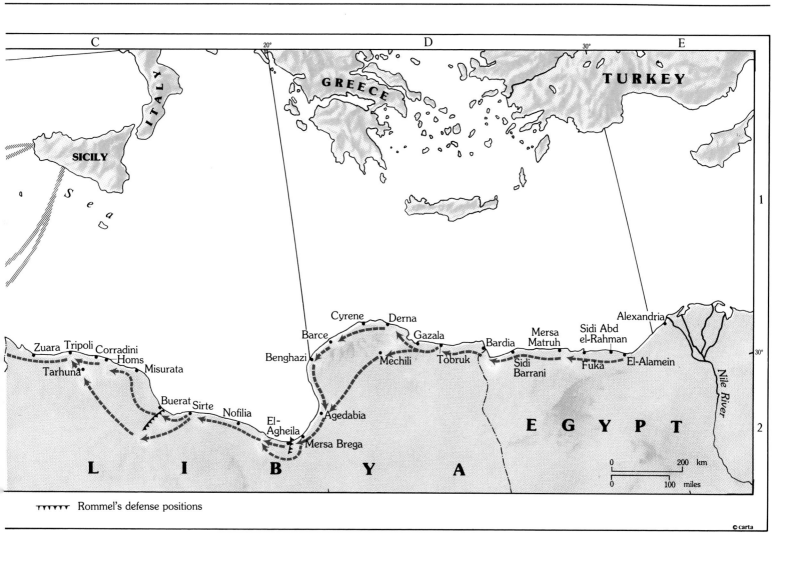

TTTTTT Rommel's defense positions

follow up the retreat.

The first major American military commitment now began. Together with the British First Army, the Americans began landing in Morocco and Algeria on 8 November. Sporadic Vichy French resistance was easily overcome. North Africa from Morocco as far as the Tunisian border was now in Allied hands. The Germans poured in reinforcements and halted the Allied advances by December. Montgomery's Eighth Army now regrouped and on 23 January 1943, it entered Tripoli. Hastily constructed German defenses halted the Eighth Army on a line of hills on the southern Tunisian border, the Mareth Line. After some difficulty the British were able to penetrate the edge. By 14 April the Americans and the British First and Eighth Armies had surrounded the Germans and Italians. After a month of bitter fighting the latter surrendered on 12 May with 250,000 troops. Rommel had already returned to Germany on 12

March and was held responsible for a failure that, in reality, was caused by Hitler, who had refused to allow German or Italian units to withdraw. Hitler's refusal had cost him not only a seasoned army, but men who could have been used on the Russian and Italian fronts. Hitler was now engaged in a struggle for Stalingrad and was about to defend Sicily and Italy, the "soft under-belly of the Axis," as Churchill described it. Rommel committed suicide on 14 October 1944.

In all these Allied battles African troops had played an important but inconspicuous part on the lines of communications. The march of Senegalese troops across the desert from Chad is one of the epics of military history. In the Western Desert of Egypt the West African frontier forces, from Nigeria and Ghana, had played an essential supportive role without which victory would not have been achieved.

98. DECOLONIZATION OF THE MIDDLE EAST, 1946–1967

At the end of World War II Allied troops controlled the area from Morocco to the borders of Iran. The Americans held Morocco, Algeria, and Tunisia; the British held all the rest. Egypt had a nominal independence, which was nullified in practice by the presence of British troops in the Delta and on the Suez Canal; Iraq had been recognized as a kingdom in 1927; Lebanon and Syria had had their mandates terminated in 1943 and were declared independent republics; Saudi Arabia, Yemen, and Turkey had never acknowledged dependence.

In Morocco, Algeria, and Tunisia large French populations, together with Spaniards and Italians, presented problems. In Algeria local French resistance continued until independence was granted in 1962; the others became independent in 1956. In Libya the emir was recognized as King Idris I in 1951, but for a time continued to have British advisers. In order to forestall Egyptian demands, the Sudan became independent in 1956. In spite of tension, the British stayed in the Canal Zone, regarding it as a safeguard of free passage to India. The weakness of this policy was shown when President Nasser nationalized the canal in 1956, and compelled evacuation.

Farther east, the emir of Transjordan was recognized as King Abdullah of Jordan in 1946. The British remained in Palestine until 1948, failing to make arrangements for successor government when they repudiated the mandate. Israel was thus born with an empty treasury and under attack from Lebanon, Syria, Iraq, Jordan, and Egypt. The Persian Gulf states, which had been protectorates, declared independence during the 1960s and 1970s; Aden, after a bloody civil war between opposing would-be successor factions, became an independent republic in 1968. If it was the end of one era, it was the beginning of another, with many problems as yet unresolved.

99. THE FIRST ARAB-ISRAELI WAR, 1948

War between Israel, its Arab neighbors, and other Arab states both far and near — whether as open warfare, armed truce, or a state of war without active hostilities — has continued since 1948. During a period of over forty years Israel has consolidated its position and even expanded its boundaries. In addition, since 1967, it has occupied the West Bank, formerly Jordanian territory, and the Gaza strip which was part of Palestine and held by Egypt from 1948 until 1967. The succession of events, and the consequent boundary changes, are traced in maps 101, 102, and 103. Juridically Jordan has relinquished all claim to the West Bank, but since it has not been annexed by Israel — other than East Jerusalem and the Old City — it has the suspended status of occupied territory under international law. The annexation of parts of Jerusalem has not been accorded international recognition.

On 15 May 1948, at midnight, David Ben-Gurion proclaimed the establishment of the State of Israel. The following morning the armies of Egypt, Jordan, Lebanon, and Syria invaded the former Palestine, but soon lost impetus. They had neither common command nor cohesion, inspite of overwhelming superiority in men, arms, tanks, and aircraft. An Israeli army was assembled from organizations that had carried on underground warfare against the British, but that had acted hitherto without coordination. The Israeli army, with massive American financial support and with arms gathered from many sources was able to establish itself, and, in spite of its weakness, to bring about a military stalemate. Although the very irregular boundaries and the displacement of some one million Palestinian Arabs pleased no one, an armistice was signed in February 1949.

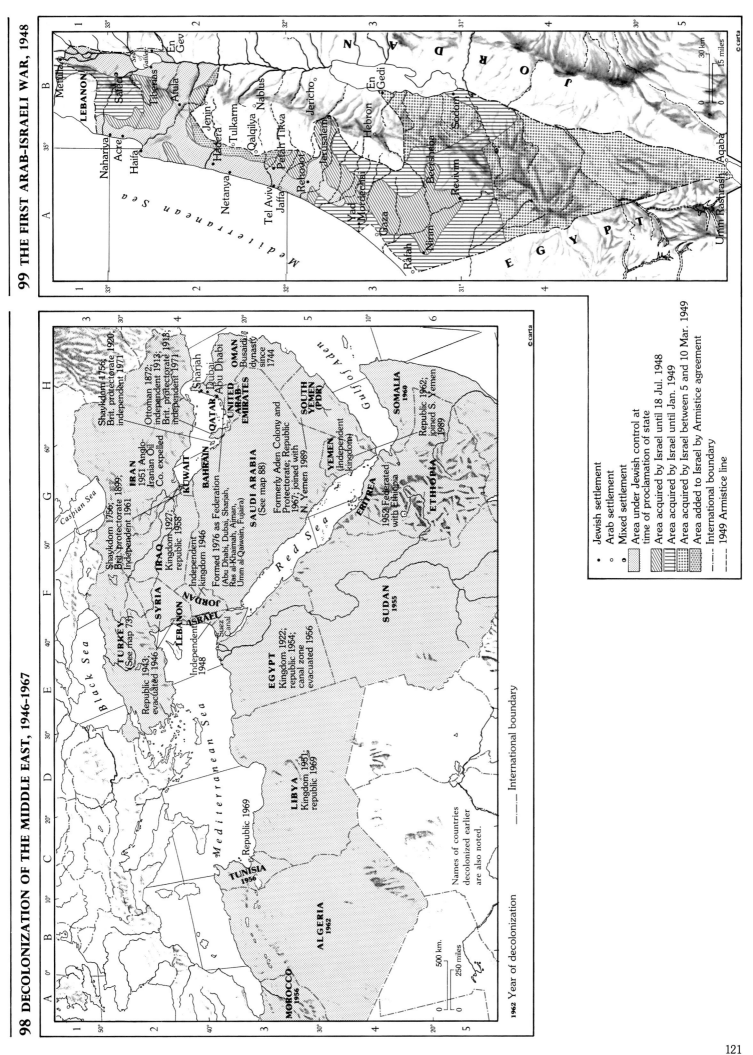

99 THE FIRST ARAB-ISRAELI WAR, 1948

LEBANON

Metulla
Safad
Tiberias
Afula
Nahariya
Acre
Haifa
Jenin
Tulkarm
Qalqilya
Nablus
Hadera
Petah Tikva
Netanya
Rehovot
Tel Aviv
Jaffa
Yad
Mordechai
Jerusalem
Hebron
En Gedi
En Gev
Jericho
Gaza
Nirim
Beersheba
Revivim
Sodom
Rafah
Umm Rashrash
Aqaba

Mediterranean Sea

E G Y P T

J O R D A N

30 km
15 miles

© carta

98 DECOLONIZATION OF THE MIDDLE EAST, 1946-1967

Black Sea

Caspian Sea

TURKEY
(See map 73)

Shaykdom 1756; Brit. protectorate 1899; independent 1961

IRAN
1951 Anglo-Iranian Oil Co. expelled

Shaykdom 1756; Brit. protectorate 1920; independent 1971

Sharjah
Dubai
Abu Dhabi

OMAN
Busaidi dynasty since 1744

Ottoman 1872; independent 1913; Brit. protectorate 1918; independent 1971

QATAR

UNITED ARAB EMIRATES
Formed 1976 as Federation (Abu Dhabi, Dubai, Sharjah, Ras al-Khaimah, Ajman, Umm al-Qaiwain, Fujaira)

BAHRAIN
Independent kingdom 1946

SYRIA
Republic 1943; evacuated 1946

IRAQ
Kingdom 1927; republic 1958

KUWAIT

SAUDI ARABIA
(See map 88)

SOUTH YEMEN (PDR)
Formerly Aden Colony and Protectorate; Republic 1967; joined with N. Yemen 1989

YEMEN
(Independent kingdom)

SOMALIA
1960
Republic 1962; joined S. Yemen 1989

Gulf of Aden

Red Sea

LEBANON
JORDAN
ISRAEL
Independent 1948

Suez canal

EGYPT
Kingdom 1922; republic 1954; canal zone evacuated 1956

SUDAN
1955

ERITREA
1953 Federated with Ethiopia

ETHIOPIA

LIBYA
Kingdom 1951; republic 1969

Republic 1969

Mediterranean Sea

TUNISIA
1956

ALGERIA
1962

MOROCCO
1956

500 km.
250 miles

Names of countries decolonized earlier are also noted.

1962 Year of decolonization

—·—·— International boundary

© carta

Legend

- • Jewish settlement
- ○ Arab settlement
- ◉ Mixed settlement

Area under Jewish control at time of proclamation of state

Area acquired by Israel until 18 Jul. 1948

Area acquired by Israel until Jan. 1949

Area acquired by Israel between 5 and 10 Mar. 1949

Area added to Israel by Armistice agreement

—·—·— International boundary

— — — 1949 Armistice line

100. IMMIGRATION INTO ISRAEL, FROM 15 MAY 1948

There have been four major *aliyot* (immigrations) to Israel. Under Abraham and then under Moses, the whole people moved. When the exiles returned from Babylon in 538 B.C. only part of the community moved; the remainder stayed in Iraq until 1948. The final return had already gathered momentum when the modern Zionist movement was inaugurated and increased only slowly between the two world wars.

In 1947 few people in Britain, the seat of the mandatory power, had much understanding of what was to unfold. A vague goodwill toward Arabs and Jews alike held that, once the mandatory power had departed, they would settle down together in some manner.

The British departure on 14 May 1948 unloosed Pandora's box. Both Jordan and Egypt seized Palestinian territory. A rump was left to Israel, which immediately had to defend itself against its neighbors. It was not only a military war of survival. Under Britain a rigorous quota system was maintained. "Illegal" immigrants were denied entry; either they were returned whence they came or interned in Cyprus.

What took place is unparalleled in human history. Between 15 May 1948 and the end of the year 101,819 immigrants were admitted; 239,576 entered in the following year. In each of the two following years more than 170,000 people were admitted. No other state has more than doubled its population within four years or absorbed, housed, and provided for heterogeneous immigrants from forty-four different countries, and divided by as many languages, from Europe, Asia, and northern Africa. It was an extraordinary feat of national construction, accomplished without serious bloodshed, but resulting, in some 1.5 million Arab refugees for whom, after more than forty years, no resolution is yet in sight.

101. THE SUEZ WAR, 1956

The Suez War — between Britain, France, and Israel on the one hand, and Egypt on the other — was short in duration and failed to lead to any lasting solution of the problems addressed. On 18 June 1956, Britain had withdrawn from the Suez Canal Zone, leaving Egypt free after a period of eighty-four years of foreign occupation. President Gamal Abdel Nasser had been elected on 3 June, and on a tide of external military support from the U.S.S.R. Because of this support, on 19-20 July, Britain and the United States informed Egypt that they would not finance the Aswan High Dam. Nasser promptly countered by nationalizing the Suez Canal and seizing all foreign assets owned by the Canal Company. Nasser's actions were clearly contrary to existing agreements with Britain and France, the principal participants in the company. Acting in concert with Israel, war began on 29 October with the Israeli occupation of Sinai, and, on 31 October, with the Anglo-French bombardment of Egyptian military installations. On 5 November British troops landed in Egypt and could easily have overcome the Egyptian forces. Acting on an initiative by the United States, the United Nations compelled an Anglo-French cease-fire on 7 November and sent a UN emergency force on 15 November. The compelling factor had been the American threat to withdraw support for the pound sterling.

Several unsatisfactory results followed. Stationing UN peace-keeping forces between Israel and Egypt solved nothing. The British and French lost all control of the canal, and both lost power and prestige vis-à-vis the Arab nations. American intervention enabled President Nasser, in spite of his military disaster, to claim a moral victory, which was confirmed by his overwhelming reelection. The U.S.S.R. thereby gained, for the time being, a preponderance in the Middle East to the detriment of all the other concerned powers.

100 IMMIGRATION INTO ISRAEL, FROM 15 MAY 1948

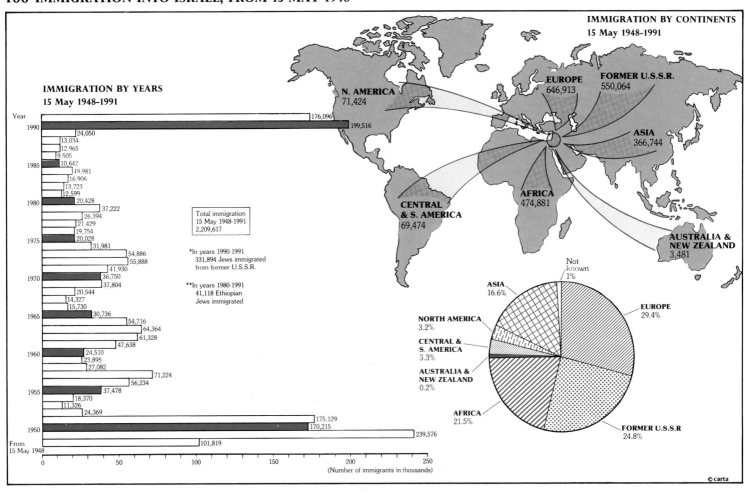

IMMIGRATION BY CONTINENTS
15 May 1948-1991

N. AMERICA
71,424

EUROPE
646,913

FORMER U.S.S.R.
550,064

ASIA
366,744

CENTRAL & S. AMERICA
69,474

AFRICA
474,881

AUSTRALIA & NEW ZEALAND
3,481

IMMIGRATION BY YEARS
15 May 1948-1991

Year

1990 — 176,096 / 199,516
24,050
13,034
12,965
9,505
1985 — 10,642
49,981
16,906
13,723
12,599
1980 — 20,428
37,222
26,394
21,429
19,754
1975 — 20,028
31,981
54,886
55,888
41,930
1970 — 36,750
37,804
20,544
14,327
15,730
1965 — 30,736
54,716
64,364
61,328
47,638
1960 — 24,510
23,895
27,082
71,224
56,234
1955 — 37,478
18,370
11,326
24,369
1950 — 175,129 / 170,215 / 239,576
From 15 May 1948 — 101,819

0   50   100   150   200   250
(Number of immigrants in thousands)

Total immigration
15 May 1948-1991
2,209,617

*In years 1990-1991
331,894 Jews immigrated
from former U.S.S.R.

**In years 1980-1991
41,118 Ethiopian
Jews immigrated

Not known 1%

ASIA 16.6%

NORTH AMERICA 3.2%

CENTRAL & S. AMERICA 3.3%

AUSTRALIA & NEW ZEALAND 0.2%

AFRICA 21.5%

EUROPE 29.4%

FORMER U.S.S.R. 24.8%

© carta

101 THE SUEZ WAR, 1956

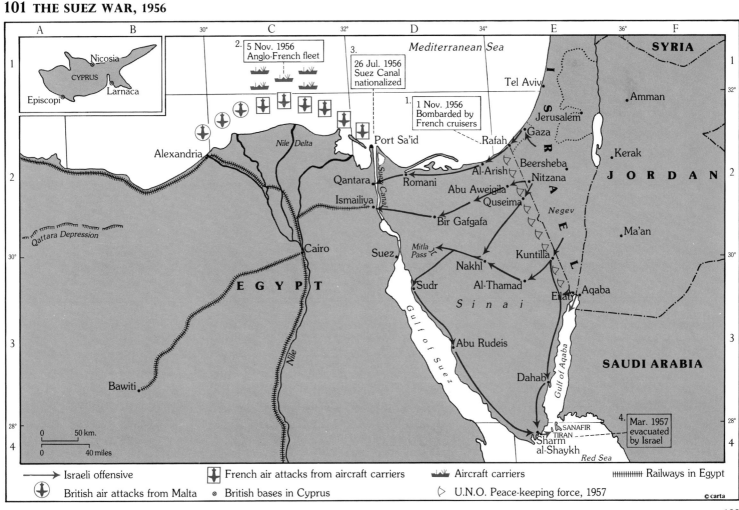

2. 5 Nov. 1956 Anglo-French fleet

3. 26 Jul. 1956 Suez Canal nationalized

1. 1 Nov. 1956 Bombarded by French cruisers

4. Mar. 1957 evacuated by Israel

CYPRUS — Nicosia, Larnaca, Episcopi

Mediterranean Sea

SYRIA

Tel Aviv, Amman, Jerusalem, Gaza, Rafah, Al-Arish, Beersheba, Nitzana, Kerak, Abu Aweigila, Quseima, Bir Gafgafa, Ma'an, Kuntilla, Nakhl, Al-Thamad, Elat, Aqaba

Port Sa'id, Qantara, Romani, Ismailiya, Suez, Mitla Pass, Sudr

Alexandria, Nile Delta, Qattara Depression, Cairo, Bawiti

EGYPT

Suez Canal, Gulf of Suez, Nile, Sinai, Negev

ISRAEL, JORDAN, SAUDI ARABIA

Abu Rudeis, Dahab, Sharm al-Shaykh, SANAFIR, TIRAN, Gulf of Aqaba, Red Sea

→ Israeli offensive   ⬇ French air attacks from aircraft carriers   Aircraft carriers   ╫╫╫╫ Railways in Egypt
⬇ British air attacks from Malta   • British bases in Cyprus   ▷ U.N.O. Peace-keeping force, 1957

© carta

123

102. THE SECOND ARAB-ISRAELI WAR, 1967

This war is known by such names as the "Lightning War" and the "Six-Day War" because of its short duration, from 5 to 10 June 1967. It was a moment of high tension in the Middle East, for the persistent propaganda of President Nasser had precipitated violent riots against the British in Aden, and service families had been withdrawn. Nasser took the opportunity to demand the withdrawal of the UN peace-keeping force in Sinai. When the secretary-general of the UN temporized, Nasser replied by closing the Strait of Tiran and the Gulf of Aqaba to Israel. The effect was to deny oil supplies to Israel.

The Israeli government regarded this as an act of war. On 5 June air attacks were mounted against Egypt, Jordan, and Syria, and, within six days, the whole of the Sinai peninsula, with its oil deposits, had been occupied. The Jordanian West Bank was seized and occupied, and the Golan Heights, which overlook the upper reaches of the Jordan River, were occupied. At the same time the Old City of Jerusalem was taken and declared to be annexed to the capital of Israel. These acts, which have not received international recognition, and the creation of some 1.5 million Palestinian refugees, constitute issues of bitter contention between Israel and its Arab neighbors.

The Six-Day War was not only a demonstration of Israeli military strength and capability. It destabilized the Nasser regime in Egypt, and by so doing it ultimately prepared the ground for agreement between Egypt and Israel. It also provoked the emergence of the Palestine Liberation Organization, which Israel would have to take into account.

103. THE THIRD ARAB-ISRAELI WAR, 1973

The Six-Day War was felt as a deep humiliation not only by the three nations that had been defeated — Egypt, Jordan, and Syria — but by the entire Islamic world. Arabs, preponderant in population, wealth, and arms, had been defeated by, as they saw it, a puny and illegitimate nation. Bitterness, which went back to the times of the British mandate, now overflowed.

On 22 November 1967, the United Nations passed Resolution 242, recognizing the Arab territories occupied by Israel to be truly Arab possessions, but demanding that the Arab powers recognize the State of Israel. This they would not do.

Nasser died in 1970. His successor, Anwar al-Sadat, sought to restore Egyptian self-confidence, particularly that of his army. In 1972 he expelled eighteen thousand Russian military advisers and broke off diplomatic relations with the U.S.S.R.

On 6 October 1973, on the Day of Atonement (Yom Kippur), when every devout Jew was fasting in repentance, Egypt and Syria attacked Israel in Sinai and on the Golan Heights. Their combined forces had a tremendous superiority in tanks — 3,000 against 1,700. The effect of the surprise attack and this superiority gave the Egyptians a series of victories. After the expulsion of the Russians from Egypt, the power vacuum had been filled by the United States — a position that was contrary to U.S. policies and interests. Secret negotiations brought the hostilities to a close on 22 October and led ultimately to talks between Egypt and Israel, which eventuated in the Camp David Agreement of 1979.

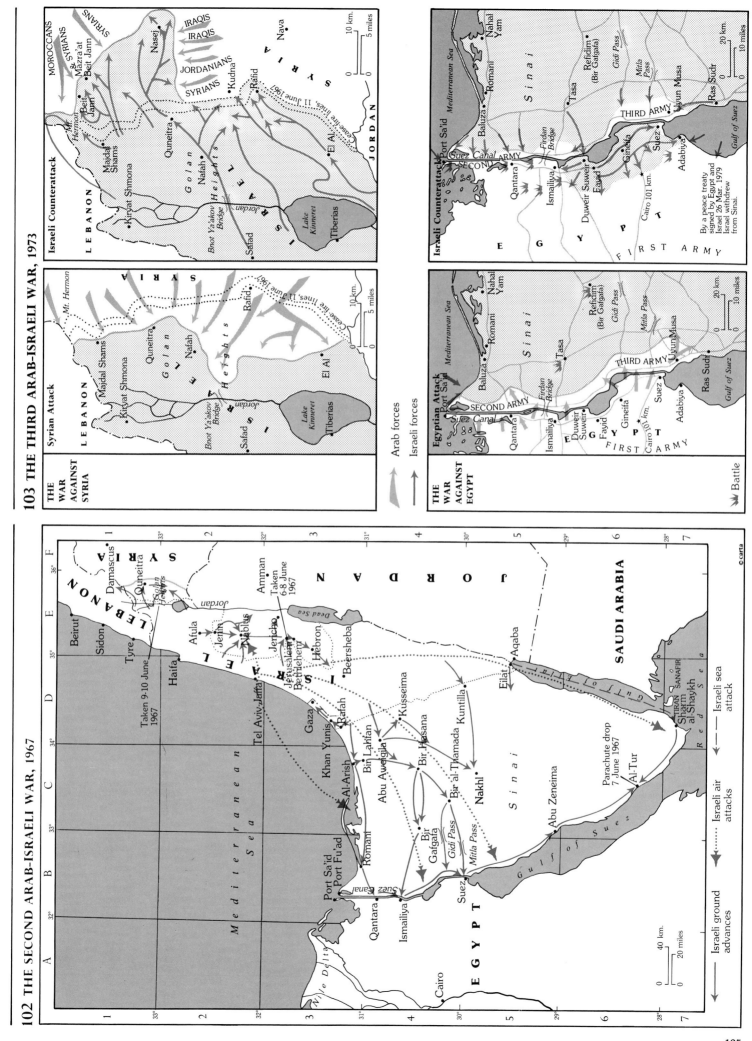

103 THE THIRD ARAB-ISRAELI WAR, 1973

THE WAR AGAINST SYRIA

Israeli Counterattack

Syrian Attack

THE WAR AGAINST EGYPT

Israeli Counterattack

Egyptian Attack

By a peace treaty signed by Egypt and Israel 26 Mar. 1979 Israel withdrew from Sinai.

Arab forces
Israeli forces

Battle

102 THE SECOND ARAB-ISRAELI WAR, 1967

Israeli ground advances
Israeli air attacks
Israeli sea attack

© Carta

104. THE UNITED ARAB EMIRATES AND THE GULF STATES

The states of the Persian Gulf, include Oman, Kuwait, Bahrain, and Qatar, together with the United Arab Emirates — a federation of states that was formed by treaty in 1971, consisting of Abu Dhabi, Dubai, Sharjah, Ajman, Umm al-Qaiwan, and Fujairah, to which Ras al-Khaimah was added in 1972. Their importance, which is disproportionate to their population or size, stems from both their ownership of a great proportion of the world's oil reserves and their strategic position.

Oman had a separate history from quite early times, but the remaining states were formed during the eighteenth century in response to the growth in East-West trade and the weakening power of the Ottoman Empire. In the nineteenth century they were taken under British protection in a series of treaties, partly because of their need for assistance against Wahhabi expansion in what is now Saudi Arabia (see map 88). All these states are located on the western side of the Gulf; the strategical crux is Hormuz Island on the Iranian side, from which the

Portuguese controlled the Gulf from 1518 until Dutch, English, and French East Indies Companies set up nearby in the seventeenth century. In 1650 the Omanis freed the seaport of Masqat, their best port, from Portuguese control, and by 1698 they had established a seaborne empire down the eastern African coast from Mogadishu to the border of Mozambique.

The shaykhdoms and emirates of the inner gulf had no part in these events. Some derived riches from pearl fisheries; others derived a meager living from fishing, and, in some places, agriculture. By 1800 wood was being imported from India to service a boatbuilding industry. It was but a short step from building vessels for commercial purposes to using them for piracy, the seaborne counterpart of the Bedouin *ghazzu* (raids in search of booty). It was because of this that on 8 January 1800 Britain compelled the acceptance of a general treaty of peace.

105. THE LEBANON, ISRAEL, AND SYRIA

From 1516 until 1917 Lebanon formed part of the Ottoman Empire. After the Treaty of Versailles in 1919, it became a League of Nations mandate, entrusted to France. In 1926 it became a republic, but in 1941 it was occupied by Free French forces. It regained a nominal independence in 1943 and actual independence in 1946.

Made up of the rich Bekaa valley lying between two mountain ranges — the Lebanon and the Anti-Lebanon — and a fertile coastal belt, this country is a museum of Christian and Muslim sects. Among the latter, apart from Sunni Orthodox, there are Ismaili, the survivors of Assassins; the Alawi (Nusayri); and the Druze, warlike mountaineers who practice graduated secret rites. The greatest number of Christians is found in the region north of Beirut, Sunnis occupy the south, with Shi'ites of different sects in the Bekaa valley and the mountains on the east.

Hostility among the different groups led to protracted civil war and intervention by Syria in 1976. The Palestine Liberation Organization took advantage of the situation to establish a base from which to attack Israel. This led to full-scale Israeli intervention in 1978 and the occupation of the southern part of the country as a cordon sanitaire. Israel again intervened in 1982 and expelled the Palestine Liberation Organization. A UN peace-keeping force has been virtually powerless. Syria again intervened in 1987, with an army of 37,000 men and assisted by Iranian troops.

In the earlier stages of the conflict Syria was backed by the U.S.S.R., which opposed American support for Israel. The withdrawal of the U.S.S.R. from such activities gives rise to some hope that some solution to the many problems will be found within the context of a general Middle Eastern settlement.

104 THE UNITED ARAB EMIRATES AND THE GULF STATES

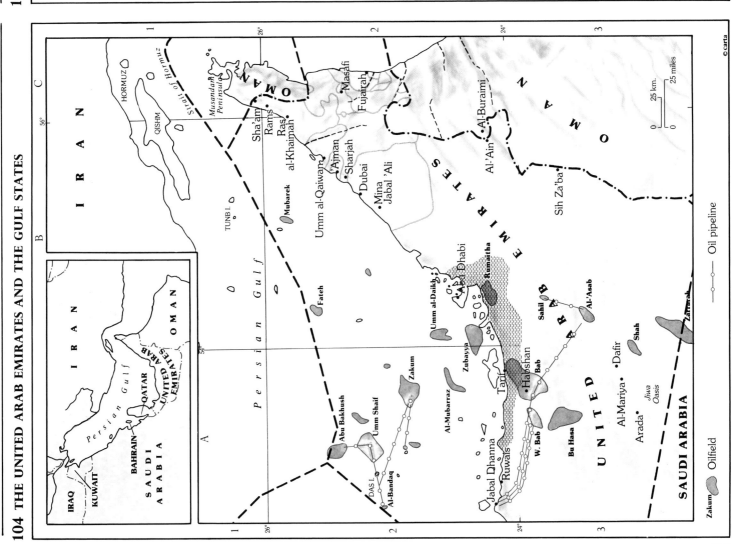

Zakum ▒ Oilfield

○—○—○ Oil pipeline

Inset map labels:
IRAQ
KUWAIT
IRAN
BAHRAIN
QATAR
UNITED ARAB EMIRATES
SAUDI ARABIA
OMAN
Persian Gulf

Main map labels:
IRAN
QISHM
HORMUZ
Strait of Hormuz
Musandam Peninsula
OMAN
Persian Gulf
TUNB I.
Mubarek
Sha'am
Rams
Ras al-Khaimah
Umm al-Qaiwain
Ajman
Sharjah
Dubai
Mina Jabal 'Ali
Masafi
Fujairah
Al-Buraimi
Al'Ain
Sih Za'ba
OMAN
Fateh
EMIRATES
Umm al-Daikh
Abu Dhabi
Rumaitha
Sahil
Al-Asab
Zubayya
Habshan
Bab
Shah
UNITED
Tarif
Al-Mariya
Dafir
Arada
Jiwa Oasis
Al-Mubarraz
W. Bab
Bu Hasa
Zakum
Umm Shaif
Abu Bakhush
DAS I.
Al-Bandaq
Jabal Dhanna
Ruwais
Zarrara
SAUDI ARABIA
0   25 km.
0   25 miles

© carta

105 THE LEBANON, ISRAEL, AND SYRIA

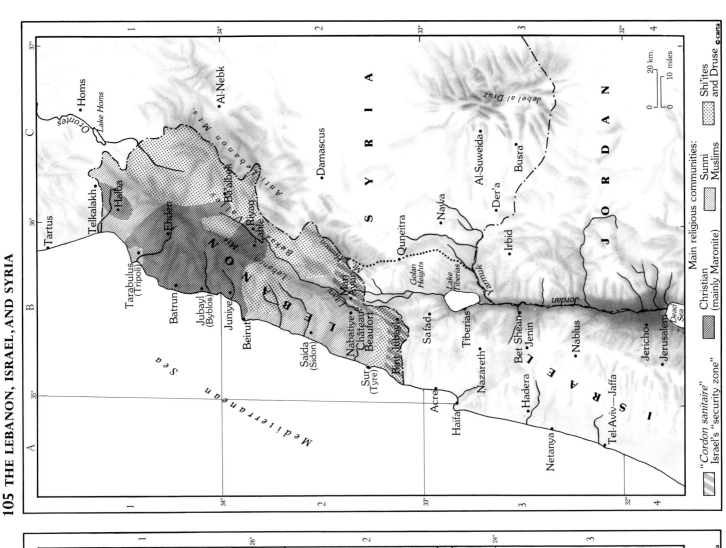

Main map labels:
Homs
Lake Homs
Orontes
Al-Nebk
Tartus
Telkalakh
Safita
Hama
Baalbek
Riyaq
Lake
Anti-Lebanon Mts.
Lebanon Mts.
Tarabulus (Tripoli)
Batrun
Jubayl (Byblos)
Juniye
Beirut
Saida (Sidon)
Sur (Tyre)
Nabatiye
Chateau Beaufort
Bint Jbail
LEBANON
Bekaa
Damascus
SYRIA
Quneitra
Golan Heights
Nawa
Al-Suweida
Der'a
Busra
Irbid
JORDAN
Jebel al-Druz
Yarmuk
Lake Tiberias
Safad
Tiberias
Nazareth
Acre
Haifa
Hadera
Netanya
Tel-Aviv—Jaffa
Bet Shean
Jenin
Nablus
Jericho
Jerusalem
Jordan
Dead Sea
ISRAEL
Mediterranean Sea

Main religious communities:

Christian (mainly Maronite)

Sunni Muslims

Shi'ites and Druse

"Cordon sanitaire" Israel's "security zone"

0   20 km.
0   10 miles

© carta

127

106. THE IRAQ-IRAN WAR, 1980–1988

At the end of World War I, with the dissolution of the Ottoman Empire and the creation of the new state of Iraq in 1921, certain boundary questions with neighboring Persia (Iran) were left unresolved. These questions involved the confluence of the Tigris and Euphrates rivers below Basra, which is known as Shatt-al-Arab, annd the three Tunb Islands in the Strait of Hormuz. The former thus controls access to Iraq's only port, Basra. Through the latter, 35 percent of the world's oil trade passes, not only from Iran and Iraq, but also from the Gulf States (see map 104).

In 1979 the return of the Shi'ite leader Ayatollah Khomeini to Iran led to anxiety in Baghdad, for the southern two-thirds of Iraq were controlled by Shit'ites, whereas the north and the government were Sunni Muslims. In 1980 the Iraqi president, Saddam Hussein, abrogated the 1973 agreement with Iran, which had granted to Iran some 518 square kilometers (200 square miles) north of Shatt-al-Arab, and demanded the return of the Tunb Islands. Hussein's actions led to border skirmishes on the part of Iraq, and finally to wholesale war, in which the Iraqis had some initial success. Iraq had superior air power (600 to 100 aircraft) and ground power (1,000 to 3,500 tanks), although a much smaller population (16 million as compared to Iran's 45 million). A war of attrition followed, with the bombing of oil installations and cities and with an estimated 1.5 million casualties. In the northeast of Iraq, where the majority of the population are Kurds by race and Sunnis by faith, rebellions erupted among the Kurds that were put down by the Iraqi government with napalm and poison gases in a manner so cruel as to be unsurpassed since Chingiz Khan.

In order to secure the free passage of oil supplies to the West an international naval force of seventy-five vessels controlled the waters on both sides of the Strait of Hormuz — United States, U.S.S.R., and France on the west side, and Great Britain, Italy, Belgium, and the Netherlands on the east , with seventy-five vessels in all. A peace was patched up in 1988.

107. THE RUSSO-AFGHAN WAR, 1979–1988

In the nineteenth and twentieth centuries Afghanistan has been a focus of conflicting British and Russian political interests. The Treaty of Gandamak gave Britain control of the Khyber Pass, a principal commercial route between India and Soviet Central Asia, and of Afghan foreign policy. This treaty was effective until 1948. In 1953 General Mohammed Daoud Khan seized power and a parliamentary democracy was instituted. Economic and military assistance was obtained from the U.S.S.R. A military coup overthrew the monarchy in 1973, and installed Daoud as president. In 1977 he made Afghanistan a one-party state. Shortly thereafter he was assassinated, and a democratic republic with a Communist constitution was proclaimed.

The Afghans do not form a single people. They are divided ethnically among Pashtuns, Baluchis, Tajiks, Nuristanis, Hazaras, Turkmen, Uzbeks, and Kirghiz; they are divided by religion between Sunni and Shi'ite Muslims. Eleven separate resistance movements erupted, with opposing religious characteristics, from Islamic fundamentalism, traditionalism, and Wahhabism to moderates, royalists, and, among the Hazaras, pro-Iranian unionists. It was in the face of this chaos that on 27 December 1979 the Soviet Army entered Afghanistan at the request of a government that was no longer able to maintain order. As in the nineteenth century, when the British Indian forces had been baffled by the skill and resources of Afghan guerillas, so now Soviet forces with tanks, aircraft, and vastly superior equipment were able to cause devastation without succeeding in conquest. The devastation was so vast that three million persons fled to Iran and Pakistan. The last Soviet soldier did not leave the country until 1987.

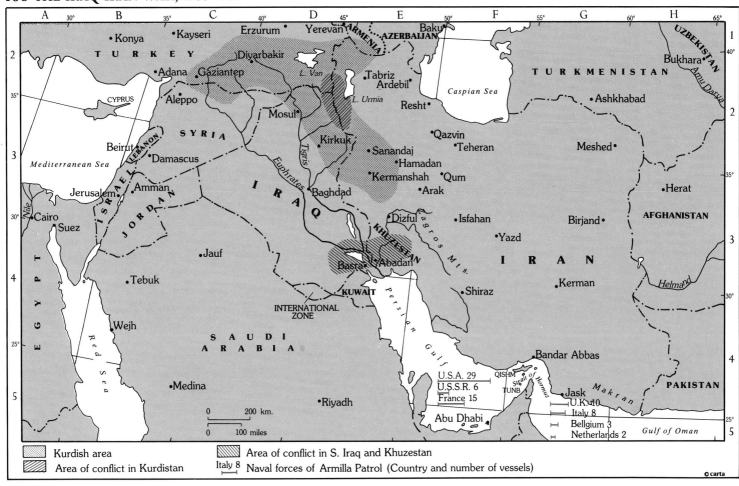

Kurdish area
Area of conflict in Kurdistan
Italy 8

Area of conflict in S. Iraq and Khuzestan
Naval forces of Armilla Patrol (Country and number of vessels)

U.S.A. 29
U.S.S.R. 6
France 15
U.K. 10
Italy 8
Bellgium 3
Netherlands 2

© carta

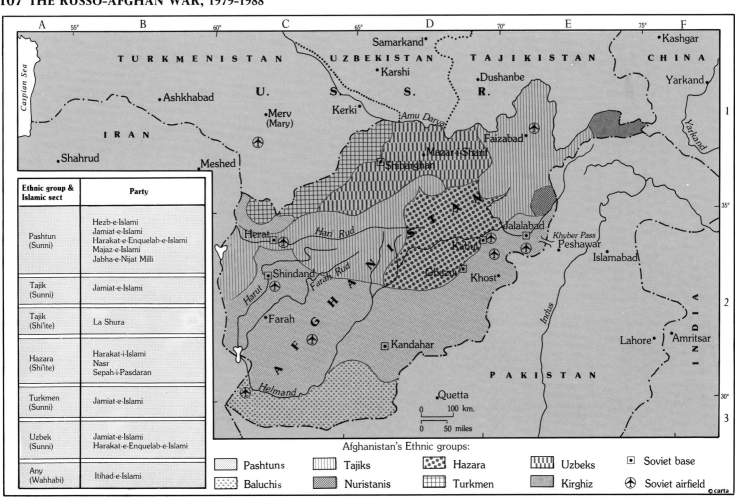

Ethnic group & Islamic sect	Party
Pashtun (Sunni)	Hezb-e-Islami Jamiat-e-Islami Harakat-e-Enquelab-e-Islami Majaz-e-Islami Jabha-e-Nijat Milli
Tajik (Sunni)	Jamiat-e-Islami
Tajik (Shi'ite)	La Shura
Hazara (Shi'ite)	Harakat-i-Islami Nasr Sepah-i-Pasdaran
Turkmen (Sunni)	Jamiat-e-Islami
Uzbek (Sunni)	Jamiat-e-Islami Harakat-e-Enquelab-e-Islami
Any (Wahhabi)	Itihad-e-Islami

Afghanistan's Ethnic groups:

Pashtuns Tajiks Hazara Uzbeks ⊡ Soviet base
Baluchis Nuristanis Turkmen Kirghiz ✈ Soviet airfield

© carta

108. THE UNION OF NORTH AND SOUTH YEMEN, 1990

Yemen, known to the Romans as Arabia Felix, ("Happy Arabia"), is a prosperous agricultural area in the mountains of southwest Arabia. From around 950 to 45 B.C. it was known as the kingdom of Saba, the realm of the biblical queen of Sheba. In the arid lower zone grew the best of the frankincense and myrrh used in the temples of the ancient world. A series of ports, of which Aden was the chief, served as entrepôts for trade between India, Africa, and the Far East.

Converted to Islam in the seventh century, and nominally subject to the caliphate, local dynasties of sultans sprang up in both the highland and lowland areas. Under the Ottoman Empire a tenuous allegiance was honored as much in the breach as in the observance. Between 1839 and 1962 Britain, in a series of advisory treaties, converted the lower area into a series of protected states. Until the 1960s life in both areas continued much as it had been in

the Middle Ages, except in the port of Aden.

Backed by Egyptian troops, a revolution took place in northern Yemen in 1962. Under British pressure, a federation (Arabic, *al-Ittihad*) of all the sultanates was formed in the southern area. From 1962 to 1967 a civil war, largely confined to Aden, contested which party should succeed to power after British departure, promised for 1967. A Marxist party gained the upper hand, making Aden a Russian naval base in 1967.

Of the two areas the northern was the more stable. A catalyst was the discovery of oil and gas in the Marib/Wadi al-Jawf area in the north and in much greater quantities near Shabwa in the south. Export began in 1987, taking advantage of a refinery in Little Aden built in British times. The south is greatly dependent on the agriculture of the north, and the unification on 22 May 1990 was to the advantage and prosperity of both areas.

109. MINORITIES IN THE MIDDLE EAST, 1993

The Middle East is a kaleidoscope of races and religions, in the center of which Arabs predominate. Ottoman Turkish law gave each *millet* (religious community) the right to its own domestic law. Within this framework rigidly separate communities evolved, their boundaries seldom crossed in marriage. Thus, in spite of Turkish overlordship and Arab predominance, Armenians, Assyrians, Circassians, Georgians, Greeks, Jews, Kurds, Mandaeans (Sabeans), Syrians, Turkmen, and others formed obvious divisions. Among Christians Pre-Chalcedonians (Armenians, Assyrians, Copts, Ethiopians and Syrians), and Greek Orthodox all had Catholic counterparts, or Uniate bodies, under the wing of the Latins and united in their obedience to the Pope in Rome. In the nineteenth century a number of Protestant denominations added their missionaries, under the protection of their respective consuls, but they did not form recognized *millets*.

Among Jews exclusive national synagogues ca-

tered to differing national origins, with subdivisions that ranged from ultraorthodox to liberal. Ladino was spoken by Sephardim, Yiddish by Ashkenazim, each a lingua franca apart from the Hebrew of liturgy. Further divisions formed a kaleidoscope of their own, the extreme being proclaimed even today by a wall graffito in ultraorthodox Mea Shearim: "Judaism and Zionism are diametrically opposed."

While the great majority of Muslims are Sunni (orthodox), Shi'ites (sectarians) are divided into many sects. Ithna'asharis predominate over Alawis (Nusayris), Ibadhis, Ismailis, and Zaydites, with further fractions such as the Druzes. Mandaeans and Yezidis (Manichaeans) are esoteric syncretistic sects. In Iran Zoroastrians are a relic of what was once the national religion.

The problem of the Kurdish minority in Iran, Iraq, Russia, Syria, and Turkey is considered in map 111. No consistent statistics for this group are available.

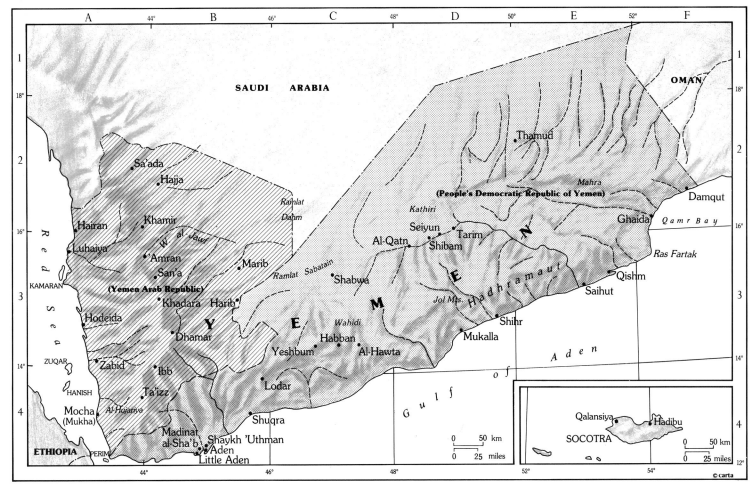

SAUDI ARABIA

OMAN

Thamud

Mahra

(People's Democratic Republic of Yemen)

Kathiri

Damqut

Ghaida

Qamr Bay

Sa'ada

Hajja

Ramlat Dahm

Seiyun

Tarim

N

Ras Fartak

Khamir

Al-Qatn

Shibam

Hairan

W. al Jawf

Marib

Ramlat Sabatain

Shabwa

E

Qishm

Luhaiya

Amran

San'a

Jol Mts.

Hadhramaut

Saihut

KAMARAN

(Yemen Arab Republic)

Khadara Harib

Y

E

M

Shihr

Hodeida

Dhamar

Wahidi

Habban

Al-Hawta

Mukalla

Aden

ZUQAR

Zabid

Yeshbum

Gulf

of

Ibb

Ta'izz

Lodar

HANISH

Al-Hujariya

Mocha (Mukha)

Shuqra

ETHIOPIA

PERIM

Madinat al-Sha'b

Shaykh 'Uthman

Aden

Little Aden

0   50 km
0   25 miles

SOCOTRA
Qalansiya   Hadibu
0   50 km
0   25 miles

© carta

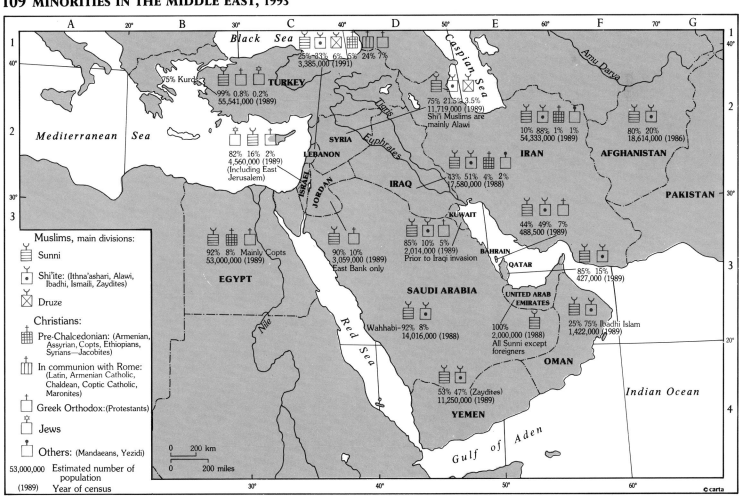

Black Sea

Caspian Sea

Amu Darya

75% Kurds

25% 33% 6% 5% 24% 7%
3,385,000 (1991)

TURKEY

99% 0.8% 0.2%
55,541,000 (1989)

75% 21.5% 3.5%
11,719,000 (1989)
Shi'i Muslims are mainly Alawi

10% 88% 1% 1%
54,333,000 (1989)

IRAN

80% 20%
18,614,000 (1986)

AFGHANISTAN

Mediterranean Sea

82% 16% 2%
4,560,000 (1989)
(Including East Jerusalem)

SYRIA

Tigris

Euphrates

LEBANON

ISRAEL

JORDAN

IRAQ

43% 51% 4% 2%
17,580,000 (1988)

PAKISTAN

92% 8% Mainly Copts
53,000,000 (1989)

EGYPT

90% 10%
3,059,000 (1989)
East Bank only

KUWAIT

85% 10% 5%
2,014,000 (1989)
Prior to Iraqi invasion

44% 49% 7%
488,500 (1989)

BAHRAIN

QATAR

85% 15%
427,000 (1989)

Nile

SAUDI ARABIA

UNITED ARAB EMIRATES

100%
2,000,000 (1988)
All Sunni except foreigners

25% 75% Ibadhi Islam
1,422,000 (1989)

Red Sea

Wahhabi-92% 8%
14,016,000 (1988)

OMAN

Indian Ocean

53% 47% (Zaydites)
11,250,000 (1989)

YEMEN

Gulf of Aden

Muslims, main divisions:
- Sunni
- Shi'ite: (Ithna'ashari, Alawi, Ibadhi, Ismaili, Zaydites)
- Druze

Christians:
- Pre-Chalcedonian: (Armenian, Assyrian, Copts, Ethiopians, Syrians—Jacobites)
- In communion with Rome: (Latin, Armenian Catholic, Chaldean, Coptic Catholic, Maronites)
- Greek Orthodox: (Protestants)
- Jews
- Others: (Mandaeans, Yezidi)

53,000,000   Estimated number of population
(1989)   Year of census

0   200 km
0   200 miles

© carta

110. ISLAM IN 1993

While Islam continues to have its spiritual roots in the holy cities of Mecca, Medina, and Jerusalem and its intellectual roots in the al-Azhar university mosque in Cairo, its greatest numerical strength is in Indonesia (80% of a population of 149,451,000), Pakistan (97% of a population of 84,501,000), India (12% only out of a population of 684,000,000), Bangladesh (85% of a population of 90,660,000), and the U.S.S.R., (44,236,000 Muslims, or 16.87 percent of a total population of 262,084,654 according to the 1979 census). Religious statistics, however, are notoriously misleading, for they can state only a declared religious allegiance.

Revivalist movements have arisen from time to time among, for example, the Wahhabis (map 88) and, in earlier times, the Ibadhis of Oman and Tunisia. The Senusi movement arose in the nineteenth century in Libya; the Muslim Brotherhood formed in Egypt; and what is known as Muslim fundamentalism has arisen during the present time.

A unique feature of the growth of Islam has been the work of the Sufi brotherhoods since the twelfth century. Originating among Persian mystics in Baghdad, the Sufi teachings spread Islam to the courts of Malaysia and Indonesia in the twelfth century. With a succession of sultans who were themselves Sufis, they provided the religious impulse for the Ottoman Empire. Shortly after the beginning of the nineteenth century, the Sufis spread Islam among the ordinary people in western and eastern Africa (map 86). Membership in these fraternities, as indeed in Islam itself, gave adherents a sense of belonging to an international fellowship, preserving cherished values in spite of war and colonization. With or without Sufi membership, that sense is very much alive today, especially when the community as a whole appears to be threatened.

Strictly defined, Islam has no organized church or hierarchy. Each Muslim is a priest for himself. Nevertheless, there is a "clergy," whose primary function is to interpret and declare the religious law, for in Islam all law derives from the Koran and the *hadith* (the traditional sayings or decisions of the Prophet Muhammad). This structure is by no means necessarily a weakness, for the interpretations of the lawyers adhere strictly to precedent, enabling a decision given in Cairo to be the same as one given in Canada, Bangladesh, or Indonesia. This uniformity and solidarity of law notwithstanding the Sufi brotherhoods never actively opposed the atheistic communism in Soviet Russia; they have simply ignored its proponents in their practical and spiritual lives.

Among Muslims, there are, however, wide variations in contemporary attitudes and practices. In al-Azhar women are admitted as pupils, and in many parts of the Muslim world they practice as teachers, whether of religion or of secular subjects in schools and universities. While this adaptation has not kept pace with social changes in other parts of the world, it is reaching its goals in its own fashion.

110 ISLAM IN 1993

For Shi'ites in the Middle East, see map 109

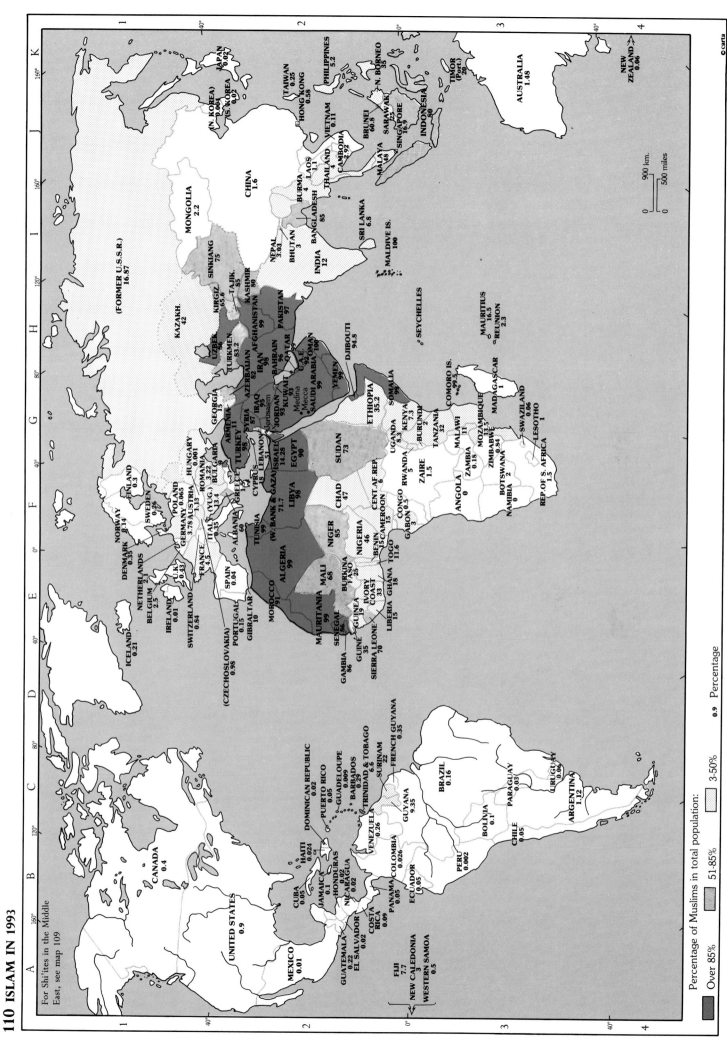

Percentage of Muslims in total population:

Over 85%

51-85%

3-50%

0.9 Percentage

Ccarta

111. KUWAIT

At the end of the seventeenth century a group of Arabs expelled from Iraq by the Ottoman government for brigandage and piracy settled in Kuwait. Led by the Al Sabah family, by 1758 they numbered ten-thousand, owned eight-hundred vessels and engaged in trade, fishing, and pearling. The Ottomans exercised no effective control over them. In 1898 the British government learned that Russia wished to construct a coaling station there. Acting promptly, the British made a treaty in 1899 in which Kuwait agreed not to dispose of any territory to a foreign power without British consent. This treaty effectively introduced British protection, which terminated only on 2 June 1961, when a new treaty gave Kuwait independence.

When oil was discovered in Kuwait in the 1930s, Iraq immediately laid claim to it. This claim was renewed by armed force in July 1961, when General Kassim proclaimed Kuwait "an integral part" of Iraq. British troops were sent in accordance with the treaty, and the claim was disallowed by the United Nations.

Following the war between Iraq and Iran (map 106), President Saddam Hussein of Iraq was left with an immense quantity of arms, including biological, neurological, and nuclear weapons, and the largest air force in the Middle East. When he attacked and seized Kuwait in August 1990, contrary to UN warnings, it appeared that nothing could stop his advance to seize all the Gulf States, and even Saudi Arabia and thus possess the greatest part of the oil production and reserves of the world. King Faysal of Saudi Arabia appealed to the UN for aid, and a UN force, the largest contingent of which was from the United States, was speedily assembled and sent to Saudi territory. An overwhelming and swift campaign compelled a cease-fire after five days of fighting (24-28 February 1991).

The core of the Iraqi army escaped, but a UN mission is still (1993) engaged in destroying biological and nuclear devices as agreed at the time of the cease-fire. The Iraqi government that initiated the attack survived in office.

112. NATURAL RESOURCES AND HIGHER EDUCATION

Since 1907, when oil was first exported from southwest Persia, the exploitation of oil resources has come more and more to dominate the economy of the Middle East. The discovery of fresh resources is perhaps not yet at an end, given the discovery of oil in the Marib and Shabwa areas of Yemen in 1987 and in central Saudi Arabia in 1991. The Gulf has long been the predominant oil-producing region, with 40 percent of the world's oil produced in Iraq and Kuwait. So rich is the world in oil resources that the stoppage of these two sources in 1990 had only temporary effect upon world economy.

In other respects the distribution of natural resources is very uneven, varying from the relative richness of Morocco and Algeria to the sparsity of the Gulf region, where petroleum is by far the largest source in natural wealth.

Much of the development in this respect has been the work of American and British oil companies, and French companies in northern Africa. In Egypt and Lebanon, and more recently Israel, secular institutes of higher learning have long provided the infrastructure. In very recent times universities have developed in Saudi Arabia and the Gulf, where much of the infrastructure has been maintained by the migration of Palestinian Arabs. In Kuwait until very recently these immigrants greatly outnumbered the native-born populations, by at least two to one. The growth in numbers of a highly educated native-born population must now be expected to transform the character of the region and to produce new problems. This, among other causes, has led to considerable emigration, especially to the United States.

111 KUWAIT

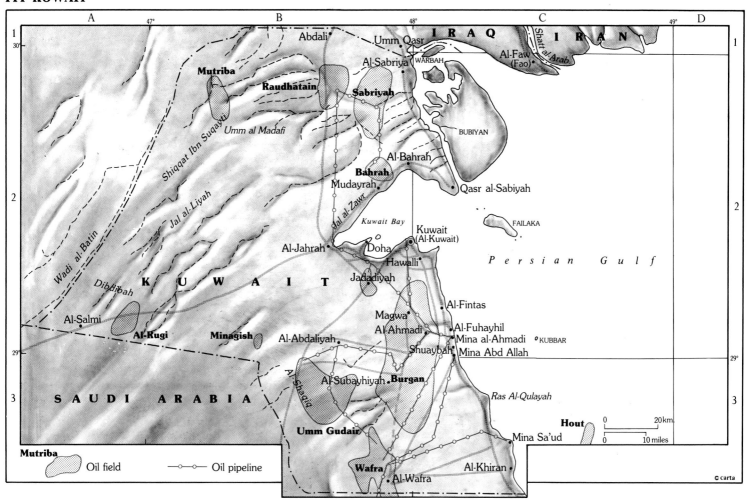

Mutriba	Oil field	

Oil pipeline

Map labels:
- Abdali
- Umm Qasr
- **I R A Q**
- **I R A N**
- Al-Sabriya
- WARBAH
- Al-Faw (Fao)
- Shatt al-Arab
- **Mutriba**
- **Raudhatain**
- **Sabriyah**
- Shiqqat Ibn Suqayti
- Umm al Madafi
- BUBIYAN
- Al-Bahrah
- **Bahrah**
- Mudayrah
- Jal al-Zawr
- Qasr al-Sabiyah
- Jal al-Liyah
- **K U W A I T**
- Kuwait Bay
- FAILAKA
- Kuwait (Al-Kuwait)
- Doha
- Al-Jahrah
- Hawalli
- *P e r s i a n   G u l f*
- Wadi al-Batin
- Dibdibah
- Jadadiyah
- Al-Fintas
- Al-Salmi
- **Al-Kugi**
- **Minagish**
- Magwa
- Al-Ahmadi
- Al-Fuhayhil
- Mina al-Ahmadi
- KUBBAR
- Al-Abdaliyah
- Shuaybah
- Mina Abd Allah
- **S A U D I   A R A B I A**
- Al-Shaqiq
- Al-Subayhiyah
- **Burgan**
- Ras Al-Qulayah
- **Umm Gudair**
- **Hout**
- Mina Sa'ud
- **Wafra**
- Al-Wafra
- Al-Khiran

Scale: 0 — 20 km / 0 — 10 miles

© carta

112 NATURAL RESOURCES AND HIGHER EDUCATION

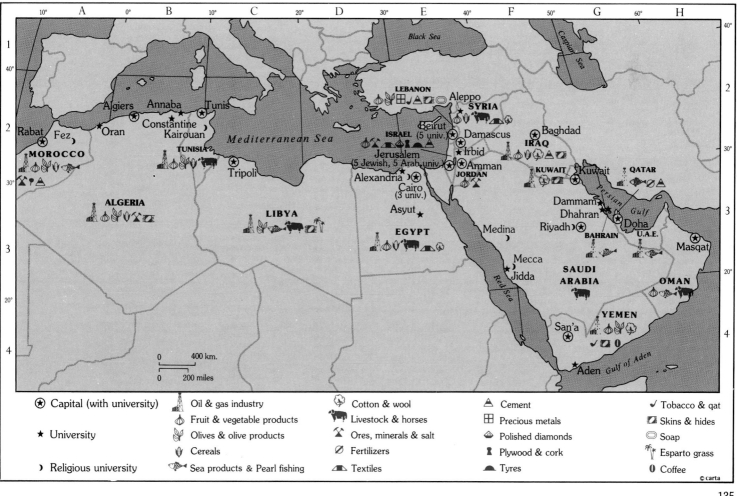

Legend:
- (★) Capital (with university)
- ★ University
- ⟩ Religious university
- Oil & gas industry
- Fruit & vegetable products
- Olives & olive products
- Cereals
- Sea products & Pearl fishing
- Cotton & wool
- Livestock & horses
- Ores, minerals & salt
- Fertilizers
- Textiles
- Cement
- Precious metals
- Polished diamonds
- Plywood & cork
- Tyres
- Tobacco & qat
- Skins & hides
- Soap
- Esparto grass
- Coffee

© carta

135

113. THE MIDDLE EAST, 1993 — POLITCAL AND POPULATION

The map includes all members of the Arab League, together with Israel and the six Islamic republics that were part of the U.S.S.R. The population figures shown are chiefly United Nations estimates. The figures for Kuwait, recorded on 1 August 1990 include foreign nationals, many of whom were longstanding Kuwaiti residents with children born in Kuwait. A similar distortion of population figures is probably true of other oil-producing states. Following the Gulf War many foreign nationals were repatriated from Kuwait, and the population figures estimated by UN for Kuwait also reflect the indiscriminate murders that took place on a large scale during the Iraqi occupation. In spite of possible distortions, many of the percentages represent genuine trends of population growth. In 1917, Egypt had a population of 12,750,918; by 1992 it had passed fifty-three million. In 1912, Syria had a population of 2,626,160 as against 11,719,000 in 1993. Ottoman Palestine numbered only about 700,000 persons. The population of Israel has, of course, been greatly increased by Jewish immigration, principally since 1948, and reached, in 1993, about five million. During the same period Palestinian Arabs have emigrated to many different countries, especially to the oil-producing countries of the Gulf.

The boundaries of a majority of these countries can be regarded as stable, though that of Kuwait is still disputed by Iraq. The boundaries of Israel contain former Jordanian territories, which were acquired in 1967 and are administered as occupied territory in accordance with international and Jordanian law. The Golan Heights and the Old City of Jerusalem have been annexed by Israel, but these claims have not been accorded formal international recognition. In these occupied territories Palestinian Arabs form a majority.

At the Conference of Paris, 1919, the participants professed policies of self-determination for small nations, but these policies were unevenly applied in the Middle East. The former Ottoman provinces were carved up between Britain and France, and the claims of small nations disregarded. A short-lived Armenian republic was swallowed up by Russia, and Kurds found themselves divided between Iran, Iraq, Syria and Turkey, and what in 1923 became the U.S.S.R. Migrations of Kurds in the early 1990s from Iraq, following genocidal persecution, into Iran and Turkey, are too recent to be brought to account here. The newly created Iraq of 1919, containing the oil-bearing *wilayet* of Mosul, was one-third Kurdish, one-third Sunni (being the former *wilayet* of Baghdad) and one-third Shi'ite (the former *wilayet* of Basra). The settlement reflected British imperial oil interests rather than any genuine political realities. Indeed, so unreal was this creation that until 1957 cabinet meetings were conducted in the Turkish language.

The crumbling of the U.S.S.R. into twelve independent republics during 1991 brought into being no less than six Muslim republics whose ancestry made them heirs of the caliphate at its greatest expansion (map 23). These six republics have small populations compared with those to the south and west of them, but all possess nuclear facilities. In Kazakhstan one-tenth of the whole nuclear armament of the former U.S.S.R. is to be found. Thus these nations can have a military potential out of all proportion to their population figures. In them too the growth of Islamic fundamentalism, hostile to western European countries, further complicates the complex political situation that is present from Pakistan and Iran to Libya and Algeria. Fifty years ago Islamic countries as a whole had little or no economic strength. The wealth that oil production has brought and the development of education and professional expertise in its wake, have transformed the Middle East as a whole into a most potent factor in global politics.

113 THE MIDDLE EAST, 1993 — POLITICAL AND POPULATION

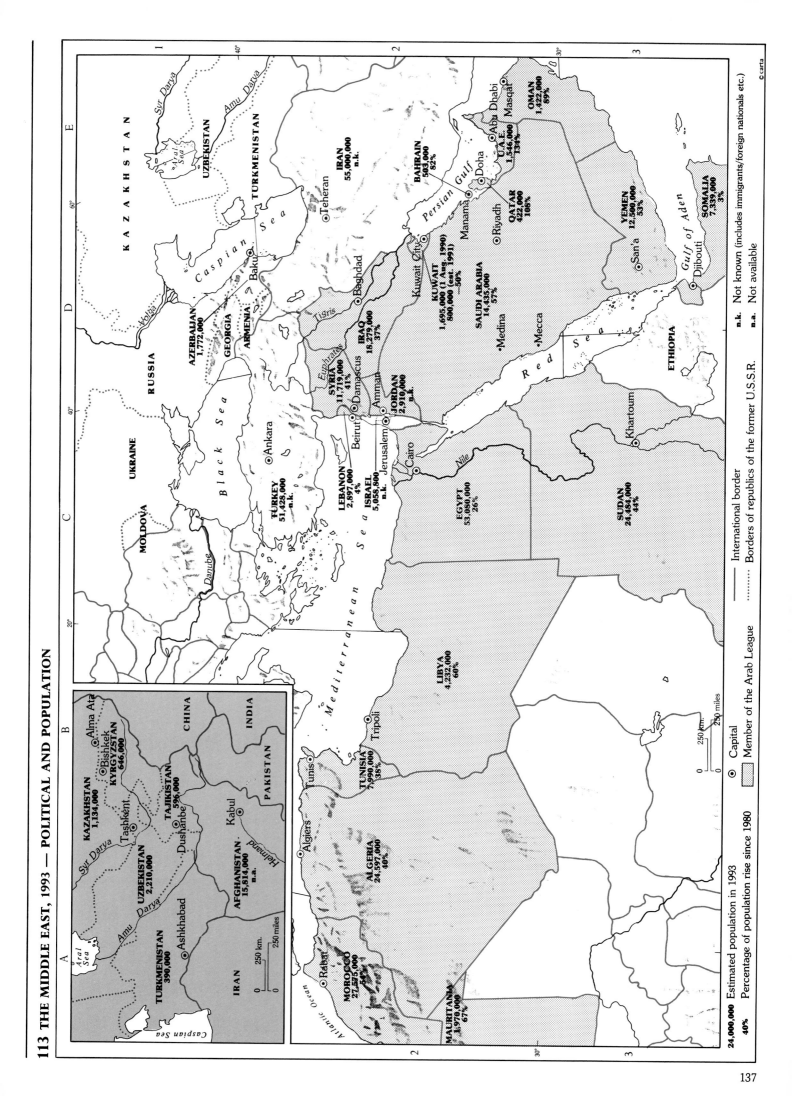

KAZAKHSTAN

UZBEKISTAN

TURKMENISTAN

RUSSIA

UKRAINE

MOLDOVA

Aral Sea

Sur Darya

Amu Darya

Volga

Caspian Sea

Black Sea

AZERBAIJAN
1,772,000

GEORGIA

ARMENIA
⊙Baku

⊙Teheran

IRAN
55,000,000
n.k.

⊙Ankara

TURKEY
51,428,000
n.k.

Mediterranean Sea

LEBANON
2,897,000
4%

ISRAEL
5,058,800
n.k.

Beirut⊙
Damascus⊙

SYRIA
11,719,000
41%

Amman⊙

JORDAN
2,910,000
n.k.

Jerusalem⊙

⊙Cairo

Nile

EGYPT
53,080,000
26%

Baghdad⊙

IRAQ
18,279,000
37%

Tigris

Euphrates

Kuwait City⊙

KUWAIT
1,695,000 (1 Aug. 1990)
500,000 (est. 1991)
-50%

⊙Riyadh

•Medina

•Mecca

SAUDI ARABIA
14,435,000
57%

Red Sea

ETHIOPIA

Khartoum⊙

SUDAN
24,484,000
44%

BAHRAIN
503,000
82%

Manama⊙

Doha⊙

QATAR
422,000
108%

Persian Gulf

⊙Abu Dhabi
Masqat⊙

U.A.E.
1,546,000
131%

OMAN
1,422,000
89%

YEMEN
12,500,000
53%

⊙San'a

Gulf of Aden

Djibouti⊙

SOMALIA
7,339,000
3%

Tripoli⊙

LIBYA
4,232,000
60%

Tunis⊙

TUNISIA
7,990,000
38%

Algiers⊙

ALGERIA
24,597,000
40%

Rabat⊙

MOROCCO
27,575,000
54%

MAURITANIA
1,970,000
67%

Atlantic Ocean

0   250 km.
0   250 miles

Inset map (lower left)

TURKMENISTAN
390,000

Aral Sea

Caspian Sea

IRAN

Ashkhabad⊙

Amu Darya

Syr Darya

UZBEKISTAN
2,210,000

Tashkent

⊙Alma Ata

⊙Bishkek

KYRGYZSTAN
646,000

KAZAKHSTAN
1,134,000

TAJIKISTAN
596,000

Dushanbe⊙

Helmand

Kabul⊙

AFGHANISTAN
15,814,000
n.a.

CHINA

INDIA

PAKISTAN

0   250 km.
0   250 miles

Legend

International border

Borders of republics of the former U.S.S.R.

⊙ Capital

Member of the Arab League

24,000,000 Estimated population in 1993
40% Percentage of population rise since 1980

n.k. Not known (includes immigrants/foreign nationals etc.)
n.a. Not available

© carta

137

SELECT BIBLIOGRAPHY

Agatharcides of Cnidus: *On the Erythraean Sea*, ed. & trans. S.M. Burstein, Hakluyt Society, London, 1989.

Ahmad ibn Majid [al-Najdi]: *Tri Neizvestnye Lotsii Akhmada Ibn Madzhida* ed. & trans. T.A. Shumovskii, Russian Academy of Sciences, 1957; Portuguese trans. as *Três Roteiros Desconhecidos*, [Three Unknown Logbooks], Lisbon, 1960.

The Annual Register, from 1768, various editors, to date.

Anstey, V.: *The Trade of the Indian Ocean*, London, 1929.

Arberry, A.J., ed.: *The Legacy of Persia*, London, 1953.

Arkell, A.J.: *History of the Sudan: from the earliest times to 1821*, 2nd edn., 1961.

Atiya, Aziz A.: *A History of Early Christianity*, London, 1968.

Atkinson, W.C.: *A History of Spain and Portugal*, London, 1960.

al-Azhary, M.S., ed.: *The Iran-Iraq War*, London, 1984.

Baedeker, K.: *Guide to Spain and Portugal*, Leipzig, 1908.
　　The Mediterranean: Seaports and Sea Routes, Leipzig, 1911.
　　　Palestine and Syria, Leipzig, 1912.
　　　Egypt and the Sudan, Leipzig, 1929.

Bahat, D.: *The Illustrated Atlas of Jerusalem*, New York, 1991.

Baker, J.N.L.: *History of Geographical Discovery and Exploration*, London, 1931.

Beckingham, C.F.: *Atlas of the Arab World and the Middle East*, London, 1960.

Belhaven, Lord: *The Eagle and the Sun*, London, 1951.

Bidwell, R.: *Travellers in Arabia*, London, 1976.

Boswell, C.E.: *Islamic Dynasties*, Edinburgh, 1967.

Bovill, E.W.: *Caravans of the Old Sahara*, London, 1933.
　　The Golden Trade of the Moors, London, 1958.

Bowersock, G.W.: *Roman Arabia*, Harvard, 1983.

Bréhier, L.: *L'Egypte de 1798 à 1900*, Paris, 1900.

Brice, W.C.: *An Historical Atlas of Islam*, Leiden, 1980.

Bright, J.: *History of Israel*, 2 vols., London, 1967.

Burckhardt, J.L.: *Travels in Arabia*, London, 1829.

Burn, A.R.: *Alexander the Great and the Hellenistic Empire*, London, 1947.

Butler, A.J.: *The Arab Conquest of Egypt*, Oxford, 1902.

Buzurg ibn Shahriyar al-Ramhormuzi: *The Book of the Wonders of India: Mainland, Sea and Islands*, ed. & trans. G.S.P. Freeman-Grenville, London, 1981.

Cambridge Ancient History, various editors, 12 vols., 1925–.

Cambridge History of Africa, ed. F.D. Fage and R.A. Oliver, 8 vols., 1975–1986.

Cambridge History of India, various editors, 6 vols., 1922–1937; 2nd edn., 5 vols. to date from 1960.

Cambridge History of Iran, 6 vols., from 1968–.

Cambridge History of Islam, 2 vols., 1970 ff.

Cambridge Medieval History, various editors, 1913–1936.

Casson, L. ed. & trans.: *The Periplus Maris Erythraei*, Princeton, 1989.

Cary, M. and Warmington, E.H.: *The Ancient Explorers*, London, 1952.

Chadwick, H.: *The Early Christian Church*, London, 1967.

Chitty, Derwas A.: *The Desert a City*, Oxford, 1966.

Clark, C.M. and Horton, M.C., "Archaeological Survey of Zanzibar", *Azania* 20, pp.167–171.

Cook, M.A., ed.: *A History of the Ottoman Empire to 1730*, Cambridge, 1976.

Cornevin, R.: *Histoire de l'Afrique*, 3 vols., Paris, 1962.

Cresswell, K.A.C.: *Early Muslim Architecture*, 2 vols., Oxford, 1932, 1940.

Daniel-Rops, J.: *Ces Chrétiens nos frères*, Paris, 1965.

Dauphin, J.: *Incertain Irak, 1914–1953*, Paris, 1991.

Davies, C.C.: *An Historical Atlas of the Indian Peninsula*, Oxford, 1949.

Diringer, D.: *The Alphabet, a Key to the History of Mankind*, 3rd edn., London, 1968.

Doe, D.B.: *Southern Arabia*, London, 1972.

Dols, M.W.: *The Black Death in the Middle East*, Princeton, 1977.

Doughty, C.M.: *Travels in Arabia Deserta*, Cambridge, 1988.

Dozy, R.: *Spanish Islam*, London, 1913 (from the French edn. of 1861).

Encyclopaedia of Islam, 1st edn., 1913–1938.

Encyclopaedia of Islam, 2nd edn., in progress (to Mo), 1954-.

Fauvel, J.J. ed.: *Maroc*, Hachette Guides Bleus, Paris, 1983.

Fisher, G.: *Barbary Legend: War, Trade and Piracy, 1415–1830*, Oxford, 1957.

Fliche, A. and Martin, V.: *Histoire de l'Eglise*, 12 vols., Paris, 1934–1964.

Fox, R.L.: *Pagans and Christians*, London, 1988.

Freeman-Grenville, G.S.P.: "The Gulf States", *Burke's Royal Families of the World*, II, *Africa and Asia*, London, 1980.
　　The Beauty of Cairo, London, 1980.
　　The East African Coast: Select Documents, repr., London, 1977.
　　　The Beauty of Jerusalem, 2nd edn., London, 1987.
　　　The Swahili Coast, 2nd to 19th Centuries, London, 1988.
　　　The New Atlas of African History, London and New York, 1991.

Freeth, S. and Winston, V.: *Explorers in Arabia*, London, 1978.

Frend, W.H.C.: *The Donatist Church*, Oxford, 1952.

Friesel, E.: *Atlas of Modern Jewish History*, Oxford, 1990.

Gardiner, A.: *The Egypt of the Pharaohs*, Oxford, 1961.

Gaury, G. de: *Rulers of Mecca*, London, 1951.

Gibb, H.A.R. and Bowen, H.: *Islamic Society and the West*, 2 parts, 1950, 1957.

Glubb, J.B.: *The Great Arab Conquests*, London, 1983.

Gomra, I.: *A Historical Chart of the Muslim World*, Leiden, 1972.

Goodwin, G.: *Islamic Spain*, London, 1991.

Gray, J.M.: *History of Zanzibar*, Oxford, 1962.

Grousset, R.: *L'Empire des Steppes*, Paris, 1969.

Guillaume, A.: *Islam*, London, 1954.

Gurney, O.R.: *The Hittites*, Harmondsworth, 1981.

Hamdun, S. and King, N.: *Ibn Battuta in Black Africa*, London, 1975.

Hazard, H.W.: *Atlas of Islamic History*, Princeton, 1951.

Healey, J.E.: *Reading the Past: the Early Alphabet*, London, 1990.

Heers, J.: *Gênes au XVe siècle*, Paris, 1961.

Herodotus: *The Histories*, ed. J.E. Powell, 2 vols., Oxford, 1949.

Herzog, C.: *The Arab-Israeli Wars*, London, 1982.

Hill, R.: *Egypt in the Sudan, 1820-1881*, London, 1959.

Hitti, P.K.: *History of Syria*, London and New York, 1951.
    Lebanon in History, London and New York, 1962.
    History of the Arabs, 8th edn., New York, 1963.

Hogarth, D.G.: *The Penetration of Arabia*, London, 1904.

Hogben, S.J. and Kirk-Greene, A.H.M.: *The Emirates of Northern Nigeria*, Oxford, 1966.

Holmes, R.: *World Atlas of Warfare*, London, 1988.

Holt, P.M.: *A Modern History of the Sudan*, London, 1961.
    Egypt and the Fertile Crescent, London, 1966.
    The Age of the Crusades, London, 1986.
    and Daly, M.H.: *The History of the Sudan*, 3rd edn., London, 1979.

Horton, M.C.: *Preliminary reports on excavations on Shanga, Manda Is., Kenya; Mtambwe Mkuu, Pemba Is.; and on Tumbatu Is., Zanzibar*, circulated privately, 1984 ff.

Horton, M.C., Brown, H.M., and Oddy, W.A.: "The Mtambwe Hoard", *Azania* XXI, 1986, 115–123.

Hourani, A.H.: *Minorities in the Arab World*, London, 1947.

Hourani, G.F.: *Arab Seafaring*, Oxford, 1951.

Huntingford, G.W.B.: *Periplus of the Erythraean Sea*, Hakluyt Society, London, 1980.

Hurgronje S.: *Mekka in the latter part of the nineteenth century*, English trans., 1931, repr. 1971.

Ibn Battuta: *Les Voyages d'Ibn Battuta* (Rihla), ed. & trans. C. Defremery and B.R. Sanguinetti, 4 vols., Paris, 1858 ff.
    The Travels of Ibn Battuta, ed. & trans. H.A.R. Gibb, Hakluyt Society, 3 vols., 1956 ff.; vols. 4 and 5, ed. & trans. C.F. Beckingham, have not yet been published.

al-Idrisi: *Kitab Rujar* (c.1155), ed. C.F. Beckingham et al., 9 parts, Naples, 1971.

Ibn Hawqal: *Kitab Surat al-Ard* (c.988), 2 vols., trans. G. Wiet, Paris, 1964.

Inalcik, H.: *The Ottoman Empire*, London, 1973.

Ingrams, D. *A Survey of social and economic conditions in the Aden Protectorate*, Asmara, 1949.

Irwin, P.: *The Middle East in the Middle Age: The Early Mamluk Sultanate, 1250-1382*, London, 1986.

Jonquière, C. de la: *L'Expédition d'Egypte, 1789-1801*, Paris, 2 vols., 1899, 1901.

Josephus, Flavius: *Complete Works*, ed & trans. H. St.J. Thackeray, 17 vols., New York, 1926–1965.

Julien, Ch.-A.: *Histoire de l'Afrique du Nord*, 2 vols., Paris, 1956, 1961.

Keay, J.: ed. *Royal Geographical Society History of World Exploration*, London, 1991.

Keesing's Contemporary Archives, monthly, 1931 to date.

Khaldun, Ibn: *The Muqaddimah: an Introduction to History*, trans. F. Rosenthal, 3 vols., London and New York, 1958.

Khowaiter, A.A.: *Baibars the First: his Endeavours and Achievements*, London, 1978.

Kollek, T.: *For Jerusalem*, Tel Aviv, 1978.

Lammens, H.: *L'Arabie occidentale avant l'Hégire*, Beyrouth, 1928.

Lane, E.: *Manners and Customs of the Modern Egyptians* (1836) (1866 edn.), London, 1936.

Lane-Poole, S.: *History of Egypt in the Middle Ages*, London, 1901.
    The Moors in Spain, London, 1887, repr. Beyrouth, 1967.

Leroy, J.: *Monks and Monasteries of the Near East*, London, 1963.

Lessner, J.: *The Topography of Baghdad in the Early Middle Ages*, Detroit, 1970.

Le Strange, G.: *Lands of the Eastern Caliphate*, Cambridge, 1905.
    Baghdad during the Abbasid Caliphate, Oxford, 1900.
    Palestine under the Moslems, London, 1890.

Lévi-Provençal, E.: *Histoire de l'Espagne musulmane*, 3 vols., Paris, 1932.

Lewcock, R.: *Wadi Hadramawt and the Walled City of Shibam*, Paris, 1986.

Lewis, B.: *The Arabs in History*, London, 1964.
    The Middle East and the West, London, 1964.

Liddle, P.: *Men of Gallipoli*, Warmington, 1988.

Little, E.: *History and Historiography of the Mamluks*, London, 1986.

Lomrigg, S.H.: *History of Iraq, 1900-1950*, London, 1956.
    The Middle East – A Social Geography, London, 1963.

Longworth, P.: *The Rise and Fall of Venice*, London, 1974.

Lorimer, J.G.: *The Gazetteer of the Persian Gulf, Oman and Central Arabia*, Bombay, 6 vols., 1908-1915.

Lybyer, A.H.: *The Government of the Ottoman Empire in the time of Suleiman the Magnificent*, Cambridge, Mass., 1913.

Mahaffy, J.: *Alexander's Empire*, 3rd edn., London, 1887.
    A History of Egypt under the Ptolemaic Dynasty, London, 1899.

McLaurin, R.D.: *The Political Role of Minority Groups in the Middle East*, New York, 1979.

al-Maqrizi: *Description Historique et Topographique de l'Egypte*, trans. P. Casanova, Cairo, 1906.

al-Mas'udi: *Les Prairies d'Or (Muruj al-Dhahab)*, ed. & trans. C. Barbier de Meynard et Pavet de Courteille, 10 vols., Paris, 1861-1877.

Milne, J.G.: *A History of Egypt under Roman Rule*, 2nd edn., London, 1913.

Minorsky, V.: *Hudud al-Alam*, Oxford, 1937.

Morgan, D.: *The Mongols*, Oxford, 1986.
    Medieval Persia, 1046–1797, Oxford, 1988.

Moscati, S.: *The World of the Phoenicians*, London, 1973.

Munro-Hay, S.C.H.: *Aksum: an African Civilisation of Late Antiquity*, Edinburgh, 1991.

Naval Intelligence Division: *Western Arabia and the Red Sea*, HMSO, 1945.

Neill, S.: *A History of Christian Missions*, London, 1964.

Norwich, J.J.: *History of Venice*, 2 vols., London, 1982.

Oliver, R.A. and Mathew, A.G.: Oxford *History of East Africa*, Vol. I, Oxford, 1963.

Peel Report: *Palestine Royal Commission: Report*, July 1937, HMSO, London.

Peters, R.E.: *Histoire des Turcs*, Paris, 1966.

Petrie, W.M.F.: *A History of Egypt under the Pharaohs*, 3 vols., London, 1894.

Philby, H.St.J.B.: *The Empty Quarter*, London, 1933.

Pitcher, D.: *Historical Geography of the Ottoman Empire*, London, 1968.

Pliny: *The Natural History*, trans. H Rackham, 6 vols., 1940–1963.

Powell-Price, J.C.: *A History of India*, London, 1955.

Procopius: *History of the Wars*, trans.H.D. Dewing, New York, 1914.

Ptolemy, Cl.: *The Geography*, trans. E.F. Robbins, New York, 1940.

Rabinovich, A.: *Jerusalem: The Measure of the Year*, Jerusalem, 1985.

Ramsay, W.M.: *Historical Geography of Asia Minor*, London, 1890.

Riley-Smith, J. ed.: *The Atlas of the Crusades*, London, 1990.

Roolvink, R.: *Historical Atlas of the Muslim Peoples*, Amsterdam, 1957.

Roux, G.: *Ancient Iraq*, London, 1962, second edition 1980.

Runciman, S.: *History of the Crusades*, 3 vols., Cambridge, 1951–1954.

Russell, D.: *Medieval Cairo*, London, 1962.

Rutter, E.: *The Holy Cities of Arabia*, London, 1928.

Strabo: *The Geography*, trans. H.L. Jones, 8 vols., New York, 1917–1932.

Setton, K.M.: *History of the Crusades*, 5 vols., Philadelphia, 1958–.

Sabini, J.: *Armies in the Sand*, London, 1981.

Salt, H.: *A Voyage to Abyssinia*, London, 1814.

Sanders, N.K.: *The Sea Peoples*, 2nd edn., London, 1985.

Schrader, F.: *Atlas de Géographie Historique*, Paris, 1922.

Schofield, R.: *Kuwait and Iraq: Historical Claims and Territorial Disputes*, London, 1991.

Schwartzberg, J.F.: *A Historical Atlas of South Asia*, Chicago, 1978.

Searight, S.: *The British in the Middle East*, London, 1979.

Sellassie, S.H.: *Ancient and Medieval Ethiopian History to 1270*, Addis Ababa, 1972.

Serjeant, R.B.: *The Portuguese off the South Arabian Coast*, Oxford, 1963.

Shaw, S.J. and E.K. Shaw: *History of the Ottoman Empire and Modern Turkey*, Cambridge, 1977.

Shboul, A.M.H.: *al-Mas'udi and his World*, London, 1979.

Slot, B.J.: *The Origins of Kuwait*, Leiden, 1991.

Smail, R.C.: *Crusading Warfare, 1097–1193*, Cambridge, 1976.

Smith, V.A.: *History of India*, revised edn., Oxford, 1958.

Souidi, Dj.: *Cahiers d'Achir*, Centre National d'Etudes Historiques, Algiers, I, 1992; II, 1993.

Sprenger, A.: *Die Alte Geographie Arabiens*, Bern, 1875.

Stanwood, F., Allen, P., and Peacock, L.: *Gulf War*, London, 1991.

Sykes, P.M.: *The History of Persia*, 2 vols., London, 1930.

Tamrat, T.: *Church and State in Ethiopia, 1270–1527*, Oxford, 1972.

Tariq al-Janabi: "Recent Excavations in Samarra" *World Archaeology*, 14, 3, 1983.

Tarn, W.W.: *Alexander the Great*, 2 vols., Oxford, 1948.

Tibbetts, G.R.: *Arab Navigation in the Indian Ocean before the Coming of the Portuguese*, London, 1971.

Thesiger, W.: *Arabian Sands*, London, 1959.

Thomas, B.: *Arabia Felix: Across the Empty Quarter*, London, 1938.

The Times Atlas of the World, London, 1985.

Toussaint, A.: *Histoire de l'Ocean Indien*, Paris, 1961.

Trimingham, J.S.: *Islam in the Sudan*, Oxford, 1949.
Islam in West Africa, 1962.
Islam in East Africa, 1964.
Islam in Ethiopia, 1965.

Vallaud, P. ed.: *Atlas des Guerres du XXe Siècle*, Paris, 1990.

Vassiliev, A.A.: *Histoire de l'Empire Byzantin*, 2 vols., Paris, 1932.

Vlekke, B.H.M.: *Nusantara: A History of Indonesia*, The Hague, 1965.

Volkoff, O.V.: *Le Caire, 969–1969*, Cairo, 1971.

Watt, W.M.: *Muhammad at Mecca*, Oxford, 1953.
Muhammad at Medina, Oxford, 1956.
and Cachia, P.: *A History of Islamic Spain*, Edinburgh, 1965.

Webster, G.: *The Roman Imperial Army*, 3rd edn., London, 1981.

Wellard, J.: *Babylon*, New York, 1974.

Wellsted, J.R.: *Travels in Arabia*, London, 1838.

Whitaker's Almanack, annually, London, from 1868 to date.

Winder, R.B.: *Saudi Arabia in the nineteenth century*, New York, 1965.

Wissman, H. von: *Southern Arabia*, two sheets, London, 1957/1958.

Wittek, P.: *The Rise of the Ottoman Empire*, London, 1938.

Zambaur, E.de: *Manuel de Généalogie et de Chronologie pour l'Histoire de l'Islam*, Hanover (1927), repr. 1977.

Zanzibar Guide, Government Printer, Zanzibar, 1952.

Ziegler, P.: *The Black Death*, London, 1969.

INDEX TO THE MAPS

Note: the list of maps serves as a subject index. This index of countries, place names and persons, is necessarily selective. Thus, after map 1, the first occasion on which a name occurs is usually recorded, and thereafter only those occasions on which that name is of importance. In some instances names will only be found in the texts accompanying the maps.